Muscogee County Georgia
Superior Court Minutes
1838-1840

- Volume #1 -
(Part 1)

By:
Michael A. Ports

Southern Historical Press, Inc.
Greenville, South Carolina

Copyright 2021
By: Michael A. Ports

All rights reserved. No part of this publication may be reproduced, stored in a retrieval system, transmitted in any form, posted on to the web in any form or by any means without the prior written permission of the publisher.

Please direct all correspondence and orders to:

www.southernhistoricalpress.com
or
SOUTHERN HISTORICAL PRESS, Inc.
PO BOX 1267
375 West Broad Street
Greenville, SC 29601
southernhistoricalpress@gmail.com

ISBN # 978-1-63914-010-7

Printed in the United States of America

Introduction

On December 11, 1826, the Georgia General Assembly created Muscogee County from lands recently ceded by the Creek Indians and designated Columbus as the seat of its government. Portions of Muscogee County were taken to form Chattahoochee, Harris, Marion, and Talbot Counties. The judges of the Superior Courts, elected to serve three-year terms, held court in each county at least twice per year, as they traveled from county to county within their circuit. The Superior Court held jurisdiction over all criminal matters, most civil cases, especially those involving title to land, appeals from Inferior Court and Justices Court decisions, divorces, admissions to the bar, grand juries, and registration of land deeds.

The following transcription comes from the microfilm photographed in 1965 at the courthouse in Columbus, Georgia, by the Genealogical Society of Salt Lake City, Utah, and available at the Georgia Archives in Morrow, Georgia. The heading on the microfilm reads

**Muscogee
County
Georgia
Superior Court**

and

**Superior Court
Court Minutes**

**Book 1
No Index**

1838 - 1840

On nthe spine of the original volume is printed the following

**MINUTES I MUSCOGEE
SUPERIOR
COURT**

One front cover of the original volume is printed the following

MINUTES
I
MUSCOGEE
SUPERIOR
COURT

On the first inside sheet the clerk wrote the following

Minutes
1838-1839

The next two inside pages are blank. One the next inside unnumbered page, the clerk wrote the following

Minutes of the Superior Court
Muscogee County Commencing 15th day of October ~~term~~ 1838

And on the next subsequent unnumbered page, the clerk wrote

    Grand Jury Presentment Oct Term 1838   121
                "   May 1839   387
                "   Oct 1839   594

While the original record volume contains no index, a complete full-name index follows the transcription. The reader should know that a lone surname in the index indicates that no first name appears in the minutes, for example Mr. Smith or Smith & Company. An index entry such as Smith, ___ indicates that a first name was entered into the minutes, but has been obscured by an ink blot, smear, tear, or other imperfection. The numbers in brackets, for example [263], are the original page numers and are placed in the upper lefthand corner of each original page.

The courthouse burned in October 1838, resulting in the destruction of virtually all the county records. The first surviving volume of minutes begins on October 15, 1838, at the start of the October Term, and continue in chronological order through the end of the October Term 1839. The minute book contains 623 pages of minutes, too many to be transcribed into one volume. The following transcription includes the first 234 pages.

Joseph Sturgis presided as judge during the first day, thereafter Marshall J. Wellborn presided during the remainder of the time. Gerard Burch served as clerk and Thomas H. Burch served as deputy clerk during the entire period covered by the minutes. Based upon the different handwriting, as many as six or possibly more deputy clerks entered some of the proceedings, but their names are not recorded. The original signatures of the four men appear many times throughout the minutes. The minutes contain numerous other original signatures, mostly of attorneys filing various motions, petitions, and affidavits as well as those parties confessing judgment, signing affidavits, and filing bonds for appeals and stays of execution, as well as their securities.

For the most part, the handwriting is legible, and the quality of the microfilm is good, making the reading and transcription process straightforward and not too difficult, although the handwriting of one particular clerk is not much better than a scrawl. The occasional ink blot, smear, or other imperfection is noted within brackets, for example [blot] or [faint]. The transcription follows Sperry's recommended guidelines for reading early American handwriting.[1] Generally, the transcription maintains the overall format of the minutes, but presents the case citations, jury panels, lists of witnesses, signatures, and other court proceedings in a standard and consistent format. No grammar or spelling errors are corrected in the transcription, although a few commas, semicolons, apostrophes, and periods are added for clarity. The clerks entered a vertical squiggly line to delineate case citations, affidavit and petition headings, and signature citations, replicated by the symbol } in the transcription. Following many of the original signatures, the clerk entered a symbol consisting of the capital letters "L" and "S" encircled by a squiggly line, evidently indicting the individual's seal, as follows

---

[1] Sperry, Kip, *Reading Early American Handwriting*. Genealogical Publishing Company, Baltimore, Maryland, Sixth Printing, 2008.

Sometimes, after an original signature the clerk entered the following

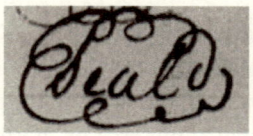

Neither symbol is included in the transcription.

Sometimes the clerk formed the letters "a" and "o" in a very similar manner, making abbreviations like Jas. and Jos. and surnames Bagg and Bogg or Shannan and Shannon difficult to distinguish. At other times, the letters "a" and "u" are too similar to differentiate such names as Burton and Barton or Barnett and Burnett, or Barns and Burns. In a similar manner, the names Edmond and Edmund can be difficult to distinguish. The formation of the letters "n" and "r" at the end of surnames sometimes appear to be the same. Inavariably, the formation of the capital letters "I" and "J" are identical. Determining which letter usually not difficult when the first letter of a name, but almost entirely a guess when a lone middle initial. The clerk often crossed the letter "t" by extending the horizontal line across the entire word, making it difficult to distinguish between such surnames as Walters and Watters. Compounding the problem, he sometimes neglected to cross any "t" in a word, making a "t" appear to be an "l." Careful researchers will consult the original record or the microfilm copy to either confirm the transcription or formulate an alternative interpretation of the clerk's handwriting.

The book is dedicated to the memory of the author's relatives Cullen and Edna (Harrell) Harp, who were early residents of Muscogee County during this period. Many thanks are offered the kind, patient, and generous staff of the Georgia Archives for their assistance and suggestions, not only in locating the original records, but in understanding their historical context. Thanks also are offered LaBruce Lucas of the Southern Historical Press for his sage professional advice and counsel. Special thanks are offered to Marcia Tremonti for her patience and encouragement throughout the entire process of transcription and publication.

Superior Court Minutes

[1] Muscogee Superior Court
Monday 15th October 1838

This Court met according to adjournment, present the Honorable Joseph Sturgis, Judge of the Superior Courts of the Chattahoochee Circuit.

The names of the following persons being called and answered to, when the Oaths of Grand and Special Jurors were Administered to them by the Solicitor General.

1. John Johnston
2. Hudson A. Thornton
3. Anderson Hunt
4. Augustus Hayward
5. Carnot Woodruff
6. Emanuel Ezekiel
7. Mansfield Torrence
8. Frederick Toby
9. Hiram Fuller
10. Thomas Hoxey
11. William Clarke
12. ~~William~~ Geo A. Norris
13. William L. Jeter
14. William P. Malone
15. Henry K. Hill
16. Henry Mims
17. Seymour R. Bonner, Tallisman
18. Wm S. Chipley, T.
19. William W. Pool
20. John H. Colquitt
21. John R. Boon, Regular P
22. Charles King
23. Jonathan P. Jackson

The names of the following persons being called and answered to, when the Oath of Petit Jurors were administered to them by the Solicitor General.

N° 1
1. ~~Richard~~ Umphrey Rowell
2. Daniel Brown
3. Edmund Kelly
4. Randol Tillery
5. Willson Culpepper
6. James Ryals
7. Robert Higdon
8. Zepheniah Parker
9. Isaac H. Webb
10. John McGough
11. Rhode L. Smith
12. Joseph Phelps

Nº 2
1. James Jernigan
2. Seaborn Eley
3. Jacob Johnson
4. ~~Stephen Beck~~ Bird B. Mitchell
5. William C. Morris
6. Seth Tatum
7. John Benton
8. Hiram Yonge
9. Thomas Motley
10. Price Davis
11. Willson Gordy
12. Elias Howell

[2] Muscogee Superior Court Monday 15th October 1838

Ordered, That the Grand Jurors Summoned to attend this Court on the monday after the fourth monday in October are Ordered to attend said Court on the fourth monday in December next. And that the petit Jurys Subpoenaed to attend the said Court on the thursday after the fourth monday in this Ins^t will atend said Court on thursday after the third monday in December next. And that the Clerk do cause this order to be published in the several Gazetts in this place.

Muscogee Superior Court October Term 1838

To the Honorable Joseph Sturgis, Judge of the Superior Courts in and for the Chattahoochee circuit in said State, the said Court being a Court of Record having a Clerk and Seal. The Petition of James Graham respectfully Sheweth that he is a native of the Kingdom of Ireland, a part of her Majesties dominions, the Queen of Great Brittain and Ireland, that he is aged thirty years, and by profession a Catholic Clergyman, that he sailed from the City of Liverpool in England on the twentieth day of September eighteen hundred and thirty three and landed in the City of Charleston in the state of Southcarolina on the seventh day of November of the same year. That it is bonafide his intention to become a citizen of the United States, being Sincerely attached to the well being and good order of the Same. That he hereby forever renounces all allegiance to all and every foreign Prince, potentate, State, or Kingdom whatever, and particularly to Victoria Alexandria, Queen of Great Brittain and Ireland, whereof he was late a Subject, and that he will Support and defend the Constitution of the United States, being Sincerely attached to the principles thereof.

James Graham

We, the undersigned Citizens of the United States, do hereby Certify that we have been for Some time past acquainted with Dr James Graham, the within declarant, and that during that time he has behaved himself as a moral upright man and that he believes from our knowledge of his Character that it is bonafide his intention to become a citizen of the United States. October 15th 1838

James H. Campbell
Th° C. Evans

Georgia }
Muscogee County } Personally appeared in Open Court James Graham, the within declarant, who after being duly sworn deposeth & Saith that the facts Stated in the within declaration are true in Substance and in fact.

James Graham

[3] Muscogee Superior Court
Monday the 15th October 1838

Sworn to and Subscribed in Open Court this 15th day of October Eighteen hundred and thirty eight.

(copy furnished) Joseph Sturgis, J. S. C. C. C.

The Court adjourned to meet again on the Second monday in December next.

Muscogee Superior Court Monday 10th December 1838

The Court met according to adjournment, present the Honorable Marshall J. Wellborn, Judge of the Superior Courts in the Chattahoochee Circuit.

The following persons whose names are hereto annexed appeared anwered to their names as Special and Grandjurors.

1. John Johnson
2. Anderson Hunt
3. Augustus Hayward
4. Emanuel Ezekel
5. Mansfiel Torrence
6. Frederick Toby
7. Thomas Hoxey
8. William Clark
16. Jonathan P. Jackson
17. James M. Russel
18. Jeremiah McCoy
19. John D. Jordon
20. Charles King
21. Theophilus P. Bryan
22. George Smith
23. Hiram Fuller

9. George A. Norris
10. Wm L. Jeter
11. Wm P. Malone
12. Henry K. Hill
13. Henry Mims
14. William S. Chipley
15. ~~John H. Colquitt~~ Willis P. Baker

[4] Muscogee Superior Court Monday December 10th 1838

Petit Jury N° 1 Sworn

1. ~~Richard~~ Umphry Rowel
2. Daniel Brown
3. Edward Kelly
4. Randol Tillory
5. Willson Culpepper
6. James Ryals
7. Robert Higdon
8. Zepheniah Parker
9. Isaac Webb
10. John McGough
11. Rhode L. Smith
12. Joseph Phelps

N° 2

1. Alfred T. Brannon
2. James Jernigan
3. Seaborn Eley
4. Jacob Johnson
5. Stephen Beck
6. Thomas Motley
7. Price Davis
8. ~~William~~ Willson Gordy
9. Elias Howell Francis Jepson T.
10. Thomas V. Miller
11. Abner Hill
12. Charles F. Spillers

Bank of Milledgeville }
     vs   } Assumpsit
Alexander McDougald }

Jury N° 1. We, the Jury, find for the Plaintiff the sum of four thousand dollars principal & three dollars protest fee, with interest & cost of suit.

                              John McGough, Foreman

James Harril   }
     vs   } Assumpsit
Roberson & Holcomb }

Jury N° 1. We, the Jury, find for the Plaintiff the sum of four hundred & twenty eight dollars and forty cents principal, with interest & cost of suit.

John McGough, Form

Bank of Milledgeville }
     vs   } Assumpsit
Alfred Iverson   }

Jury N° 1. We, the Jury, find for the Plaintiff the Sum of four thousand dollars principal and three dollars protest fee, with interest and Cost of Suit.

John McGough, Form

[5] Muscogee Superior Court December adjourned term 1838 Monday 10 Decr 1838

William & W. Toney }
     vs   } Assumpsit
William H. Smith   }
Surviving Copartner }
of Ge° W. Pinhorn   }

Jury N° 1. We, the Jury, find for the Plaintiff two hundred and forty dollars & eleven cents, with interest & cost.

John McGough, Form

Hampton S. Smith }
     vs   } Debt
William P. M.   }

I confess Judgment to the plaintiff for five hundred and thirty dollars, with interest & cost.

Wm P. McKeen

Walter T. Colquitt }
     vs   } Assumpsit
Theobald Howard }

We, the Jury, find for the plaintiff fifteen hundred & six dollars, with interest & cost.

John McGough, F. M.

Hampton W. Hill }
    vs   } Assumpsit
George W. Pinhorn }
& John H. Ware }

We, the Jury, find for the plaintiff One hundred & Seventy five dollars, with interest & Cost.

John McGough, F. M.

S. P. Church & Co }
    vs   } Asumpsit
Carnes & Tatum }

We, the Jury, find for the Plaintiff four hundred & fifty three dollars, with interest & Cost.

J^{no} McGough, F. M.

E. S. Greenwood }
    vs   } Debt
Philo D. Woodruff }

I confess Judgment to the plaintiff for Two hundred and ninety two dollars & fifty six cents, with interest & cost of suit.

J. N. & J. M. Bethune, Def^{ts} At^{ys}

Hampton S. Smith }
    vs   } Debt
W. B. Robinson & Co }

We, the Jury, find for the Plaintiff one hundred & twenty five dollars, with interest & Cost.

         Jnº McGough, F. M.

[6]

Fellows, Wadsworth & Cº }
   vs   } Assumpsit
John G. Mulford }

We, the Jury, find for the Plaintiff Three hundred & forty one dollars & sixty six cents, with interest & Cost.

         Jnº McGough, F. M.

Packer, Prentice & Cº }
   vs   } Assumpsit
John G. Mulford }

We, the Jury, find for the Plaintiff Three hundred & thirty two dollars & sixty cents, with interest & Cost of suit.

         Jnº McGough, F. M.

Wright & Harris, for the }
use of Hardy Moy }
   vs   } Debt
Abraham Gilbert }

We, the Jury find for the Plaintiff Three hundred & twenty three dollars & sixty cents, with interest & cost.

         Jnº McGough, F. M.

D. Hungerford & Cº }
   vs   } Debt
Alpha K. Ayer }

I Confess Judgment to the Plaintiff for fifty two dollars & thirty nine cents, with interst & Cost of

A. K. Ayer

McClary, Asher & C º }
    vs   } Debt
Ayer & Hogg   }

I Confess Judgment to the Plaintiff for fourteen hundred & seventy two dollars & sixty six cents, with interest & Cost.

Campbell, McDougald, & Watson, Def^ts Att^ys

Lewis J. Davis }
    vs   } Debt
John D. Howell }

Settled.

Bank of Milledgeville }
    vs   } Assumpsit
Alfred Iverson   }

We, the Jury, find for the Plaintiff the sum of four thousand dollars principal and three dollars protest fee, with interest & cost of suit.

Jn º McGough, F. M.

Foster & Fogle }
    vs   } Debt
Isaac Mitchell }

I Confess Judgment to the Plaintiffs for four hundred dollars, with interest & cost.

J. N. & J. M. Bethune, Def^ts Att^ys

[7] Muscogee Superior Court December Adjourned term Monday 10th December 1838

George L. Middlebrook }
    vs   } Assumpsit & Bail
A. Turner & C°   }

We, the Jury, find for the Plaintiff three hundred and fifty dollars 12½ Cts, interest & cost.

                        Jn° McGough, F. M.

James N. Bethune }
    vs   } Assumpsit
Slaton Henly   }

We, the Jury, find for the Plaintiff ninety six dollars & twenty Eight Cents principal debt, with interest & cost of suit.

                        Jn° McGough, F. M.

Francis Jepson, who }
sues for the use &c }
    vs   } Assumpsit
Allen G. Bass   }

I Confess Judgment to the Plaintiffs for one hundred and twenty nine dollars principal, with interest & cost of suit.

                        Thomas G. Gordon, Defts Atty

Henry Matthews }
    vs   } Debt
Thomas C. McKeen}

We, the Jury, find for the plaintiff sixty three dollars principal, with interest & cost of suit.

                        Jn° McGough, F. M.

William McBride }
    vs   } Debt
Kensey & Short }
& T. A. Brannon }

We, the Jury, find for the Plaintiff three hundred dollars principal, with interest & cost of suit.

                                  Jnº McGough, F. M.

Walter T. Colquitt }
    vs   } Assumpsit
Morgan Jones   }

I Confess Judgment to the Plaintiff for the sum of one hundred & fifty nine dollars, with interest & cost of suit & consent that this copy stand in lieu of the Original declaration & process.

                                  Morgan Jones

Samuel Hooper }
    vs   } Assumpsit
William Pace, Jʳ }

I Confess Judgment to the plaintiff for three hundred dollars, with interest & cost.

                              J. N. & J. M. Bethune, Def Attʸ

[8]

Elias B. Crane }
    vs   } Assumpsit
Luther Blake }

We, the Jury, find for the Plaintiff five hundred dollars & three dollars protest fee, with interest & cost.

                                  John McGough, F. M.

Francis Jepson }
    vs   } Assumpsit
Jacob D. Paul & }
Eli B. W. Spivey }

We, the Jury, find for the Plaintiff Two Hundred dollars, with interest & Cost of suit.

                            Jn° McGough, F. M.

Lewis Dowdle }
    vs   } Debt
Henry C. Phelps }

We, the Jury, find for the Plaintiff Two hundred and eighty dollars, with interest & cost.

                            Jn° McGough, F. M.

James Abbercrombie }
    vs   } Assumpsit
Philo D. Woodruff }
& Ja^s N. Bethune }

We Confess Judgment to the Plaintiff for the sum of three thousand Eight hundred and forty dollars, with interest & cost of suit.

                            J. N. & J. M. Bethune, Def^t Att^{ys}

Crawford & McKim }
    vs   } Assumpsit
Richard Hooper }

We, the Jury, find for the Plaintiffs Twenty six hundred and ninety five dollars & eighty one cents, with interest & Cost of suit & Six dollars for cost of protest.

                            John McGough, F. M.

Turentine, Andrews & Watson }
      vs   } Debt
William Brazil   }

We, the Jury, find for the Plaintiff forty six dollars & ninety three cents principal, with interest & cost of suit.

                                      John McGough, F. M.

Turentine, Andrews & Watson }
      vs   } Debt
Slaton Henly   }

We, the Jury, find for the plaintiffs seventy three dollars principal, with interest & cost of suit.

                                      Jn° McGough, F. M.

[9]   Monday December 10th 1838

Jacob Fogle   }
      vs   } Assumpsit
James H. Shorter, Admtr. & }
Sophia H. Shorter, Admtrx. }
of Eli S. Shorter, Dec^d }

We, the Jury, find for the Plaintiff Two hundred & eight dollars & seventy eight cents, with interest & cost.

                                      John McGough, F. M.

Lewis Dowdle   }
      vs   } Debt
Henry C. Phelps }

We, the Jury, find for the Plaintiff Three hundred & thirteen dollars & thirty eight cents, with interest & cost.

                                      Jn° McGough, F. M.

Ordered that all cases upon Open accounts be set down for trial on friday next unless Continued.

Edward W. Wright } Debt in the Superior Court of Muscogee County
      vs   } returnable to the April Term of said Court
Edward Delony   } for the year 1838

It appearing to the Court that the declaration & process in the above stated case was regularly sued out, copied, & served, & that said case was placed on the docket of said Court, and Judgment by default entered thereon at the last April Term of said Court, and it further appearing to the Court that said Original declaration & process, with the Sheriff entry of service thereon, together with the Clerk's docket of said case, were destroyed by fire. And it appearing to the court that the Copy declaration now filed in court is in substance a true Copy of said Original declaration & process, Sheriff's entry thereon. It is therefore ordered by the Court that the same be established in lieu of said Original as destroyed & that said case be docketed & the entry of "Judgment by default" be made thereon.

Samuel A. Bailey }
    vs   } Assumpsit
H. Mims & C° }

same }
    vs   } Assumpsit
Thomas Hoxey }

Same }
    vs   } Assumpsit
Hampton S. Smith }

Same }
    vs   } Assumpsit
Same }

Same }
    vs   } Assumpsit
Walter H. Weems }
& John Fontaine }

Same }
    vs   } Assumpsit
Same }

[10]

Same }
    vs   } Assumpsit
William P. Malone }

Same }
    vs   } Assumpsit
Isaac Mitchell }

Same }
  vs } Assumpsit
Same }

Same }
  vs } Assumpsit
Henry Mims }

Same }
  vs } Assumpsit
Same }

Same }
  vs } Assumpsit
John Warren }

Same }
  vs } Assumpsit
Wm H. Mitchell }

Same }
  vs } Assumpsit
Thos A. Brannon }
William P. Malone }
& H. Mims & Co }

Same }
  vs } Assumpsit
Alfred M. Terry }
John Johnson }
securities }

Joseph Poythress }
  vs } Debt
Isaac Mitchell }

Georgia }
Muscogee County } Personally Samuel A. Bailey, Plaintiff, and Plaintiff's Attorney in the above mentioned cases, who being sworn in open Court, saith that the Original declarations in the above mentioned cases were filed to the April Term last past of this Court, that the same were destroyed by the late Conflagration of the Clerk's office in the City of Columbus, that the Copies herewith filed with the process and the entries of the Sheriff thereon are to the best of the recollection, information, and belief of the deponent Copies of the said Originals as they existed in the Clerk's office at the time of the destruction thereof, and the deponent further saith that shortly after the Calling of the appearance docket at the last term of this Court this deponent examined the said docket, and that the entry of default was made in each & every of said Cases in the hand writing of the presiding Judge of said Court. Sworn to & Subscribed in open Court this 10th day of December 1838.

Gerard Burch, Clk   Saml A. Bailey

It Appearing to the Court by the foregoing Affidavit that the Original declarations, together with the process and entries thereon, were destroyed at the late Burning of the Clerks office in the city and that said cases were regularly called and defaulted at the last Term of this Court. It is on motion ordered that the Copies herewith filed be established, taken, and held in lieu of said Originals and that the said cases be returned to the docket in the same situation in which they Stood at the time of their destruction.

[12] Monday 10th December 1838

Seaborn Jones }
    vs } Assumpsit
Wm H. Harper, Admtr }
of Ja^s J. Hill }

We, the Jury, find for the Plaintiff one hundred dollars principal, with interest & Cost of suit.

                Jn° McGough, F. M.

Augustus Howard, Guardn }
    vs } Assumpsit
M. N. Clarke & }
J. P. Jackson }

We, the Jury, find for the Plaintiff Two hundred & sixty three dollars & fifty cents principal, with interest & cost of suit.

                Jn° McGough, F. M.

Crawford & McKim }
    vs } Assumpsit
H. Mims & C° }

We Confess Judgment to the Plaintiffs for the sum of two Two thousand six hundred & ninety five dollars and Eighty one cents, with interest & Cost of suit and three dollars Cost of protest.

                J. N. & J. M. Bethune, Def^{ts} Att^{ys}

E. S. Greenwood & C° }
    vs   } Debt
Philo D. Woodruff }

I Confess Judgment to the Plaintiffs for the sum of Three thousand six hundred and fifty seven dollars and forty one cents, with interest & Cost of suit.

                        J. N. & J. M. Bethune, Def^{ts} Att^{ys}

Stewart & Fontaine }
    vs   } Debt
Bluford Sanders }

We, the Jury, find for the plaintiffs forty one dollars & fifty two cents principal, with interest & cost of suit.

                        Jn° McGough, F. M.

Justices of the Inferior }
Court of Talbot County }
    vs   } Assumpsit
Edward Delony }

Shaham, Beall & Reynolds }   Daniel Davis }
    vs   } Assumpsit   vs   } Assumpsit
A. B. Worsham }   Josiah Roberts }

Georgia }
Muscogee County } Decr adjourned Term Superior Court

Personally came Alexander W. Sneed into open Court and, after being duly sworn, deposeth & saith that the Original declarations in the above stated cases have been destroyed, that the annexed Copies are in substance Copies of said Originals, and that he has been informed by the Sheriff that the same were served within the time prescribed by law.

Sworn to and Subscribed   A. W. Sneed

[13] Ordered by the Court that the accompanning Copies be established in lieue of the lost Originals and that the same be entered on the Docket.

It Appearing to the Court, that the Original declaration & process in the case of John S. Robertson vs James N. Bethune brought to the April Term of this Court hath been lately destroyed by fire, & it further appearing that the annexed is a substantial Copy of said Original papers. On Motion, ordered that said Copy be established in lieue of said lost Original & that said case be reinstated upon the docket.

Henry King }
  vs   } Assumpsit
Lemuel Jepson }

We, the Jury, find for the Plaintiff sixty five dollars principal, with interest & cost of suit.

          Jn° McGough, F. M.

Samuel Lytle }
  vs   } Debt
Andrew P. Jones }

I Confess Judgment to the Plaintiff for forty five dollars & thirteen cents principal, with interest & cost of suit.

        Campbell, McDougald & Watson, Def^{ts} Att^{ys}

Muscogee Superior Court April Term 1838

James H. Shorter }		Same }	
vs } Assumpsit		vs } Assumpsit	
Asa Bates & }		William P. Malone }	
Thomas C. Evans }			

Same }		Same }	
vs } Assumpsit		vs } Assumpsit	
Asa Bates }		Charles L. Bass }	

Same }		Same }	
vs } Assumpsit		vs } Assumpsit	
Elisha S. Norton }		Thomas Hoxey }	

Same vs Peter V. Guerry, Senr Richard Jones S. R. Bonner & J. B. Green	} Assumpsit	Same vs Thomas C. Evans } Assumpsit

Same
   vs   } Assumpsit
Ben^j P. Tarver }

Same
   vs   } Assumpsit
Thomas G. Gordon }

Same
   vs   } Assumpsit
John D. Jordan }

[14] Monday 10th December 1838

Dana Hungerford, for the }
use of James H. Shorter }
   vs   } Assumpsit
Lucian A. Boudre }

Same
   vs   } Assumpsit
Charles L. Bass }

James H. Shorter }
   vs   } Assumpsit
Isaac Mitchell, Pr. }
& B. A. Cosby }
Endorser }

Same
   vs   } Assumpsit
James S. Calhoun }

Same
   vs   } Assumpsit
Timothy Collins, Principal }
& T. & M. Evans, Endorser

Dana Hungerford, for the use of
James H. Shorter }
   vs   } Assumpsit
   John A. Urquhart }

Same
   vs   } Assumpsit
Thomas C. McKeen }

James H. Shorter }
   vs   } Assumpsit
Richard Hooper }

Same }
  vs } Assumpsit
Timothy Collins, Prin. }
Underwood, Torrance & C° }
Endrs,. & Ben^j P. Tarver }

Same }
  vs } Assumpsit
Henry Mims }

Same }
  vs } Assumpsit
Calhoun & Bass, Princpl. }
& J. L. Lewis, Endr. }

Same }
  vs } Assumpsit
John B. Peabody }

Same }
  vs } Assumpsit
Wm B. Robinson & C° }

Same }
  vs } Assumpsit
Moore & Tarver }

Same }
  vs } Assumpsit
Same }

Same }
  vs } Assumpsit
T. & M. Evans }

Same }
  vs } Assumpsit
John Warren }

Same }
  vs } Assumpsit
Battle A. Sorsby, Princpl. }
Read & Talbot, Endorsers }

[15]

Same }
  vs } Assumpsit
James S. Calhoun }

Same }
  vs } Assumpsit
James H. Campbell, Pr. }
John D. Howell, End. }
& Theobald Howard }

Same }
  vs } [blot] Asspt
Dana Hungerford }

Same }
  vs } Assumpsit
William J. Rylander }

Same }
  vs } Assumpsit
Thomas Hoxey }

Same }
  vs } Assumpsit
H. C. Phelps & C° }

Same }
   vs } Assumpsit
John T. Walker }

Same }
   vs } Assumpsit
Wm W. Pooll }

Same }
   vs } Assumpsit
Kenneth McKenzie }

Same }
   vs } Assumpsit
Timothy G. McCrary }

Same }
   vs } Assumpsit
Edward Cary }

Same }
   vs } Assumpsit
James Rankin }

Same }
   vs } Assumpsit
Calhoun & Bass }

James H. Shorter, Admtr. & }
Sophia H. Shorter, Admtrx. }
of Eli S. Shorter, Dec^d }
   vs }
Daniel McDougald }

Same }
   vs } Assumpsit
Same }

Same }
   vs } Assumpsit
Moore & Tarver }

Same }
   vs } Assumpsit
M. W. Thweatt & }
Thacker B. Howard }

Same }
   vs } Assumpsit
Thos C. Evans }
Matt R. Evans }
& John H. Ware }

[16]   Monday 10th December 1838

James H. Shorter, Admtr. & }
Sophia H. Shorter, Admtrx. }
of Eli S. Shorter, Dec^d }
   vs }
Solomon Averitt }

James H. Shorter, Admtr. & }
Sophia H. Shorter, Admtrx. }
of Eli S. Shorter, Dec^d }
      vs   }
Philo D. Woodruff &   }
Carnot Woodruff   }

Muscogee Superior Court October Adjourned Term 1838

David Golightly, Attorney for Plaintiffs in the case above &within stated, being in Open Court duly sworn, saith that the Originals, declarations, & process In Each of said cases has been lost by fire, & that the Copies here shown to the Court are true Copies in substance of the original declarations, process, & Sheriff's return in said Cases to the best of his knowledge & belief.

Sworn to in open Court this 11th Decr 1838.

Gerard Burch, Clk   D. Golightly

It is therefore ordered by the Court that the said Copies be established in lieue of said Originals.

Thomas Grant   }   Wittich, Greenwood & Co }
      vs   } Assumpsit   for the use of Thomas Grant }
Isaac Mitchell   }   vs   } Assumpsit
                                             Isaac Mitchell   }

The death of the plaintiff having been suggested in each of the above cases & Sci fas having issued Making Mary P. Grant Admtrx. & Thomas F. Foster Admtr. Ordered that they be made parties & the actions proceed.

Battle A. Sorsby   }
      vs   } Debt
Daniel D. Ridenhour }

We, the Jury, find for the plaintiff one hundred and fifty three dollars & twelve cents, with interest & cost of suit.

                                            Jno McGough, F. M.

Battle A. Sorsby }
    vs   } Debt
Eli B. W. Spivey }

We, the Jury, find for the Plaintiff one hundred & sixty four dollars & seven cents, with interest & cost of suit.

                              Jnº McGough, F. M.

Thomas Moore }
    vs   } Case
Garland B. Terry }
Endorser   }

We, the Jury, find for the plaintiff two hundred dollars principal, with interest & cost of suit.

                              Jnº McGough, F. M.

[17]

The State   }
    vs   } Simple Larceny
Lorenzo Dow Glenn }

True Bill.   Mansfield Torrance, Foreman

The State   }
    vs   } Passing a forged Check
Thomas Thustand }

True Bill.   Mansfield Torrance, Foreman

Battle A. Sorsby }
    vs   } Debt & Bail
Thomas B. Ozment }

We, the Jury, find for the plaintiff thirty one dollars & ninety five cents, with interest & cost.

Jn° McGough, F. M.

J. W. & R. Leavitt }
    vs   } Debt
Cary & Day   }

I Confess Judgment to the Plaintiffs for the sum of four hundred and forty eight dollars and forty four cents, with interest & cost of suit, and three dollars cost of Protest.

Colquitt, Holt, & Echols, Att^{ys} for Def^t Cary

The Court adjourned to meet again tomorrow morning at nine O'clock.

Marshall J. Wellborn, J. S. C. C. C.

[18] Muscogee County Superior Court Tuesday 11th December 1838

The Court met according to Adjournment, present the
Honorable Marshall J. Wellborn

Homer Hurd   }
    vs   } Assumpsit
John D. Jordan }

Jury N° 1. We, the Jury, find for the Plaintiff the sum of four hundred dollars, with protest & interest & cost of suit.

Jn° McGough, Form.

Sterling Edwards }
    vs   } Assumpsit
Mansel H. Torrence}

Jury Nº 1. We, the Jury, find for the Plaintiff the Sum of thirty five dollars, with interest & costs of suit.

           Jnº McGough, Form.

James E. Sloan }
  vs   } Assumpsit
Theobald Howard }
& John Taylor   }

Jury Nº 1. We, the Jury, find for the Plaintiff the sum of Five hundred dollars, with interest & cost of suit & protest fee.

           Jnº McGough, Form.

George Cooper   }
  vs   } Assumpsit
Thomas G. Gordon }
& Allen G. Bass, makers }
& J. S. Calhoun, indorser }

Jury Nº 1. We, the Jury, find for the Plaintiff the Sum of One thousand dollars, with interest & cost of suit.

           Jnº McGough, Form.

D. Hungerford & Cº }
  vs   } Debt
Pool, Lively & McCrary}

Jury Nº 1. We, the Jury, find for the Plaintiff against William W. Pool and Peleg R. McCrary Three thousand eight hundred and twenty seven dollars & eighty cents, with interest from the thirteenth day of August eighteen hundred & thirty eight and cost of suit.

           Jnº McGough, Form.

The State   }
  vs   } Assault & Battery
Bird F. Robertson}

True Bill.   Mansfield Torrence, foreman

[19]   Tuesday 11ᵗʰ December 1838

George Hargraves   }
    vs   } Assumpsit
William B. Roberson }

Jury Nº 1. We, the Jury, find for the Plaintiff thirteen hundred and sixty one dollars & Sixty three cents principal, with interest & cost of suit.

                          Jnº McGough, Form.

George Hargraves }
    vs   } Assumpsit
Charles L. Bass }

~~We, the Jury find~~ I confess Judgment for the Plaintiff for thirteen hundred and sixty one dollars & Sixty three cents, with interest and cost of reserving the right of Appeal.

                       Thoˢ G. Gordon, Defᵗˢ attʸ

William Nelms   }
    vs   } Attachment in assumpsit
Thomas R. Gold }

Jury Nº 1. We, the Jury, find for the Seven hundred dollars, with interest & cost of suit and three dollars cost of Protest.

                          Jnº McGough, Form.

John W. Rinaldi, indorsee   }
    vs   } Assumpsit
Robison & Hand ~~& James Kirlin~~ }

James Kirlin ~~Jacob M. Guerry~~ }
    vs   } Debt
Jacob M. Guerry   }

James Kirlin }
    vs   } Debt
Lemuel Jepson }

Georgia, Muscogee County It appearing to the Court that the original petitions & process's in the above stated cases were destroyed in the burning of the Court House & Clerk's Office & that the Copies Submitted to the Court are in Substance Copies of the Originals, except the dates of the processes not put in, and that the defendants were duly served with Copies. It is on Motion ordered that Said copies be established in Lieu of the originals.

William Roswell }
    vs   } Attachment
James Suddith }

In Muscogee Superior Court April term 1838.

It appearing to the court that the original Attachment & petition &c were destroyed in the burning of the Court House & Clerk's Office & that the Copy Submitted to the Court, except dates, is a Copy of the Original burned, it is on Motion ordered that the Said Copy be established in lieu of the Original.

[20] Tuesday December 11th 1838

The Court Adjourned to meet again tomorrow morning at Nine O'Clock.

Wednesday December 12th 1838

The Court met according to Adjournment. Present, the Honorable Marshall J. Wellborn.

The Insurance Bank of Columbus }
    vs   } Assumpsit
Burton Hepburn }

We, the Jury, find for the Plaintiff Twenty Six thousand dollars, with interest & cost of suit and three dollars cost of Protest.

                                      Jn° McGough, F. M.

The Insurance Bank of Columbus }
        vs   } Assumpsit
Edward Cary   }

I Confess Judgment to the Plaintiff for the sum of three thousand five hundred dollars, with interest & cost of suit and three dollars for cost of Protest.

                                       Edwd Cary

The Insurance Bank of Columbus }
        vs   } Assumpsit
Calhoun & Bass   }

I Confess Judgment to the Plaintiffs for three thousand and five hundred dollars, with interest & cost of suit and three dollars for cost of Protest.

John B. Guedron }
     vs   } Debt
James M. Mitchell }

We, the Jury, find for the Plaintiff the sum of forty five dollars and fifty cents, with interest & costs of suit.

                                  Jn° McGough, F. M.

John B. Guedron }
     vs   } Debt
Jacob M. Guerry   }

We, the Jury, find for the Plaintiff one hundred & twenty nine dollars and fifty cents, with interest & cost of suit.

                                  Jn° McGough, F. M.

John B. Guedron }
     vs   } Debt
Henry C. Anderson }

We, the Jury, find for the Plaintiff the sum of forty nine dollars, with interest & cost of suit.

Jn° McGough, F. M.

Henry Matthews }
     vs   } Debt
James H. Jones, Jr }

We, the Jury, find for the Plaintiff for ninety one dollars & 94 cents, with interest & cost of suit.

Jn° McGough, F. M.

[21]

The State   }
    vs   } Passing a forged Check
Thomas Thustand }

Nollo Prossequi, 1838.   Henry L. Benning, Sol. Genl. C. C.

William Dougherty }
    vs   } Assumpsit and verdict for the Plaintiffs for twenty two
William P. McKeen } hundred & ten dollars, with interest & Costs & three dollars for protest fee

The defendant, being dissatisfied with the verdict of the Jury rendered in the above cause and having paid all Costs and demanded an Appeal, brings ~~Randal~~ James R. Jones and tenders him as his security, and they, the said William P. McKeen & James R. Jones acknowledge themselves Jointly & Severally bound to William Dougherty, the Plaintiff, for the payment of the eventual condemnation money in said Cause.

In Testimony whereof, they have hereunto Set their hands & Seals the 12th day of December 1838.

Test. Gerard Burch, Clk   Wm P. McKeen
                                            J. R. Jones

William Dougherty }
     vs   } Assumpsit and verdict for the Plaintiffs for twenty two
James R. Jones   } hundred & ten dollars, with interest & Costs & three
dollars for Protest fee

The defendant, being dissatisfied with the verdict of the Jury rendered in the above cause and having paid all cost and demanded appeal, brings William P. McKeen and tenders him as his Security, and they, the said James R. Jones & William P. McKeen, acknowledge themselves Jointly & Severally bound unto William Dougherty, the Plaintiff, for the payment of the eventual condemnation money in said Cause.

In Testimony whereof, they have hereunto Set their hands & Seals the 12th day of December 1838.

Test. Gerard Burch, Clk   J. R. Jones
                                         Wm P. McKeen

William Roswell }
     vs   } Attachment
James Suddith   }

Georgia, Muscogee County. Order to apply money raised on attachment to Judgment in said October adjourned Term 1838. It appearing to the Court that Seventy one dollars has been raised on Said Attachment by the Sale of perishable property. It is on motion ordered that the Clerk pay over Said Amount to Plaintiff's fi fa, deducting therefrom the Costs & Charges.

[22]   Tuesday December 12th 1838
        Muscogee Superior Court October adjourned term 1838

Personally appeared in Open Court Nathan P. Willard, who after being duly sworn, deposeth & saith that a number of Copy notices to Creditors filed by this deponent in the Clerk's Office of the Superior Court of said County of Muscogee have been destroyed by the late Conflagration and that the Copies now filed are true & correct Copies of them so destroyed. And that the said notices were so filed in due time and in terms of the Law.

Sworn to in Open Court December 12th 1838. N. P. Willard

The State   }
    vs   } Purjury
James R. Lyons   }

It appearing to the Court that Daniel McDougald & James C. Watson were Bail for defendant in the above Stated Case for his appearance at this term of the Court. And whereas, it appears to the Court that they have Surrendered into the Custody of the Sheriff of said County their principal, James R. Lyons, in Satisfaction of said Bond. It is on motion Ordered by the Court that said Bail be discharged & that a exhonerater be entered on Said Bail Bond.

Charles D. Stewart   }   Grieve & Rankin   }
        vs   } Debt   vs   } Debt
Jonathan P. Jackson } 665   Jonathan P. Jackson   } 671

Garret Hallenbeck   }   James Rankin, bearer }
        vs   } Debt   vs   } Assumpsit
Jacob M. Guerry &   } 672   John J. Willson   } 677
Luther Blake   }

Garret Hallenbeck   }   John Logan   }
        vs   } Debt   vs   } Assumpsit
Jacob M. Guerry &   } 678   Benjamin G. Kenny, maker } 681
Edward Delany   }   Thomas A. Brannon &   }
                                             George W. Short, Guarantees }

[23]

James S. Norman, Admtr. &   }
Henrietta White, admtrx. of }
John S. White, deceased   }
        vs   } Assumpsit
John J. Willson   }

Georgia   }
Muscogee County   } It appearing to the Court from the admissions of parties defendants that the Copies Submitted in the above stated cases for April term 1838 are true Copies of the Original petitions &c lost or destroyed by fire in the burning of the Court house and Clerk's Office and that said defendants were

duly & legally Served with Copies of the same. It is on motion ordered that the said Copies be established in lieu of the Originals.

The State }
    vs } Perjury
James R. Lyons }

True Bill.   Mansfield Torrance, Forman

William Williamson }
    vs } Ca sa
Absalom Echols }

It Appearing to the Court that the above stated ca sa has been lost & destroyed & that defendant has been arrested & that he gave Michael W. Pearry as security on said Ca sa Bond & that said Ca sa Bond has been lost or destroyed. It is therefore on motion ordered by the Court that the annexed Copies be established instanter in lieu of said lost Originals.

Henry Matthews }
    vs } Debt
James H. Jones, J^r }

We, the Jury, find for the Plaintiff for ninety one dollars & ninety four Cents principal, with interest & cost of suit.

                                       Jn° McGough, F. M.

Samuel Lytle }
    vs } Assumpsit
Thos J. Reed }

We, the Jury, find for the Plaintiff for one hundred & fifty nine dollars sixty seven & half cents principal, with interest & cost of suit.

                                       Jn° McGough, F. M.

William P. McKeen, Cr. }
  vs   } Case
James R. Jones & }
Elisha S. Norton }

We, the Jury, find for the Plaintiff for one hundred & twenty four dollars & twenty Cents principal, with interest & cost of suit.

         Jn° McGough, F. M.

The Court adjourned to meet again tomorrow morning at nine O'clock.

         Marshall J. Wellborn, J. S. C. C. C.

[24}   Muscogee Superior Court October Term 1838
     Wednesday the 12th December 1838

The Court met according to adjournment, present the Honorable Marshall J. Wellborn.

James S. Calhoun}   James S. Calhoun }
  vs   } assumpsit   vs   } Assumpsit
M. D. Roberson }   C. W. Buckley &C}
& Thos J. Hand }

The Farmers Bank of Chattahoochee }
    vs   } assumpsit
William D. Hargroves   }

The Sames }
  vs   } assumpsit
James Rankin }

Same   }   The Same }
  vs   } assumpsit   vs   } assumpsit
Richard Hooper }   Joseph Davidson }

The Same vs John J. Willson. assumpsit

Fort, Townsend & C° vs Roberson & Williams. Assumpsit

Calhoun & Bass vs John J. Willson. Assumpsit

Calhoun & Bass vs M. W. Thweatt. Assumpsit

The Same vs Nicholas M. Lewis. Assumpsit

James S. Calhoun vs John Rounds. assumpsit

The Same vs William McGee. assumpsit

The Farmers Bank of Chattahoochee vs John A. Campbell. Assumpt

[25] It appearing to the Court that the Original declarations of which the foregoing is a list of the Copies for Muscogee Superior Court at April term 1838 have been all burnt with the Clerk's Office with all the papers therewith attached. It is ordered by the Court that the Copies as above Stated be established instanter in lieu of the said Originals so destroyed and that the dates of process and service on said Copies be established in lieu of said Originals.

Declarations returnable to October Term 1838

George Field vs Seaborn Jones. Assumpsit

The Same vs The Same. Assumpsit

The Same vs T. & M. Evans. Assumpsit

The Same vs The Same. Assumpsit

The Same vs John Fontaine. Assumpsit

The Same vs The Same. Assumpsit

Benedict & Wetmore vs A. F. Brannon & Co. Assumpsit

Alexander Moss vs James W. Glenn. Assumpsit

Benedict & Wetmore vs Wm S. Hartsfield & Co. Assumpsit

Same vs W^m & W. Toney. Assumpsit

Bostwick & Taylor vs T. T. Gammage & C°. Assumpsit

John Schley vs George C. Hodge. Assumpsit

The Same vs The Same. Assumpsit

Elizabeth Billups vs H. D. Baldwin. Attachment

Declarations returned to April Term 1838

Dikeman & Mills vs John G. Mulford. Assumpsit

Lemuel H. Hamilton vs E. S. Greenwood. Assumpsit

[26]　　　　　　　Wednesday December 12th 1838

Lemuel H. Hamilton vs Isaac Mitchell. Assumpsit

Michael Harned vs Jacob M. Johnson. Assumpsit

Olcott, McKisson & C° vs W^{m} & W. Toney. Assumpsit

The Same vs The Same. Assumpsit

John Cowart, Junr vs Allen J. Mims & James S. Walker.

Crawford & McKim vs W^{m} & W. Toney.

Samuel Thompson vs Calhoun & Bass.

William G. Porter vs Moore & Tarver.

Greenway, Henry & C° vs W^{m} & W. Toney. Assumpsit

George Field vs Sullivan & Ryder. Assumpsit

The Same vs Chisholm & Collins. Assumpsit

D. Hungerford & C° vs William Rogers. Assumpsit

The Same vs Pool, Lively & McCrary. Assumpsit

Georgia }
Muscogee County } Personally appeared John Schley, Attorney at Law in the above cases, in open Court and, being duly sworn, deposeth & saith that the declarations in the above stated cases were burnt when the Clerk's office was burned and that the Copies hereunto annexed he believes to be Copies in substance of the declaration, processes, and returns of the Sheriff in said Cases so far as it comes to his own knowledge and such as is derived from the knowledge or information of others he belives to be Correct in substance. Sworn to in open Court this 11th December 1838.

Gerard Burch, Clk						John Schley

It appearing to the Court that the original declarations in the cases stated above were destroyed by fire at the time the Clerk's Office of said County was burned and from the affidavit of John Schley, Attorney at Law in said cases, that the Copies hereunto annexed and presented are Copies in substance of said declarations, process, and Sheriff's returns thereon. On Motion, ordered by the Court that said Copies hereunto annexed

[27] and presented be and are hereby established in lieu of said Originals so burned and destroyed.

John Doe, on the several Demises }
of Allen Davis & Thomas Motley }
      vs } Ejectment
Richard Roe, casual ejector & }
Henry Mann, tenant in possession }

We, the Jury, find for the Plaintiff the premises in dispute & twenty four dollars mean profits.

                          John McGough, F. M.

Howard & Wittich }
    vs } Case
Alpha K. Ayer }

Settled at Def[s] Cost.

Richard W. Morris }
     vs   } Debt
Joseph Davidson }

We, the Jury, find for the Plaintiff for the sum of Two hundred & seventy six dollars and eighty seven cents, with interest & cost of suit.

                            Jn° McGough, F. M.

Edward Cary }
     vs   } Attachment
A. H. Falconer }

We, the Jury, find for the Plaintiff the sum of three hundred dollars, with interest and cost of suit.

                            Jn° McGough, F. M.

Lewis J. Dowdle }
     vs   } Assumpsit
James H. Shorter, Admtr. & }
Sophia H. Shorter, Admtrx. }
of Eli S. Shorter, Dec^d }

We, the Jury, find for the plaintiff two hundred and eighty dollars, with interest & Cost of suit.

                            Jn° McGough, F. M.

Gardner Ford }
     vs   } Debt in Muscogee Superior Court October Term 1838
James R. Jones & }
James Boykin }

It appearing to the Court that the Original declaration in the above stated case has been lost or destroyed & also that it was duly & legally served & that the annexed is a substantial Copy of the same. On motion, it is ordered that said Copy be established & the same is hereby established in lieue of the Originals so lost or destroyed. October 12th 1838

Cicero D. Hudson }
  vs } Assumpsit
William Sullivan }

We Confess Judgment to the Plaintiffs for four hundred & twenty three dollars, with interest and cost of suit.

        Campbell & McDougald, Def[ts] Att[ys]

[28]   Wednesday December 12th 1838

The Insurance Bank of Columbus }
  vs   } Assumpsit
James S. Calhoun }

I Confess Judgment to the Plaintiff for the sum of Six thousand two hundred & fifty dollars, with interest & costs of suit and three dollars for cost of Protest, reserving right of appeal.

        Tho[s] G. Gordon, Def[ts] Att[y]

Thomas Hunt & C[o], Endorsees }
  vs   } Assumpsit
Keeler & Sherwood }

We, the Jury, find for the Plaintiff the sum of six hundred & twenty six dollars & twenty five cents, with interest & cost of suit.

        Jn[o] McGough, F. M.

Tho[s] Hunt & C[o], endorsees }
  vs   } Assumpsit
Keeler & Sherwood }

We, the Jury, find for the Plaintiff the sum of Two hundred & twenty six dollars and sixty eight cents, with interest & cost of suit.

        Jn[o] McGough, F. M.

Bogert & Kneeland }
      vs   } Assumpsit
Seaborn Jones, endorser }

We, the Jury, find for the Plaintiffs the sum of Two thousand Six hundred and Eighty two dollars and forty two cents, with interest & costs of suit, also one hundred and seven dollars & twenty nine cents for the difference of Exchange between Columbus in the State of Georgia and the City of New York at the time the note Sued on became payable, and three dollars for cost of Protest.

                                      Seaborn Jones, Def^t

Allen Mims vs M. D. Roberson. Debt

Henry Mims & Co vs Umphrey Rowell. Debt

John Logan vs Timothy Collins & David E. Walker. Debt

Ann Reid vs Elijah Corley, Benjamin Howard, & Eli B. W. Spivey. Assumpsit

It appearing to the Court upon the Oath of Jesse P. Hitchcock, the Plaintiff's Attorney in the above cases, that each of the above Cases was Commenced and the Declarations filed in legal time before & returnable to the last april term of this Court and that the Same was to the best of his knowledge & belief in the Clerk's Office at the time the same was burnt & consequently the Said papers appertaining to the above mentioned cases are lost or destroyed. It is therefore on motion ordered that that the copies of the said declarations & processes, together with the returns of the Sheriff in each of the above cases herewith filed, be and the same are hereby established in lieu of the said lost originals.

[29] $10,000 Twelve months after date, we promise to pay to the order of Felix Lewis at either of the banks in Columbus, Georgia Ten thousand dollars for value recieved without defalcation.

Columbus, Geo. February 15th 1836   Bonner & Jones

I indorse the within to ~~Felix Lewis~~ Eli S. Shorter.

                                      ~~Eli S. Shorter~~ Felix Lewis

I indorse the within to Daniel McDougald.

Eli S. Shorter

I indorse the within to the Insurance Bank of Columbus.

D. McDougald

It appearing to the Court that the above is a Copy of a note consumed by fire in the Clerk's Office of the Superior Court of Muscogee County and that suits are progressing on the same. Ordered that said copys be established in lieu of said Originals.

Burton Hepburn, for the use of }
The Insurance Bank of Columbus}
     vs   } October Term 1838
John Dillingham   }
William A. Garland   }
& Robert P. Guyard   }

Insurance Bank of Columbus }
     vs   } April Term 1838
James H. Shorter, Admtr.   }
Sophia H. Shorter, Admtrx. }
of Eli S. Shorter, dec[d]   }

Insurance Bank of Columbus }
     vs   } April Term 1837
Seymour R. Bonner   }
& Richard Jones   }

Insurance Bank of Columbus }
     vs   } October Term 1837
Seymour R. Bonner   }
& Richard Jones   }

Insurance Bank of Columbus }
   vs   } October Term 1837
John D. Howell   }
William S. Chipley   }
Luther Blake   }
& Daniel McDougald }

It appearing to the Court that the Original declarations were consumed in the Clerk's office of the Sup^r Court by fire & that the foregoing are copies. Ordered that said Copies be established in lieu of the lost Originals.

Egbert B. Beall }
  vs   } Assumpsit
William Pace, J^r }

I Confess Judgment to the Plaintiff for two hundred & eighty seven dollars & ninety seven cents, with interest & cost of suit, with stay of Execution Six months.

          Wm Pace, J^r

The Court adjourned to meet again tomorrow morning at nine O'clock.

         Marshall J. Wellborn, J. S. C. C. C.

[30]   Muscogee Superior Court October term adjourned
       Thursday 13th December 1838

The Court met this moring according to adjournment, present the Honorable Marshall J. Wellborn, J. S. C. C. C.

Arthur B. Baker   }
  vs   } Attachment
Charles N. Jordan & }
John D. Jordan, Garnishee }

It appearing to the Court that John D. Jordan has been served with a summons of Garnishment returnable to this term of the Court in the above stated case & he having failed to appear & put in his answer. It is therefore on motion Ordered by the Court that the said John D. Jordan do appear on or before the last day of the next term of this Court & file in the Clerk's office of this Court his answer to said summons of Garnishment or shew cause to the Contrary & that a Copy of this Rule be served on the said John D. Jordan by the Sheriff at least twenty days before the next term of this Court. October Term Adjourned 1838.

Charles Bailey }
  vs   } Debt To April Term 1838
W. B. Robinson & C° } In Muscogee Superior Court
& Seaborn Jones }

R. & G. Barker   }
  vs   } Debt To April Term 1838
Timothy Collins, Principal} In Muscogee Superior Court
& Luther Blake, security }

It appearing to the Court that the Original Petitions, processes, & entries thereon which were filed in the above cases were destroyed by the late fire in the City of Columbus which Consumed the Records of said Court & that there were defaults regularly entered in said cases at the last term of said Court. On motion ordered that the Copies now offered be & the same be established in lieue of the Originals so destroyed & that the said cases proceed.

Robbins, Painter & C°}
  vs   } Assumpsit
John E. Davis   }

It appearing to the Court that the affidavit to hold to Bail in the above stated case is defective in this, that it is not regularly attested according to law. on motion of Defendant's Attorney, ordered that the bail in said case be and is hereby discharged and the proceedings against said Bail dismissed.

John B. Baird }
  vs } Assumpsit
Matt R. Evans }

I Confess Judgment to the Plaintiff for thirteen hundred & eleven dollars and twelve cents, with interest & cost of suit and three dollars for cost of Protest, reserving the liberty of Appeal.

          Seaborn Jones. Att[y] for Def[t]

[31]

John B. Baird }
  vs   } Assumpsit
Thomas C. Evans }

I Confess Judgment to the Plaintiff for thirteen hundred & eleven dollars & twelve cents, with interest & cost of suit and three dollars for cost of Protest, reserving the liberty of Appeal.

           Seaborn Jones, Def^{ts} Att^y

Wade Hill }
  vs   } Assumpsit
Alfred Iverson & }
Thomas C. Evans }

It appearin to the Court upon sufficient evidence that the Original declaration and process in this case been destroyed by fire and that the foregoing are Copies in substance of the said Original declarations and process and acknowledgement of service. It is therefore ordered that the said Copies be established and stand in lieu of said Originals.

Wade Hill }
  vs   } Assumpsit
Alfred Iverson & }
Thomas C. Evans }

We, the Jury, find for the plaintiff the sum of four hundred and thirty two dollars, with interest & Costs of suit and three dollars for protest fee.

           Jn° McGough, F. M/

Morgan Jones }
  vs   } Trespass &C
Newsome Taunton }

We Confess Judgment to the defendant for costs of suit, reserving the right of appeal.

Campbell & McDougald, Def^{ts} Att^{ys}

June 9th 1834
One day after date, I promise to pay to Elza Bland, or bearer, the Sum of four hundred and eighty dollars & twenty cents, for value received.

Signed. Jn° H. Brodnax

State of Georgia }
Muscogee County } Personally appeared in open Court Isaac Mooney, who being duly sworn, deposeth and Saith that the original promissory note of which the above purports to be a Copy was destroyed by fire in October last when the Clerk's Office of said County was burned and that the said original note was of file in Said Office in a certain Suit at the instance of this deponent against said Bland and Judgment obtained thereon. & this deponent further Saith that the above is a Copy in Substance of the Said Original so burned & destroyed.

Sworn to & Subscribed in open court Isaac X Mooney, his mark
this 13th December 1838 Gerard Burch, Clk

Georgia }
Muscogee County } It appearing to the Court that the Original note, a Copy of which is described above, was destroyed by fire at the burning of the Clerk's Office of said County and that the said Original was of file in said Office

[32]

[blot} Court October adjourned Term 1838 Thursday 13th December 1838

Office and that the Copy hereunto attached is a Copy in substance of said Original so destroyed by fire as aforesaid. On motion ordered by the Court that the Copy hereunto attached be & the same is hereby established in lieu of the said Original so destroyed by fire as aforesaid.

The Insurance Bank of Columbus}
  vs   } Assumpsit
Alfred Iverson   }

The Same vs Burton Hepburn. Assumpsit

The Same vs James C. Watson. Assumpsit

It appearing to the Court that the above named Defendants were sued as endorsers on a promissory Note of which Seth Love & William Wellborn are the makers against whom suit is now pending in the State of Alabama. It is ordered that plaintiff's Counsil have leave to withdraw said Original note from the Clerk's office.

John Doe, ex dem }	
Samuel Jackson }	
vs }	Ejectment Verdict for Plff
Richard Roe, casual ejector }	Rule Nisi for New Trial
& Umphrey Rowell & Seaborn }	
Rowell, tenants in possession }	

on motion, it is ordered that Plff shew Cause as soon as Council can be herd why the verdict in the above case should not be set aside & new trial awarded on the ground that the Court misunderstood directed the Jury as to the law, 1st Because the Court Charged the Jury that it was not necessary for the plaintiff to prove the defendant to be in the actual possession of the premises, But that the possession of his tenant was sufficient, 2nd Because the Court charged the Jury that the Gathering & the houseing the Crop on the premises by the defendant was evidence of possession. And for other causes, and that a copy of this rule be served upon the plaintiff's council.

I acknowledge Service of the within rule.

Colquitt, Holt & Echols, Plff^s Att^{ys}

E. & F. Bradley }	
vs }	Debt
John R. Lloyd }	

Jury N° 1. We, the Jury, find for the Plaintiff the Sum of fifty two dollars and thirty three cents principal, with interest & cost of Suit.

Jn° McGough, form

[33]

Insurance Bank of Columbus }
      vs   } Assumpsit
James H. Shorter, Admtr. & }
Sophia H. Shorter, Admtrx, }
of Eli S. Shorter, deceased }

We, the Jury, find for the Plaintiff ten thousand dollars principal debt, with interest & cost and also three dollars protest fees. 13th Decem 1838

                               Jn° McGough, form

John Doe, on the demise }
of Samuel Jackson }
      vs   } Ejectment
Richard Roe, Casual ejector }
& Umphrey Rowell & Seaborn }
Rowell, tenants in possession }

Jury N° 1. We, the Jury, find for the Plaintiff the premises in dispute and thirty dollars for mean profits.

                                 Jn° McGough, form

E. & F. Bradley }
      vs   } Debt
John T. Walker }

Jury N° 1. We, the Jury, find for the Plaintiff the Sum of thirty five dollars & Six cents principal, with interest & Cost of Suit.

                                 Jn° McGough, form

E. & F. Bradley }
      vs   } Debt
Phillip Lamar }

Jury Nº 1. We, the Jury, find for the Plaintiff the Sum of forty eight dollars & fifty six Cents principal, with interest & cost of Suit.

          Jnº McGough, form

E. & F. Bradley }
  vs   } Debt
James S. Normon }

We, the Jury, find for the Plaintiff the sum of one hundred & twenty nine dollars & thirty one cents principal, with interest & Cost of Suit.

          Jnº McGough, form

E. & F. Bradley }
  vs   } Debt
James S. Normon }

We, the Jury, find for the Plaintiff the Sum of One hundred dollars principal, with interest & cost of suit.

          Jnº McGough, form

[34] Superior Court ~~Wednesday~~ Thursday 13th December 1838

E. & F. Bradley }
  vs   } Debt
Daniel Walling }

Jury Nº 1. We, the Jury, find for the Plaintiffs the sum of forty three dollars & Six cents principal, with interest & cost of suit.

          Jnº McGough, form

T. M. & J. Allyn }
  vs   } Debt
D. Hungerford & Cº }

We, the Jury, find for the Plaintiffs the Sum of eleven hundred & thirty Seven dollars & thirty one Cents principal, with interest & cost of suit.

        Jn° McGough, form

E. & F. Bradley }
  vs   } Debt
John M. Patrick }

Jury N° 1. We, the Jury, find for the Plantiffs the sum of one hundred and twenty three dollars & eighty five cents principal, with interest & cost of suit.

        Jn° McGough, F. M.

E. & F. Bradley }
  vs   } Debt
James Sarenet }

Jury N° 1. We, the Jury, find for the Plantiffs the sum of thirty one dollars & fifty cents principal, with interest & cost of suit.

        Jn° McGough, F. M.

E. & F. Bradley }
  vs   } Debt
John M. Patrick, Jr }

Jury N° 1. We, the Jury, find for the Plantiffs the sum of fifty nine dollars & sixty seven cents principal, with interest & cost of suit.

        Jn° McGough, F. M.

E. & F. Bradley }
  vs   } Debt
Wm W. Nichols }

Jury N° 1. We, the Jury, find for the Plantiffs the sum of forty one dollars & fifty cents principal, with interest & cost of suit.

        Jn° McGough, F. M.

[35]

E. & F. Bradley }
    vs   } Debt
James S. Norman }

Jury Nº 1. We, the Jury, find for the Plantiffs the sum of thirty seven dollars & eighty seven & a half cents principal, with interest & cost of suit.

                                      Jnº McGough, F. M.

E. & F. Bradley }
    vs   } Debt
Anthony Levie }

Jury Nº 1. We, the Jury, find for the Plantiffs the sum of forty one dollars & fifty cents principal, with interest & cost of suit.

                                        Jnº McGough, F. M.

E. & F. Bradley }
    vs   } Debt
Thomas Jepson }

Jury Nº 1. We, the Jury, find for the Plantiffs the sum of thirty eight dollars & forty six cents principal, with interest & Cost of suit.

                                        Jnº McGough, F. M.

Arthur B. Baker }
    vs   } Assumpsit
Charles N. Jordan}

Jury Nº 1. We, the Jury, find for the Plantiff the sum of fifty three dollars, with interest & Cost of suit.

                                        Jnº McGough, F. M.

Seaborn Thorn }
    vs } Debt
John Whitesides }

Jury N° 1. We, the Jury, find for the Plantiff the sum of six hundred dollars, with interest & Cost of suit.

                              Jn° McGough, F. M.

Robert McQueen }
    vs } Assumpsit for Rent
Robinson & Hand }

Jury N° 1. We, the Jury, find for the Plantiff the sum of one hundred and twenty five dollars, with interest & cost of suit.

                              Jn° McGough, F. M.

Bogert & Kneeland }
    vs } Assumpsit
T. B. Howard }

Jury. I Confess Judgment to the Plantiff for the sum of Two thousand six hundred & Eighty two dollars & forty two cents, with interest & Cost of suit, also One hundred and Seven dollars & twenty nine cents for the diference of Echange between Columbus in the State of Georgia & the City of New York at the time the note sued on became payable, & three dollars for Cost of protest.

                              Seaborn Jones, Def[ts] Att[y]

James H. Shorter vs Benjamin P. Tarver. Asspt

I Confess Judgment to the Plaintiff in the sum of One thousand and thirty six dollars, besides interest, cost of suit, & protest fee.

                              Thomas & Shivers, Def[ts] Att[ys]

[36] Superior Court ~~Wednesday~~ Thurs 13th December 1838

Bogert & Kneeland }
     vs   } Assumpsit
Augustus Howard }

I Confess Judgment to the Plantiffs for the sum of Two thousand Seven hundred & tweny six dollars and ninety cents, with interest & cost of suit, and the further sum of One hundred and ninety dollars & eighty eight cents for the diference of echange between Columbus in the State of Georgia & the City of New York at the time the note sued on became payable, and three dollars for cost of Protest.

                                      Seaborn Jones, Def^s Att^y

Bogert & Kneeland }
     vs   } Assumpsit
Seaborn Jones   }

We Confess Judgment to the Plantiffs for the sum of Two thousand six hundred & Eighty two dollars and forty two cents, with interest.

Francis Jepson vs Turner Williams & Magirt Ivey. Case

Francis Jepson vs John R. Lloyd & Co. Case

Henry Sanford vs Rufus K. Mills. Debt

Ayer & Hogg vs William J. McMullin. Debt

Ayer & Hogg vs Bird B. Mitchell. Debt

Elizabeth Billups vs Nathaniel W. Hoell & Thomas Fleming. Debt

Elizabeth Billups vs Michael Hoffman & A. L. Heine. Debt

Elizabeth Billups vs Michael N. Clarke & J. P. Jackson. Debt

Ayer & Hogg vs John T. Walker. Assumpsit

Ayer & Hogg vs John T. Walker. Assumpsit

Elizabeth Billups vs Emanuel Ezekiel & Henry B. Horton. Debt

Elizabeth Billups vs Ja^s V. Hogg & Washington Toney. Debt

John English vs James Van Ness. Assumpsit

[37]

John English vs James N. Bethune. Assumpsit

Wiley Lewis vs William B. Roberson, Nathaniel M. C. }
      Roberson, Bird F. Roberson, & Samuel R. Andrews } Assumpsit

In Muscogee Superior Court October adjourned Term 1838

Personally appeared in open Court Nicholas L. Howard, Attorney for the Plaintiffs in the above stated cases, who being sworn, deposeth & sath that the same were sued to the April term of the Superior Court of said County and are to the best of his knowledge, information, & belief destroyed by the late burning of the Clerk's Office of said Court. And that he verily believes from all the information he has derived in each of the aforesaid cases that the same were served by the proper officers within the time prescribed by Law, and further that the copies proposed to be established in lieu of the originals are to the best of his knowledge and belief Substantial Copies of the same.

Sworn to in open Court   Nicholas L. Howard
this 11th Decem 1838. Gerard Burch, Clk

Whereupon it is on motion ordered by the Court that the proposed copies of the original petitions, processes, & Sheriff's returns be established instanter in lieu of the originals.

James Kirlin }
    vs   } Debt
Lemuel Jepson }

We, the Jury, find for the Plaintiff the sum of forty one dollars & ninety three & three fourths cents principal, with interest & cost of suit. 11th Decr 1838

                               Jno McGough, form

James Kirlin }
    vs   } Debt
Jacob M. Guerry}

We, the Jury, find for the Plaintiff the Sum of Forty five dollars & Seventy five cents principal, with interest & cost of suit. 11th Decem 1838

                                Jn° McGough, Form

John W. Rinaldi, indorser }
    vs   } Assumpsit
Robinson & Hand   }

We confess Judgment ~~We, the Jury, find~~ for the Plaintiff the sum of two hundred and fifty three dollars & ninety three cents principal, with interest & cost of suit. 11th December 1838

                                J. N. & J. M. Bethune, Def^{ts} Att^{ys}

Garrett Hallenbeck }
    vs   } Debt
Jacob M. Guerry   }
& Luther Blake   }

We, the Jury, find for the Plaintiff the sum of eighty dollars principal, with interest & cost of suit. 11th Decem 1838

                                Jn° McGough, form

[38]   Thursday 14th December 1838

The Insurance Bank of Columbus}
    vs   } Assumpsit
James S. Calhoun   }

I confess Judgment to Plaintiff for two thousand dollars, with interest & Cost of Suit & three dollars cost of protest.

                                Thos G. Gordon, Defendant's Att^y

It appearing to the Court that the original declaration & process in this case has been lost or mislaid and that the within is a copy of the same and that the defendant was regularly served with the Same within the time prescribed by law. It is ordered that this said copy be established in lieu of said lost original.

The President, Directors, & Company }
of the Bank of Augusta }
    vs } Assumpsit
Edward Cary }

I Confess Judgment to the Plaintiff for the Sum of two thousand & Sixty dollars, with interest & cost of suit & three dollars protest fee.

                        Edwd Cary

Benoni Gray }
    vs } Judgment 12th December 1837
Adoniran Treadwell }

In the Superior Court of Muscogee County for $371.00 and execution issued thereon returnable to the April Term 1838 of said Court. It appearing to the Court that the Sheriff of Muscogee County, Joseph D. Bethune, Esqr, returned said execution "No Property to be found" at the last April Term of said Court into the Clerk's Office thereof & that the same must have been burnt in the fire on the night of the 14th October last which Consumed said Clerk's Office, therefore Ordered by the Court that the Clerk of this Court do issue another execution in the place & Stead of said burnt fi fa.

John Pickett }
    vs } Assumpsit
Owners of Steam Boat Free trader }

Dismissed.

Parrish, Marshall & Co }
    vs } Assumpsit
Alfred Iverson, maker
James H. Iverson & }
Ben^j V. Iverson, indorsers }

We Confess Judgment to the Plaintiffs for the sum of thirteen hundred & ninety two dollars & seventy two cents, with interest & Cost of suit.

J. M. Guerry, Att^y for
Alfred Iverson & B. V. Iverson

[39] Jury N° 2

1. Thos V. Miller
2. James Jernigan
3. Francis Jepson
4. Bird B. Mitchell
5. Thomas Motley
6. William Gordy
7. Seaborn Ely
8. Abner Hill
9. Price Davis
10. Jacob Johnson
11. Elias D. Howell
12. Alfred F. Brannon

Wittich, Greenwood & C° }
for the use of Thomas Grant }
      vs } Debt
Isaac Mitchell }

I Confess Judgment to the Plantiffs for fifty four dollars, with interest & cost.

J. N. & J. M. Bethune, Def^{ts} Att^{ys}

Irwin, Hall, & Walton }
      vs } Assumpsit
William P. McKeen }

Settled & Cost Paid.

James Kirksey }
      vs } Debt
Thomas G. Gordon }

I Confess Judgment to the Plantiff for the sum of one hundred and twelve dollars, with interest & Costs of suit.

Thos G. Gordon

John C. Tozier }
  vs   } Trover
John Southern }

Jury N° 2. We, the Jury, find for the Plantiff the sum of one hundred & forty dollars, with Cost of suit, which may be discharged by the delivery of the watch & Chain & payment of Cost in fifteen days.

        Thos V. Miller, foreman

W. Williams & Brother }
  vs   } Assumpsit
T. H. Smith & C°   }

We Confess Judgment to the Plantiffs one hundred & fifty six dollars & ninety cents principal, with interest & cost of suit.

       Colquitt, Holt & Echols, Defendants Att^{ys}

Jacobi & Miedzielski   }
  vs   } Assumpsit
Seaborn Jones }

Dismissed.

Preston & Nelms }
  vs   } Assumpsit
Joseph Davidson }

I Confess Judgment to the Plffs for three hundred & thirty dollars & 11 cents, with interest & cost.

        J. Davidson

[40]   Thursday December 13th 1838

Insurance Bank of Columbus}
  vs   } Assumpsit
William P. McKeen   }

Dismissed.

Insurance Bank of Columbus }
    vs } Assumpsit
Edward Cary }

Dismissed.

Insurance Bank of Columbus }
    vs } Assumpsit
Calhoun & Bass }

Dismissed.

Insurance Bank of Columbus }
    vs } Assumpsit
Thomas C. Evans }
& Matthew R. Evans

Dismissed.

The Insurance Bank of Columbus }
    vs } Assumpsit
John D. Howell }

Dismissed.

The Insurance Bank of Columbus }
    vs } Assumpsit
Alfred Iverson }

Dismissed.

The Insurance Bank of Columbus }
    vs } Assumpsit
James H. Campbell }

Dismissed.

The State   }
    vs   } Simple Larceny
Maberry Howell   }
Western Harwell   }
William Harwell   }
Avery Odom &   }
John Fox   }

True Bill.   Mansfield Torrance, Foreman

The State   }
    vs   } Robbery
William Harwell   }

True Bill.   Mansfield Torrance, Foreman

The State }
    vs   } Simple Larceny
John Fox   }

True Bill.   Mansfield Torrance, foreman

[41]

The State   }
    vs   } Simple Larceny
John Fox   }
Western Harwell &   }
Lorenzo Dow Glenn   }

True Bill.   Mansfield Torrance, foreman

The State   }
    vs   } Simple Larceny
Lorenzo Dow Glenn   }

True Bill.   Mansfield Torrance, fForeman

The State   }
       vs   } Simple Larceny
Thomas Howard   }
Western Harwell   }
& Avery Odom   }

True Bill.   Mansfield Torrance, Foreman

James H. Shorter   }
       vs   } Assumpsit
William J. Rylander }

We, the Jury, find for the Plaintiff six hundred dollars, besides interest, costs of Suit, & protest fee.

                                    Jn° McGough, Form

James H. Shorter   }
       vs   } Assumpsit
H. C. Phelps   }

We, the Jury, find for the Plaintiff six hundred & fifty dollars, besides interest, Costs of Suit, & protest fee.

                                    Jn° McGough, Form

James H. Shorter, admtr. & }
Sophia H. Shorter, Admtrx. }
of Eli S. Shorter, decd   }
       vs   } Assumpsit
Philo D. Woodruff   }
& Carnot Woodruff   }

We, the Jury, find for the Plaintiffs three thousand Seven hundred & twelve dollars, besides interest & costs of Suit.

                                    Jn° McGough, form

James H. Shorter }
  vs   } assumpsit
Timothy G. McCrary}

I confess Judgment for the Plaintiff seventy five dollars, besides interest & Costs of Suit.

       Campbell, McDougald, & Watson, Def[ts] Att[ys]

H. Mims & C[o] }
  vs   } Debt
Umphrey Rowell }

We, the Jury, find for the Plaintiff for the sum of Thirty one dollars eighty nine cents, with Interest & cost of Suit.

       Jn° McGough, Fm

[42]   Thursday 13th December 1838

Ann Reid   }
  vs   } Assumpsit
Elijah Corley   }
Benjamin Howard }
& Eli B. W. Spivey }

We, the Jury, find for the Plaintiff the sum of Two Thousand dollars, with Interest and cost of suit.

       Jn° McGough, Fm

Charles C. Bailey   }
  vs   } debt
William B. Robinson & C[o]}

We confess Judgment to the Plaintiff in the Sum of Eleven Hundred and ten dollars, with interest and Cost & Suit.

       Seaborn Jones, deft[s] att[y]

Muscogee Superior Court October adjourned term 1838

Hudson A. Thornton }   Hugh Freal }
    vs } assumpt   vs } Debt
John Dillingham, Admtr of }   Thomas Harvey }
George W. Dillingham, deceased }

It appearing to trhe court upon the oath of Jesse P. Hitchcock, the Attorney for the Plaintiffs in each of the above cases, that the Declarations in said cases were in the Clerk's Office of the Superior Court of this County at the time of the late burning and destruction of the same and that said originals are lost or destroyed and also that the Copies of the together with the entries thereon are to the best of knowledge & information substantial Copies of the said Originals. It is therefore on motion ordered by the Court that said Copies of the Said declarations & entries thereon be and the same are hereby established in lieu of the lost Originals.

Edward Kellogg & C° }
    vs } Assumpsit
Isaac Mitchell }

I Confess Judgment to the Plaintiff for the Sum of Six hundred and thirty nine dollars & ninety two cents, with interest & Costs this 14th December 1838.

                                      J. N. & J. M. Bethune, Defs Attys

[43]

Andrew B. Griffin }
    vs } Debt an verdict for the Plaintiff for thirty eight
John McMurren } hundred dollars with interest & cost

The defendant, being dissatisfied with the verdict of the Jury rendered in the above cause and having paid all Cost and demanded an appeal, brings Michael L. Dent and John L. Lewis and tenders them as his Security and they, the said Michael L. Dent & and J. L. Lewis, acknowledge themselves Jointly & Severally bound to Andrew B. Griffin, the Plaintiff, for the payment of the eventual condemnation money in said cause. In Testimony whereof, they have hereunto Set their hands & Seals this [blank] day of December 1838.

Test. Gerard Burch, Clk
John Mcmurran
M. L. Dent
John L. Lewis

Battle A. Sorsby }
    vs } Assumpt
C. W. Buckley & C° }

We Confess Judgment to the Plaintiff for the sum of one hundred & eleven dollars & fifty three cents, with interest & Costs. 14 December 1838

John Schley, Def^{ts} Att^y

B. A. Sorsby }
    vs } assumpt
Asa Bates }

I confess Judgment to the Plaintiff for the sum of Eighty eight dollars & eighty eight cents, with interest & costs this [blank] day of December 1838.

Asa Bates

B. A. Sorsby }
    vs } Assumpsit
J. P. Jackson }

I confess Judgment to the Plaintiff for the sum of seventy two dollars & ninety nine cents, with interest & Costs. 14th December 1838

J. P. Jackson

B. A. Sorsby }
    vs } Assumpsit
Lemuel Jepson }

I confess Judgment to the Plaintiff for the Sum of forty two dollars, with interest & cost of suit. 14th December 1838

           Jesse P. Hitchcock, Def^{ts} Att^y

Edward Kellogg & Co }
    vs   } assumpsit
Dana Hungerford & Co }

We confess Judgment to the Plaintiffs for the sum of nine hundred & Sixty three dollars & eight five cents, with interest & cost. 14th December 1838

          T. F. Foster, for Def^t Hungerford

[44]

Wetherell, Fowl & Co }
    vs   } assumpsit
Chisholm & Collins }

We confess Judgment to the Plaintiffs for the sum of nine hundred & fourteen dollars & thirty eight cents, with interest & costs. 14th December 1838

           Jno Schley, Def^{ts} Att^y

Thomas H. Hall   }
    vs   } Assumpsit
William Pride   }
Bird F. Robison &   }
& James C. Holland, Security }

We confess Judgment to the Plff for the sum of Seventy dollars, with interest & Cost this 14 Decem 1838.

          J. N. & J. M. Bethune, Def^{ts} Att^{ys}

Richard S. Williams }
    vs   } assumpt
John B. Peabody   }

I confess Judgment to the Plff for the sum of two hundred & thirty two dollars & Seventy four Cents, with interest & costs. 14 December 1838

          Jn° B. Peabody

Edward Kellogg & C° }
   vs   } assumpsit
Hiram Fuller   }

I confess Judgment to the Plffs for the sum of eight hundred & fifty eight dollars & Sixty eight cents, with interest & costs. 14th December 1838

          Hiram Fuller

Hamilton & Cole, to the use &c }
   vs   } Assumpsit
Howard & Wittich   }

We Confess Judgment to the Plaintiffs for the sum of seventeen hundred & twenty two dollars & eighty five cents, with interest & Costs. 14th December 1838

          Nicholas L. Howard, Def^ts Att^y

Brown Brothers & C° }
   vs   } Assumpsit
Hampton S. Smith }

I confess Judgment to the Plaintiffs for the sum of thirty three hundred & thirty six dollars & fifteen cents, with interest & Costs. 14 December 1838

          H. S. Smith

Richard Kingsland & C° }
   vs   } Assumpsit
John E. Davis, indorser }

Settled & Cost Paid.

[45]

A. S. Mims }
    vs } Debt
M. D. Robinson }

We confess Judgment to the Plaintiff the sum of thirty four dollars & eighty eight cents principal and thirteen dollars and ninety cents interest, with costs of suit.

Campbell, McDougald & Watson, Def^{ts} Att^{ys}

Samuel A. Bailey }
    vs } Assumpsit
James Mitchell }

We, the Jury, find for the Plaintiff five thousand three hundred & eighty two dollars & forty cents, with interest, three dollars protest fee, & cost.

T. V. Miller, For

Samuel A. Bailey }
    vs } Assumpsit
Thomas Hoxey }

We, the Jury, find for the Plaintiff nine hundred & forty four dollars, with interest, three dollars protest fee, & costs.

T. V. Miller, For

Samuel A. Bailey }
    vs } Assumpsit
William P. Malone }

We, the Jury, find for the Plaintiff one thousand & sixty two dollars, with interest, three dollars protest fee, & cost.

T. V. Miller, for

Samuel A. Bailey }
    vs   } Assumpsit
Henry Mims   }

We, the Jury, find for the Plaintiff nine hundred and forty four dollars, with interest, three dollars Protest fee, & cost.

                          T. V. Miller, For

Samuel A. Bailey }
    vs   } Assumpsit
William P. Malone }

We, the Jury, find for the Plaintiff Eleven hundred & sixty dollars, with interest, three dollars protest fee, & cost.

                          T. V. Miller, For

Samuel A. Bailey }
    vs   } Assumpsit
H. Mims & C°   }

We, the Jury, find for the Plaintiff one thousand & sixty two dollars, with interest, three dollars protest fee, & cost.

                          T. V. Miller, For

Samuel A. Bailey }
    vs   } Assumpsit
Thomas Henry   }

We, the Jury, find for the Plaintiff Eleven hundred & sixty dollars, with interest, three dollars Protest fee, & costs.

                          T. V. Miller, For

[46]   Thursday 13th December 1838

Samuel A. Bailey }
     vs   } Assumpsit
Hampton S. Smith }

We, the Jury, find for the Plaintiff one thousand & sixty two dollars, with interest, three dollars Protest fee, & cost.

                                       T. V. Miller, For

Samuel A. Bailey }
     vs   } Assumpsit
William H. Mitchell }

We, the Jury, find for the plaintiff Five thousand three hundred & eighty two dollars & forty cents, with interest, three dollars protest fee, & cost.

                                       T. V. Miller, For

Samuel A. Bailey }
     vs   } Assumpsit
John Warren   }

We, the Jury, find for the Plaintiff Nine hundred & forty four dollars, with interest, three dollars protest fee, & Cost.

                                       T. V. Miller, For

Samuel A. Bailey }
     vs   } Assumpsit
Walter H. Weems }
& John Fontaine   )

We Confess Judgment to the Plaintiff nineteen hundred & sixty six dollars & thirty six cents, with interest & cost.

                             Thomas & Shivers, Def[ts] Att[ys]

Samuel A. Bailey }
    vs   } Assumpsit
Henry Mims   }

We, the Jury, find for the Plaintiff Eleven hundred & sixty dollars, with interest & three dollars Protest fees, & cost.

                              T. V. Miller, For

Samuel A. Bailey }
    vs   } Assumpsit
Thomas Hoxey }

We, the Jury, find for the Plaintiff five thousand three hundred & eighty two dollars, & forty cents, with interest & three dollars Protest fee, & cost.

                              T. V. Miller, For

Joseph Poythress }
    vs   } Debt
Isaac Mitchell   }

We, the Jury, find for the Plaintiff three hundred & thirty five dollars. with interest & cost.

                              T. V. Miller, For

Samuel A. Bailey   }
    vs   } Assumpsit
Thomas A. Brannon }
William P. Malone }
& H. Mims & C°   }

We, the Jury, find for the Plaintiff Eight hundred & forty one dollars, with interest, two dollars protest, & cost.

                              T. V. Miller, For

[47]

Samuel A. Bailey }
    vs } Assumpsit
Alfred M. Terry }
John Johson, security & }
Samuel R. Andrews, security}

We, the Jury, find for the Plaintiff Eleven hundred & sixty dollars, with interest, two dollars protest fee, & cost.

                                T. V. Miller, For

James H. Shorter, Admtr. &)
Sophia H. Shorter, Admtrx. }
of Eli S. Shorter, dec^d }
    vs } Assumpsit
Solomon Averitt }

Wherefore, it is ordered by the Court that this Copy be established in lieu of said Originals and that said Copy note be established & taken in place of the Original one decsribed in this declaration.

James H. Shorter, Admtr. &)
Sophia H. Shorter, Admtrx. }
of Eli S. Shorter, dec^d }
    vs } Assumpsit
Solomon Averitt }

We, the Jury, find for the plaintiff nine hundred and sixty dollars, besides interest & costs of suit.

                                Jn° McGough, F. M.

Bogert & Hawthorn }
    vs } Assumpsit
Robert A. Ware, maker & }
Seaborn Jones, endorser }

Settled at Def^t Jones Cost.

B. B. Kirtland & C° } Ca Sa in Muscogee Superior Court
      vs   } Judgment 17th April 1838
Maginnis G. Caldwell } Returned by the Sheriff not to be found

It appearing to the Court that the Original Ca Sa has been lost or destroyed, it is therefore on motion ordered by the Court that the Clerk do issue an alias Ca Sa in said case instanter. October adjourned Term 1838

Wm Fort   }
    vs   } Assumpsit
J. S. Calhoun }

I confess judgment to the plaintiff Thirty five Hundred Dollars, with interest & Cost.

                      Seaborn Jones, Defendant's Att^y

The Court adjourned to meet again tomorrow morning at nine O'clock.

                      Marshall J. Wellborn, J. S. C. C. C.

[48]   Muscogee Superior Court October adjourned term 1838
               Friday 14th December 1838

The Court met this morning according to adjournment, present the Honorable Marshall J. Wellborn, J. S. C. C. C.

William Fort   }
    vs   } Assumpsit
J. M. Woodland }

We, the Jury, find for the Plaintiff Thirty five Hundred dollars, with interest & Cost & three dollars protest fee.

                      Jn° McGough, Fm

William Fort   }
    vs   } Assumpsit
T. & M. Evans }

I confess Judgment to the Plaintiff Thirty five Hundred Dollars, with Interest & Cost.

Seaborn Jones, def[ts] att[y]

William H. Lovejoy }
     vs   } Assumpsit
James C. McGebony } Oct Adjourned Term 1838

It appearing to the Court that the Original declaration, process, & return of service have been destroyed by fire. It is ordered that the annexed & foregoing Copy be established instanter in lieu of said lost originals.

William H. Lovejoy }
     vs   } Assumpsit
James C. McGebony }

We, the Jury, find for the plaintiff One Hundred Dollars & Interest & Costs of Suit. 11th Dec[r] 1838.

Jn° McGough, Fm

Henry Moffit   }
     vs   } Assumpsit
Elijah Corley & } Oct adjourned term 1838
Benjamin Howard }

It appearing to the Court that the Original petition & process in the foregoing case have been destroyed by fire, together with the return of service. it is ordered that the foregoing be established in lieu thereof instanter, together with the endorsement of the Sheriff's return of service. We, the Jury, find for the plaintiff the sum of two thousand three Hundred & Eight dollars & fifty cents & Interest on that sum from the 22nd day of March 1838 & Costs of suit. 14th Dec[r] 1838

Jn° McGough, Fm

[49]

Bank of Milledgeville }
  vs   } Assumpsit
Seymour R. Bonner }

We, the Jury, find for the plaintiff the sum of Four Thousand dollars principal and three dollars protest fee, with Interest & Cost of suit.

        Jn° McGough, FM

Bank of Milledgeville }
  vs   } Assumpsit
Alexander McDougald }

We, the Jury, find for the Plaintiff the sum of four Thousand dollars principal and three dollars protest fee, with Interest & cost of suit.

        John McGough, Fm

Bank of Milledgeville }
  vs   } Assumpsit
Walter T. Colquit }

I Confess Judgment for the Plaintiff for Two Thousand dollars principal and three dollars protest fee, with Interest & Cost of suit.

       Colquit, Holt & Echols, def[ts] att[ys]

The State }
  vs   } Manslaughter
David Measels } Bill found at October Term 1838

On Motion of the Solicitor General, its ordered that a Nolle Proseque be entered in the above case.

Thomas J. Terry }
  vs   } debt & Bail
P. H. Smead }

It appearing to the Court that the Original Petition, Process, Bail Bond, casa Judgment, & scifa, and entries thereon in the above case were destroyed by fire & further that those now offered to the Court are true Copies in substance of those destroyed. On motion ordered that they be and are hereby established in lieu of the said Originals so lost and destroyed and that the Plaintiff's attorney have leave to enter up Judgment against the said Bail for the debt principal, Interest, & Cost.

[50]   Friday December 14 1838

Thomas J. Terry }
    vs   } Debt & Bail Casa & Scifa
P. H. Smead   }

It appearing to the Court that the Original Petition, process, Judgment, Bail Bond, Casa, & Scifa in the above case are destroyed by the fire and further that the foregoing are true copies in substance of the same, together with the entries on the same. On motion, ordered that the same be & are hereby established in lieu of the Originals so lost and that the plaintiff, by his Attorney, have leave to enter up Judgment against the Bail in terms of the Law.

William Williamson }
    vs   } Casa
Absalom Echols   }

Whereas, it appears to the Court that the defendant has been arrested on the above stated Casa & he gave bond & Security in terms of the Statute in such case made and provided for his appearance at this term of this Court on the third monday in October next, then and there to stand to and abide by such proceedings as may be had by the Court in relation to his taking the benefit of the act of the general assembly of the State of Georgia passed on the (17th) seventeenth day of December in the year of our Lord One Thousand Eight hundred & twenty three entitled an act for the relief of Honest debtors, & that the said defendant has been called & has failed to appear & that Michael W. Perry was and is security for said defendant. It is therefore, on motion, Ordered by the Court that plaintiff's Counsel be permitted to enter up Judgment upon said Casa Bond for the whole amount against the said defendant & his Securities liable to be discharged upon payment the whole amount of the principle, Interest, & cost due on said Casa. October adjourned term 1838

[51]

Austin M. Walker }
    vs } Debt
William Kirk & }
Enoch G. Brown }

[blank space}

                              William Kirk
                              E. G. Brown
                              T. J. Biggers

Brown & Dimmock }
    vs } Assumpsit & Bail
William Peabody & C° }

Cushman & C° }
    vs } Assumpsit & Bail
William Peabody & C° }

It appearing to the Court that James Y. Smith, one of the firm of Wm Peabody & C°, has been served & arrested in the above Stated Cases and that Lewis C. Allen was Bail for the said James Y. Smith and the said Lewis C. Allen having appeared in Court & delivered up his principal, the said James Y. Smith. It is therefore on motion ordered that the Said Lewis C. Allen be discharged from all further liability on said Bail Bond.

William Fort vs James M. Woodland } Assumpsit

William Fort vs James S. Calhoun } Assumpsit

the Same vs Thomas C. & Matt R. Evans } Assumpsit

Georgia }
Bibb County } Personally appeared before me Thad^s G. Holt, who after being duly sworn, saith that the above

[52] original declarations were made out by deponent returnable to the April term 1838 of Muscogee Superior Court and as this deponent believes were

regularly served & returned to said term. this deponent further saith that the accompanying copy declarations are substantial Copies of said Original declarations.

Sworn to and Subscribed to
before me this 12 Decr 1838   Thad^s G. Holt
Myron Bartlett, J. I. C.

Ordered that the said Copy declarations be established in lieu of the lost Originals.

Maclay, Asher & Co }
      vs   } Casa, arrest, and Bond Taken
Jacobi & Heine   } October adjourned Term 1838
John H. Watson, sec on appeal }
E. Goldsmith, Samuel Goldsmith & }
H. Roberts, securities on Casa Bond }

It appearing to the Court that Adolphus L. Heine, one of the defendants in the above stated Casa, has been arrested by virtue of the same and has given Bond in terms of the Statute in such cases made and provided for his appearance at this term of this Court to stand to and abide by as such proceedings as might be had by the Court in relation to his taking the benefit of an act for the relief of Insolvent debtors passed in December Eighteen Hundred & twenty three and the said Adolphus L. Heine having failed to appear at this term of this Court or to file his schedule or to give notice in terms of the Statute aforesaid. It is ordered by the Court that the plaintiff or their attorney have leave to enter up Judgment upon the Said Bond against the Securities upon said Casa for the full amount of said Bond, conditioned to be discharged upon the payment of the principle, Interest, & Cost due upon said Casa.

Lorenzo D. Buckner vs Charles L. Bass   Lorenzo D. Buckner vs Seaborn Jones
The Same vs T. & M. Evans   The Same vs Edward Cary
Barker & Morgan vs J. T. Niles & Co

Georgia   }
Muscogee County } Personally appeared in Open Court David Golightly, who being duly sworn, deposeth & saith that the Original declarations in the above

[53] Stated cases were burned with the Clerk's office and that the Copies herewith submitted are in substance Copies of said declarations. Sworn to open Court this 14th day of December 1838.

Gerard Burch, Clk   D. Golightly

It appearing to the Court that the Original declarations in the above stated cases were destroyed by fire & that the Copies submitted to the Court are in substance the same with the lost Originals. It is ordered by the Court that the said Copies be established in lieu of said Originals.

Charles H. Stewart vs Jesse Mann. Assumpsit

Arthur B. Davis, surviving copartner of Davis & Shorter vs Philo D. Woodruff & J. N. Bethune. Assumpsit

Elliott W. Gregory vs C. E. & H. Mims. Assumpsit

Arthur B. Davis, Surviving Copartner of Davis & Shorter vs Philo D. Woodruff & James N. Bethune. Assumpsit

Elliott W. Gregory vs C. E. & H. Mims. Assumpsit

Geo W. Reeves vs George W. Way & Dana Hungerford. Assumpsit

Hill, Dawson & Co vs William Crews. Assumpsit

Hill, Dawson & Co vs William B. & B. Hastings. Assumpsit

Hill, Dawson & Co vs David Man. assumpsit

Arthur B. Davis, Surviving Copartner of Davis & Shorter }
                          vs   } Assumpsit
Philo D. Woodruff & James N. Bethune   }

Hill, Dawson & Co vs Benajah Skinner. assumpsit

It appearing to the Court that the declarations in the above stated cases were destroyed by fire. It is ordered by the Court that the copies tendered by Plaintiffs' Attorney be established in lieu of the original ones.

Gerard Burch vs Robert E. Broadnax & Ephraim C. Bany. Assumpsit

Gerard Burch vs Richard Jones. Assumpsit

William B. Robison vs John T. Walker. Assumpsit

The Mayor & Counsil of the City of Columbus vs Thos C. Evans. Assumpsit

[54]   Friday December 14th 1838

Elisha S. Norton vs Timothy Collins. assumpsit

Elisha S. Norton vs Jn° R. Lloyd. assumpsit

Arthur B. Baker, for the use of James A. Bradford vs John R. Lloyd. Assumpsit

Henry King vs Robert G. Mitchell & John Mitchell. Assumpsit

Gerard Burch vs Elam W. Smith. Assumpsit

Henry King vs Robert G. Mitchell. assumpsit

Personally came in open Gerard Burch, who being duly sworn, saith that declarations were filed in the above Stated cases, that they were as he believes burnt in the Clerk's Office, that the Copies here presented to the Court to the best of his knowledge & recollection Copies in Substance.

Sworn to in Open Court   Gerard Burch
Marshall J. Wellborn, J. S. C. C. C.

It appearing to the court that the Original Declarations in the above stated cases have been destroyed by fire and that Copies in Substance are presented to the Court, it is ordered that said Copies be established in lieu of the lost originals.

I, Paulin Miedzilski, do Solemnly swear in the presence of Almighty God that I am not possessed of any real or personal estate, debts, credits, or effects, Securities or contracts whatsoever, my wearing apparel, bedding for myself & family, and the working tools ~~and~~ or implements of my trade or calling, together with the necessary equipments for a regular Soldier of the malitia, except other that are contained in the schedule now delivered, and that I have not directly or indirecty Since my imprisonment or before sold, leased, ~~or~~ assigned, or otherwise disposed of, or made over in trust for myself or otherwise any part of my lands, estates, goods, Stock, money, debts, Securities, or contracts, whereby any money may hereafter become payable, or any real or personal estate whereby to have or expect any benefit or profit to myself, my wife, or my heirs. So help me God.

Test. Gerard Burch, Clk   Paulin Miedzielski

[55]

Wells & John Godwin }
        vs   } Ca Sa Muscogee Superior Court
Nathan P. Willard   } October adjourned term 1838

And now at this term Comes Harvey Hall, one of the creditors of the said Nathan P. Willard, and objects to his taking the Oath prescribed for the relief of Honest debtors, for that there has been fraud and consealment on the part of the said Nathan P. Willard. And that the said Nathan P. Willard Since his arrest upon said ca sa and since the obtainment of the Judgment upon which the same is founded has had and still has divers property, dues, & demands which is not contained in said Schedule. And that the said Nathan P. Willard has not made an honest Surrender of all his property & effects in said Schedule. And of this the said Harvey Hall puts himself upon the Country.

                                      Colquitt, Holt & Echols, attors
                                      for Harvey Hall

And the defendant doth the like.   Campbell, McDougald & Watson
                                        att^{ys} for Def^t

A. M. Walker   }
        vs   } Debt
William Kirk, of Muscogee Co. }
& Enoch G. Brown of Harris Co. }

We, the Jury, find for the Plaintiff the sum of seven hundred & ten dollars, with interest & cost of suit.

                                        Thos V. Miller, for

The State   }
    vs   } Arson
Jacob Cunningham   }
& James R. Lyons   }

True Bill.   Mansfield Torrance, Foreman

Shipman, Crane & C° }
    vs   } Debt
G. H. & C. A. Peabody}

We, the Jury, find for the Plaintiff the sum of Seven hundred and fifty one dollars & eighty one cents, with interes & cost of suit.

Thos V. Miller, form

James Whitfield }
    vs   } Case
John B. Peabody }

We, the Jury, find for the Plaintiff the sum of nine hundred & twelve dollars & fifty cents, with interest & cost of suit.

Thos V. Miller, form

Joseph M. Terry }
    vs   } Assumpsit
Allen G. Bass   }

We, the Jury, find for the Plaintiff the Sum of One thousand & eighty eight dollars & forty six cents, with interest, protest fee, & Cost of Suit.

Thos V. Miller, form

[56]   Friday December 14th 1838

Bennedict & Witmore }
    vs   } Debt
Carnes & Tatum   }

We, the Jury, find for the Plaintiffs the sum of One thousand & ninety six dollars & Seventy eight cents, with interest & Cost of suit.

$$\text{Tho}^s \text{ V. Miller, form}$$

Eli E. Gaither }
 vs } Debt
T. & M. Evans }
Calhoun & Bass }
& Edward Cary }

We, the Jury, finf for the Plaintiff the Sum of five thousand eight hundred & eleven dollars & eleven cents, with interest & cost of suit & protest fee.

$$\text{Tho}^s \text{ V. Miller, form}$$

Joseph M. Terry }
 vs } Assumpsit
Matt R. Evans }

We, the Jury, find for the Plaintiff the Sum of One thousand eighty ~~hundred~~ eight dollars & forty six cents, with interest & cost of suit.

$$\text{Tho}^s \text{ V. Miller, form}$$

Joseph M. Terry }
 vs } Assumpsit
John J. Boswell }

We, the Jury, find for the Plaintiff the sum of one thousand & eighty eight dollars & forty six cents, with interest, protest fee, & cost of suit.

$$\text{Tho}^s \text{ V. Miller, form}$$

Joseph M. Terry }
 vs } Assumpsit
Thomas C. Evans }

We, the Jury, find for the Plff the sum of One thousand & eighty eight dollars & forty six cents, with interest, protest fee, & cost of suit.

Thos V. Miller, form

James W. Howard }
    vs   } Debt
Jacob M. Guerry }

We, the Jury, find for the Plaintiff the Sum of Seventy one dollars, with interest & Cost of suit.

Thos V. Miller, form

Simeon McKinny}
    vs   } Case
N. M. C. Robison}

We, the Jury, find for the Plaintiff the Sum of forty Six dollars, with interest & Cost of suit.

Thos V. Miller, form

[57]

James Whitfield }
    vs   } Case
William P. Malone}

I confess Judgment to the Plaintiff for the Sum of eight hundred & fifty dollars, with interest, cost of suit, & protest fee.

Wm P. Malone

James Whitfield }
    vs   } Case
Richard Hooper }

I confess Judgment to the Plaintiff for the sum of nine hundred & twelve dollars & fifty cents, with interest & cost of Suit.

        R. Hooper

James Whitfield }
  vs   } Case
Richard Hooper }

I confess Judgment to the Plaintiff for the sum of eight hundred & fifty dollars, with interest, protest fee, & cost of suit.

        R. Hooper

Hall & Moses }
  vs   } assumpsit
Calhoun & Bass }

We Confess Judgment to the Plffs the Sum of two thousand three hundred & forty three dollars & forty five cents, with interest, protest fee, & cost of suit.

        Thos G. Gordon, Defts atty

Wiley E. Jones }
  vs   } Debt & Garnishment
Joseph Davidson }

I confess Judgment to the Plaintiff in the sum of Eight hundred & fifty dollars, with interest & cost of Suit.

        Joseph Davidson

George B. Nuckolls }
  vs   } Debt
Morgan Jones }

I Confess Judgment to the Plaintiff for the Sum of two hundred & fifty dollars, with interest & Cost of Suit.

        Morgan Jones

Dana Hungerford & C° }
     vs   } assumpsit
Pool, Lively, & McCrary }

We, the Jury, find for the Plaintiffs the Sum of eight hundred & eighty four dollars & ten cents, with interest & cost of suit.

                                            Jn° McGough, form

The Court adjourned to meet again tomorrow morning at nine O'clock.

                                      Marshall J. Wellborn, J. S. C. C. C.

[58]   Muscogee Superior Court October adjourned Term
                    Saturday 15th December 1838

The Court met according to adjournment, present the Honorable Marshall J. Wellborn, J. S. C. C. C.

Hall & Moses }
     vs   } Debt
John H. Ware }

I confess Judgment to the plaintiff for the sum of two hundred & forty dollars, with interest & cost of suit.

                                                   John H. Ware

Burton Hepburn }
     vs   } Assumpsit
Joseph B. Webb }

We, the Jury, find for the Plaintiff the sum of Eight hundred dollars, with interest, protest fee, & cost of suit.

                                            Thos V. Miller, form

An Owens, bearer }
  vs   } Debt
Francis Jepson }
Benjamin Jepson }
& Thomas C. Evans }

I confess Judgment to the Plaintiff for the sum of two hundred & Seventy five dollars, with interest & cost of suit.

        Garrett Hallenbeck, Def^{ts} Att^y

J. S. Smith & Co }
  vs   } Debt
Seymore R. Bonner }

We, the Jury, find for the Plaintiffs the Sum of two hundred & one dollars & fifty cents, with interest & Cost of Suit.

        Thos V. Miller, form

Hall & Moses }
  vs   } Debt
A. L. Rutherford }

We, the Jury, find for the Plaintiff the Sum of One hundred & fifty one dollars & forty nine cents, with interest & cost of Suit.

        Thos V. Miller, form

George W. Turrentine }
  vs   } Assumpsit
Thomas Morris }

I confess Judgment for the Plaintiff the Sum of three hundred & twenty five dollars, with interest & cost of Suit.

        Thos Morris

[59]

James Boykin, Admtr. }
of John Owens, dec^d }
    vs   } Debt
Francis Jepson }
Benjamin Jepson }
& Thomas C. Evans }

We confess Judgment to the Plaintiff for the Sum of one hundred dollars, with interest & cost of Suit.

                              Garrett Hallenbeck, Def^{ts} Att^y

James Whitfield }
    vs   } case
H. Mims & Co }

We, the Jury, find for the Plaintiff the sum of nine hundred & twelve dollars & fifty cents, with interest & cost of Suit.

                              Thos V. Miller, form

Revarius H. L. Buchanan }
    vs   } assumpsit
Templeton Reid }

We, the Jury, find for the Plaintiff the Sum of Seventy nine dollars, with interest & cost of Suit.

                              Thos V. Miller, form

William L. Wynn }
    vs   } Debt
Henry C. Phelps }

We, the Jury, find for the Plaintiff the Sum of four hundred and forty eight dollars, with interest & cost of suit.

                              Thomas V. Miller, form

Robert B. Alexander }
    vs } Assumpsit
J. J. Willson, of Muscogee & }
James Rhind, of Richmond }

We, the Jury, find for the Plaintiff the sum of Six hundred & twenty dollars & Sixty three cents, with interest & cost of Suit.

                        Thos V. Miller, form

Marshall J. Wellborn }
    vs } Assumpsit
Benjamin V. Iverson, principal }
Alfred Iverson }
Jacob M. Guerry }
John J. Boswell & }
Th^o C. Evans, Securities }

I Confess Judgment to the Plaintiff in the Sum of three thousand four hundred & eighty dollars, with interest & cost of Suit.

                        B. V. Iverson, Att^y for Def^{ts}

William S. Hartsfield & Co }
    vs } Debt
Caswell Johnson }

I Confess Judgment to the Plaintiff for the Sum of one hundred & Sixty eight dollars & Sixty nine cents, with interest & cost of Suit.

                        Caswell Johnson

[60]   Saturday 15th December 1838

Robbins, Painter & Co }
    vs } Debt & Bail
John E. Davis }

We, the Jury, find for the Plaintiff the Sum of Seven hundred & twenty dollars & twenty one cents, with interest, protest fee, & cost of Suit.

Thos V. Miller, form

Burton Hepburn }
    vs   { Assumpsit
Seaborn Jones }

I Confess Judgment to the Plaintiff in the sum of eleven thousand one hundred & Seventy three dollars & twenty seven cents, with interest, protest fee, & cost of suit.

Seaborn Jones

A. M. Walker }
    vs   } Assumpsit
Carnes & Tatum }

We, the Jury, find for the Plaintiff the Sum of three hundred and twenty eight dollars, with interest & cost of suit.

Thos V. Miller, form

William L. Wynn }
    vs   } Debt
Robert W. Carnes}

We, the Jury, find for the Plaintiff the Sum of four hundred & fifty dollars, with interest & cost of Suit.

Thos V. Miller, form

Hall & Moses }
    vs   } assumpsit
Wm P. McKeen}

We, the Jury, find for the Plaintiff the sum of two thousand three hundred and forty three dollars & forty five cents, with interest, protest fee, & Cost of Suit.

        Thos V. Miller, form

William Berry }
  vs } Assumpsit
Charles L. Bass }
& Edward Cary }

We, the Jury, find for the Plaintiffs the Sum of four thousand Seven hundred & forty four dollars & fifty cents, with interest, protest fee, & cost of Suit.

        Thos G. Gordon, Def^{ts} att^y

Burton Hepburn {
  vs } assumpsit
James S. Calhoun}

I confess Judgment to the Plff the sum of eleven thousand one hundred & Seventy three dollars & twenty seven cents, with interest, protest fee, & cost of suit.

        Thos G. Gordon, Def^{ts} att^y

[61]

William Berry }
  vs } assumpsit
Seaborn Jones }

I confess Judgment for the Plaintiff in the Sum of four thousand Seven hundred & forty four dollars & fifty cents, with interest, protest fee, & cost of suit.

        Seaborn Jones

Burton Hepburn }
  vs } assumpsit
Charles L. Bass }

I confess Judgment to the Plaintiff in the sum of eleven thousand one hundred & Seventy three dollars & twenty seven cents, with interest, protest fee, & cost of suit, with the right of Appeal.

Thos G. Gordon, Def^{ts} Att^y

William W. Wellborn }
    vs   } assumpsit
A. G. Beckham, maker }
& John H. Ware, Security }

We, the Jury, find for the Plaintiff the sum of One hundred and forty five dollars, with interest & Cost of Suit.

Thos V. Miller, form

Samuel Luckie }
    vs   } assumpsit
Sanders & Powers }

We, the Jury, find for the Plaintiff the Sum of ninety dollars, with interest & cost of suit & protest fee.

Thos V. Miller, form

James B. Bishop }
    vs   } Assumpsit
D. Hungerford }

We, the Jury, find for the Plaintiff the sum of four hundred and Sixty nine dollars & twenty four cents, with interest & cost of suit.

Thos V. Miller, form

Hall & Moses }
    vs   } Debt
Ge^o W. Ross }

We, the Jury, find for the Plaintiff the sum of two hundred & eleven dollars & Seventy cents, with interest & cost of suit.

          Thos V. Miller, form

Daniel C. Crawford }
  vs   } Case
Wm S. Hartsfield & Co }

We, the Jury, find for the Plaintiff the Sum of four hundred dollars, with interest & Cost of suit.

          Thos V. Miller, form

[62]   Saturday 15th December 1838

Hall & Moses }
 vs   } assumpsit
T. & M. Evans }

We, the Jury, find for the Plaintiff the sum of two thousand three hundred & forty three dollars & fifty five cents, with interest, protest fee, & cost of Suit.

          Thos V. Miller, form

Augustus Hayward }
  vs   } Debt
Carnes & Tatum }

We, the Jury, find for the Plaintiff the sum of nine hundred & eighty Six dollars & ninety three cents, with interest & cost of suit.

          Thos V. Miller, form

Hall & Moses }
 vs   } Debt
Asa Bates }

We, the Jury, find for the Plaintiff the sum of five hundred & ninety three dollars & ninety nine cents, with interest & cost of suit.

Thos V. Miller, form

Marshall J. Wellborn }
        vs   } assumpsit
Alpha K. Ayer, prinp^l & }
Abraham B. Ragan, Security }

We, the Jury, find for the Plaintiff the sum of one thousand dollars, with interest & Cost of suit.

Thos V. Miller, form

Smith, Wright, Lyon & Co }
        vs   } Debt
William S. Hartsfield & Co }

We, the Jury, find for the Plaintiffs the sum of Seven hundred & ninety five dollars & forty four cents, with interest, Cost of Suit, & protest fee.

Thos V. Miller, form

Stout, Ingoldsby & Co }
        vs   } assumpsit
George A. Norris }

We, the Jury, find for the Plaintiff the sum of Six hundred & two dollars & thirty five cents, with interest & cost of suit.

Thos V. Miller, form

James H. Shorter vs Thomas C. McKeen. asspt

I confess Judgment the Plaintiff for One hundred & fifty dollars, besides interest & cost of suit.

Thos C. McKeen

[63]

Harper, Thornton, & Livingston }
      vs   } assumpsit
Alpha K. Ayer   }

I Confess Judgment to the Plaintiff for the sum of one hundred and ninety three dollars, with interest, cost of suit, & protest fee.

                        A. K. Ayer

Hall & Moses }
    vs   } Assumpsit
Seaborn Jones }

I confess Judgment to the Plaintiff in the Sum of two thousand three hundred and forty three dollars & forty five cents, with interest, protest fee, & cost of suit.

                        Seaborn Jones

Stout & Ingoldsby   }
      vs   } Assumpsit
Falconar & Kimbrough }

We, the Jury, find for the Plaintiff the sum of three hundred & seventy five dollars, with with interest & Cost of Suit.

                        Thos V. Miller, form

Hall & Moses }
    vs   } Debt
Luther Blake }

We, the Jury, find for the Plaintiff the sum of thirty three dollars, with interest & cost of suit.

                        Thos V. Miller, form

Hall & Moses }
    vs   } Debt
H. Mims }

We, the Jury, find for the Plaintiffs the Sum of ninety four dollars & forty three cents, with interest & cost of suit.

                Thos V. Miller, form

James Boykin, Admtr. &c }
    vs   } Assumpsit
Richard A. Owens }

We, the Jury, find for the Plaintiff the sum of fifty eight dollars & fifty cents, with interest & cost of suit.

                Thos V. Miller, form

William S. Hartsfield & C° }
    vs   } assumpsit
William B. Robison & C° }

We confess Judgment to the Plaintiff in the Sum of One hundred & Seventy one dollars & eighty seven & a quarter cents, with interest & cost of suit.

                J. N. & J. M. Bethune, Def^{ts} Att^{ys}

[64]   Saturday December 15th 1838

William S. Hartsfield & C° }
    vs   } Debt
William B. Robison & C° }

We confess Judgment to the Plff in the sum of three hundred & five dollars & fifty three cents, with interest & cost of Suit.

                J. N. & J. M. Bethune, Def^{ts} Att^{ys}

William S. Hartsfield & C⁰ }
   vs   } Assumpsit
Jeremiah McCoy   }

We, the Jury, find for the Plaintiff the sum of one hundred and fourteen dollars & forty six & one quarter cents and cost of Suit.

         Thos V. Miller, form

Stout, Ingoldsby & C⁰   }
   vs   } Assumpsit
William S. Hartsfield & C⁰ }

We, the Jury, find for the Plff the sum of one thousand & ninety Seven dollars & thirteen cents, with interest, protest fee, & cost of Suit.

         Thos V. Miller, form

Bennedict & Wetmore }
   vs   } Debt
Wm W. Pool &   }
P. R. McCrary   }

We, the Jury, find for the Plaintiff the sum of nine hundred and ninety three dollars & Seventy eight cents, with interest & cost of suit.

         Thos V. Miller, form

Hall & Moses }
  vs   } Debt
Calhoun & Bass }

I confess Judgment to the Plaintiffs the Sum of two hundred & forty one dollars & Seventy three cents, with interest & cost of Suit.

         Thomas G. Gordon, Defts Atty

Harper, Thornton & Levingston }
   vs   } assumpsit
McKee & Prickett   }

We, the Jury, find for the Plaintiffs the sum of one hundred & ninety three dollars, with interest, protest fee, & Cost of Suit.

Thos V. Miller, form

Henry Moffitt }
  vs } Assumpsit
Wiley Harris }

We, the Jury, find for the Plaintiff Sixty Seven dollars, with interest & Costs of suit. 11th Decr 1838

Jn° McGough, F. M.

[65]

Wm P. Burford   }
  vs   } assumpsit
Michael N. Clarke, prinp^l &}
Thos A. Brannon, Security }

We, the Jury, find for the Plaintiff the Sum of one hundred dollars & eighty three & three quarter cents, with interest & Cost of Suit.

Thos V. Miller, form

Wm C. Osborn }
  vs   } assumpsit
Battle A. Sorsby }

I Confess Judgment to the Plaintiff for the sum of twelve Hundred dollars, with interest, protest fee, & cost of suit.

B. A. Sorsby

Daniel Hightower}
  vs } Debt
Thomas James }

I confess Judgment to the Plaintiff for the Sum of ninety Six dollars and fifty five cents, with interest & cost of suit.

Thos James

Wm C. Osborn }
    vs   } assumpsit
W^m & W. Toney }

We, the Jury, find for the Plaintiff the sum of twelve hundred dollars, with interest, cost of suit, & protest fee.

Thos V. Miller, form

John J. Boswell }
    vs   } Debt
John T. Walker }

We, the Jury, find for the Plaintiff the sum of three thousand two hundred & forty dollars, with interest & cost of Suit.

Thos V. Miller, form

Henry Moffitt }
    vs   } Assumpsit Oc^t Adjourned Term 1838
Wiley Harris }

I appearing to the Court that the Original declaration & process in the above case has been destroyed by fire. Ordered that the foregoing Copy be established instanter in lieu of said Original & that the case proceed without delay.

Allen & Young vs Theobald Howard. Assumpsit

Lewis C. Allen & Co vs James Boykin, Adm^r of the Estate of John J. Owens, dec^d. Assumpsit

[66]   Saturday December 15th 1838

James Kirlin }
     vs   } Debt
Calhoun & Bass }

Allen & Young vs John R. Loyd & C° } Assumpsit

Peter McLarin vs Philo D. Woodruff } Debt

Brown & Dimmock vs Johnson, Nuckols, & Brother } Assumpsit

Montross & Howell vs Bernard Mathewson } Assumpsit

North, Manning, & Hoyt vs Bernard Mathewson } Debt

Marcellus Farmer vs James Hitchcock & John G. Hitchcock, Principles & Benjamin V. Iverson, Indorser }

Jacobus & Gathwaite vs John Dillingham & C° } Debt

Johnson, Nuckolls, & Brother   }
       vs   } Assumpsit
Wright & Harris, Principals }
Asel L. Watkins &   }
Randol Tillery, endorser   }

John D. Howell }
     vs   } Assumpsit
Edward Delony }

John D. Howell }
     vs   } Assumpsit
Timothy Collins }

Maltby & Starr   }
     vs   } Assumpsit
G. H. & C. A. Peabody }

Barker & Morgan }
    vs } Assumpsit
J. T. Niles & C° }

[67]

John E. Davis }
    vs } Assumpsit
Timothy Collins & }
Samuel E. Buckler }

Richard C. Baldwin }
    vs } Assumpsit
William & James Blair }

Thomas C. Winthrop }
    vs } Assumpsit
G. H. & C. A. Peabody }

John D. Howell }
    vs } Assumpsit
George W. Ross }

North, Manning, & Hoyt }
    vs } Assumpsit
William P. Malone }

Muscogee Superior Court – October adjourned term 1838

David Golightly in Open Court, being duly sworn, deposeth & saith that the Original declarations, process, & sheriff's returns in each of the above stated cases has been lost by fire and that the copies submitted to the Court are in substance true Copies of the said Originals to the best of his knowledge and belief.

Sworn to in Open Court 14 December 1838.

Gerard Burch, Clk   D. Golightly

Therefore, it is ordered by the Court that said Copies be established in lieu of the Originals.

The State }
    vs } Forgerry ~~&c~~
Edward Boynton }

True bill.   Mansfield Torrance, Foreman

The State }
    vs } Manslaughter
David Measels }

True bill.   Mansfield Torrance, Foreman

[68]   Saturday December 15 1838

Charles L. Bass }
    vs } October adjourned term 1838
Sheldon Swift }

Ca Sa and arrest of defendant and Bond given with Security. It appearing to the Court upon sufficient evidence that the defendant has personally appeared at this term of said Court and that he has served notice upon most of his creditors as we mention in the following list at last term days before the first day of the regular term of this Court of his intention to avail himself of the Benefit of an act intitled an act for the relief of honest debtors passed in the year Eighteen Hundred & twenty three and that he did also before the time of giving said notice file his schedule in terms of said act. it is therefore Ordered by the Court that the Securities of the said defendant be discharged from all further liabilitys upon said Bond and the defendant be forthwith Discharged from all further operation and effect of said Ca Sa and from all others now in Existence or which may or which may hereafter issue in favor of the Creditors or either or any of them herein after named for debts Created at any time before the giving of such notice. Nicholas Howard, Henry Mims, Charles L. Bass, Elisha Tarver, T. & M. Evans, E. & F. Bradley, L. J. Davis, Battle A. Sorsby, Daniel McDougald & C°.

Fellows, Reed, & C°, for use }
of Officers of the Court } October adjourned term 1838
       vs } Ca sa & arrest of Defendant
Paulin Miedzielski } & Bond given with Security

It appearing to the Court upon Sufficient evidence that the defendant has personally appeared at this term of said Court and that he has served notice upon all of his creditors as we mention in the following list at least ten days before the first day of the regular term of this Court of his intention to avail him self of the benefit of an act intitled an act for the relief of honest debtors Passed in the year Eighteen Hundred & twenty three and that he did also before the time of giving said notice file his schedule in terms of said act. it is therefore Ordered by the Court that the Securities of the said defendant be discharged from all further upon said Bond and the defendant be forthwith discharged from

[69] all further operations and effect of said Ca Sa and from all others now in existence or which may hereafter issue in favor of the Creditors or either or any of them herein after named for debts created at any time before the giving of such Notice. List of Creditors notified: D. McDougald, Adolphus L. Heine, Saml E. Buckler, G. W. E. Bedell, Adrew Stevens, Ben^j W. Clapp, F. Duncan, Butran & Dolliver, J. P. Spire, [blank] Brown, John George, Haytt & Tillotson, N. Smith, Prentiss Sackett, Willard & Sewell, Bridgland & Gardin, A. B. Ropes, Smith & Vanderpool, T. & J. Cox, William H. Wilson, [blank] Colfax, Nicholas Ludlum, F. & E. Bradley.

John Cowart, Junr}
      vs } assumpsit
Allen J. Mims & }
James L. Walker }

We, the Jury, find for the Plaintiff the Sum of fifty dollars, with interest & cost of suit.

                                   Jn° McGough, form

Crawford & McKim }
      vs } Debt
W^m & W. Toney }

We confess Judgment to the Plaintiff for the sum of five thousand & Sixty one dollars & fifteen cents, with interest & cost of suit, reserving the right of Appeal.

Colquitt, Holt, & Echols, Def[ts] Att[ys]

Samuel Thompson }
    vs } Assumpsit
Calhoun & Bass }

I confess Judgment to the Plaintiff for the Sum of thirteen hundred and Seventy eight dollars & eighty two cents, with interest & cost of Suit, reserving the right of Appeal.

Tho[s] G. Gordon, Def[ts] Att[y]

Olcot & McKisson & C° }
    vs } Assumpsit
W[m] & W. Toney }

We confess Judgment to the Plaintiffs for the Sum of four hundred & two dollars & Sixty six cents, with interest and cost of Suit.

Colquitt, Holt, & Echols, Def[ts] Att[ys]

The Court adjourned to meet again on monday morning next at half past nine O'clock.

Marshall J. Wellborn, J. S. C. C. C.

[70]   Muscogee Superior Court October adjourned term 1838
                Monday 17th day of December 1838

The Court met according to adjournment, present the Honorable Marshall J. Wellborn, J. S. C. C. C.

The State }
    vs } Simple Larceny
John Fox }

Copy of Bill of indictment & list of witnesses waived by Western Harwell & Lorenzo Dow Glenn, arraignment at October Adj^d Term 1838.

J. N. & J. M. Bethune, Att^y for Def^{ts}

The State }
    vs   } Robberry
William Harwell }

The Prisoner, William Harwell, is arraigned & pleads not guilty at Oc^t adj^d Term.

Henry L. Benning, So^l Gen C. C.

D. Hungerford & Co }
    vs   } Assumpsit
William Rogers }

We, the Jury, find for the Plff the sum of fifty three dollars & fifty cents, with interest & cost of suit.

Jno McGough, form

George Field }
    vs   } Assumpsit
Chisholm & Collins }

We, the Jury, find for the Plff the Sum of two hundred dollars, with interest & Cost of suit.

Jno McGough, form

George Field }
    vs   } Assumpsit
Sullivan & Ryder }

We, the Jury, find for the Plaintiff the sum of two hundred dollars, with interest & Cost of suit.

Jno McGough, form

Greenway, Henry & C⁰ }
      vs   } Assumpsit
W^m & W. Toney   }

We confess Judgment to the Plaintiff for the Sum of twelve hundred and ninety four dollars, with interest & cost of suit.

                                                  Colquitt, Holt, & Echols, Def^{ts} Att^{ys}

[71]   Monday 17th December 1838

The State   }
    vs   } Simple Larceny
John Fox   }
Western Harwell & }
Lorenzo Dow Glenn }

All the Prisoners are arraigned & plead not guilty at Oc^t Adj^d Term 1838.

                                                  Henry L. Benning, So^l Genl C. C.

The State }
    vs   } Simple Larceny
John Fox }

        1. John McGough   7. Bird B. Mitchell
        2. Zepheniah Parker   8. Thomas Motley
        3. Isaac Webb   9. Francis Jepson
        4. Joseph Phelps   10. Thomas V. Miller
        5. John C. Tozier   11. Abner Hill
        6. Seaborn Ely   12. Umphrey Rowell

We, the Jury, find the Prisoner Guilty.

                                                John McGough, Fm

The State }
    vs   } Simple Larceny
John Fox }

Evidence. Alfred M. Terry Sworn says on the third day of Nov last he lost two Horses at night, one was a dunn Sorrell four years old, the other a chestnut Sorrell five years old, both geldings of ordinary size worth $100 neach (was at the oglethorp House same evening about Sunsett Mr Wm H. Harwell came to him and asked him what he was doing there) Horses were taken from him in this town in the County of Muscogee on the 3rd Nov past. Cross Examined: prisoner requested witness to watch Ross's Saddle & Bridle and probably we might make some a discovery by watching his Saddle & Bridle. he would help him recover him by following Ross. usually has seen prisoner at the Corner where he usually Staid when he called for him.

Hamilton Perry Sworn. Mr Fox, Mr West Harvell, & Mr Dow Glenn brought two Horses described in the bill of Indictment to witness on Saturday night the third of Nov last and told him to take one of them off and sell him in Fayette County. witness took the dunn Sorrell horse. horses were brought to him near Mrs Parks in this place. Dow Glenn took the other horse. it was about 10 O'clk at night. the Horses were worth $100 each. they told me to take $65 for the one I had. West Harvell gave him three dollars to bear his Expense.

[72] they told witness to be at that place and they would bring the Horses. they were not gone many minutes before they brought them and told witness to bring back another horse with him when he sold that one.

Cross Examined. Witness became acquainted with Fox, the Prisoner, the day Owens was killed. Fox & Harwell were together when the Horses were brought. both the horses were brought at the same time by Fox & Harwell & Glenn and Harwell gave him three dollars to beare his expenses and Fox said he ought to give him five dollars. that was in the County and on the night of the third November last.

The State }
    vs   } Simple Larceny
John Fox }

       1. John McGough   7. Bird B. Mitchell
       2. Zepheniah Parker   8. Thomas Motley
       3. Isaac Webb   9. Francis Jepson
       4. Joseph Phelps   10. Thomas V. Miller

5. John C. Tozier 11. Abner Hill
6. Seaborn Ely 12. Umphrey Rowell

We, the Jury, find the Prisoner, John Fox, Guilty.

Jn° McGough, form

The State of Georgia }
    vs   } Simple Larceny
John Fox   }

Evidence.

John Bethune, Senr Sworn. I had the charge & possession of a negro man named Sovereign who belonged to General Watson. the slave was worth between five and Six hundred dollars. Witness went to Cherokee in October & returned in November & the negro was absent & he has not Seen him since. The negro is the same as described in the Bill of Indictment. Witness gave his note to General Watson for the hire of the year.

William Ross Sworn. Witness went into the lot where John Fox staid about the time of the close of the revival in Columbus in this County and found the negro described in the Indictment in the Lot. Fox was not in the lot, but at Harvil's corner about fifty yards off. the negro was in one of Foxes Stables. Witness went off and the next day Saw Fox himself. Fox told Witness that there was a great chance to make some money. Witness asked him in what way, by taking Horses or what. Fox said it was something about a negro business.

[73] Witness asked him whose and he would not tell him. the next night witness saw the negro in the possession of Mr Cunningham by a little waggon near Foxes House. never saw him afterwards. this was near two months ago in this town. have never seen the negro Since. it was about 12 O'clock in the day that Witness saw the negro in Foxes Stable. the Stable door was Shut.

William G. Porter}
    vs   } Assupsit
Moore & Tarver }

We, the Jury, find for the Plaintiff the sum of Three Hundred & thirty six dollars nineteen cents, with Interest & Cost of suit.

Jn° McGough, Fm

Olcot, McKisson, & C° }
   vs   } Assumpsit
W^m & W. Toney }

We confess Judgment to the plaintiffs for the sum of Nine Hundred & fifty seven dollars sixty seven cents, with interest & Cost of Suit.

Colquitt, Holt, & Echols, Def^{ts} Att^y

Lemuel H. Hamilton }
   vs   } Assumpsit
Eldridge S. Greenwood }

We, the Jury, find for the Plaintiff the sum of Seven Hundred & Twenty five dollars, with Interest & cost of suit.

Jn° McGough, Fm

Michael Harned }
  vs   } Assumpsit
Jacob M. Johnson}

We, the Jury, find for the Plaintiff the sum of Seven Hundred & thirty six dollars & forty four cents, with Interest & Cost of Suit.

Jn° McGough, Fm

Dekeman & Mills }
  vs   } Assumpsit
John G. Mulford }

We, the Jury, find for the Plaintiff the Sum of Two Hundred & twenty nine dollars & eighty cents, with interest & Cost of Suit.

Jn° McGough, Fm

Lemuel H. Hamilton }
     vs   } Assumpsit
Isaac Mitchell   }

I confess Judgment to the Plaintiff for Seven Hundred & twenty five dollars, with Interest & Cost of Suit.

                                                    J. N. & J. M. Bethune, def[ts] att[ys]

[74]   Monday 17th December 1838

Garrett Hallenbeck   }
     vs   } Debt
Jacob M. Guerry, Principal }
& Edward Delony, Security }

We, the Jury, find for the Plaintiff the sum of Four Hundred & twenty dollars principle, with Interest & Cost of suit. december 14 1838

                                          Jn[o] McGough, Fm

Grieve & Rankin   }
     vs   } Debt
Jonathan P. Jackson}

I confess Judgment to the plaintiff for the sum of Fifty two dollars & twelve cents principle, with Interest & Cost of Suit.

                                         (Signed) J. P. Jackson

Chares H. Stewart }
     vs   } Debt
Jonathan P. Jackson}

I confess Judgment to the Plaintiff for the sum of One Hundred & Eighty dollars principle, with Interest & Cost of Suit.

                                         (Signed) J. P. Jackson

James Rankin, bearer }
  vs   } Assumpsit
John J. Wilson   }

I confess Judgment to the Plaintiff for the sum of forty three dollars & thirty three cents principal, with interest & Cost of Suit.

        J. J. Willson

James S. Norman, Adm^r & }
Henrietta Whilte, Admr^x of }
John S. W. White, deceased}
  vs   } Assumpsit
John J. Wilson   }

I confess Judgment to the plaintiff for the sum of One Hundred & twenty one dollars principle, with Interest & costs of suit.

        J. J. Wilson

John Logan   }
  vs   } Assumpsit
Benjamin G. Kenney, Maker }
& Thomas A. Brannon & }
George W. Short, Guarantors }
& securities   }

We confess Judgment to the Plaintiff for the sum of four Hundred & forty five dollars & forty six cents principal, with with interest & cost of suit.

        G. W. Short
        T. A. Brannon
        B. G. Kinney

[75]

Samuel A. Bailey }
    vs Wrong Entry } Assumpsit
Alfred M. Terry }
John Johnson (Security &) }
Samuel R. Andrews (Security) }

We, the Jury, find for the plaintiff Eleven Hundred & Sixty dollars, with Interest, two dollars protest fee, & cost.

                                T. V. Miller, Fm

Brown, Brother, & C° }
    vs } asst
Ragan, Colquit & Grant }

We confess Judgment to the plaintiff for Thirty three Hundred & thirty nine dollars fifteen cents, with interest & Cost this 13th day of December 1838.

                          Colquit, Holt & Echols, def[s] att[y]

Levi Cook & C° }
    vs } Assumpsit
John G. Mulford }

I confess Judgment to the plaintiffs for the sum of Four Hundred & four dollars, with interest thereon from the thirty first day of January Eighteen Hundred & thirty eight & Costs this [blank] day of December 1838.

                               John G. Mulford

William Atkison }
    vs } Assumpsit
Thomas C. McKeen }

I confess Judgment to the plaintiff for the sum of Three Hundred & three dollars, with Interest & Costs this [blank] day of December 1838.

                               Nicholas L. Howard, def[s] att[y]

Joseph T. Atwell }
    vs   } Assumpsit
Adolphus L. Heine }

I confess Judgment to the plaintiff in the sum of Eleven hundred & twenty five dollars & ninety one cents, with interest & Cost this 13 of December 1838.

                              A. L. Heine

Battle A. Sorsby }
    vs   } Assumpsit
Thomas G. Gordon }

I confess Judgment to the plaintiff for the sum of Eleven hundred & twenty five dollars & ninety one cents, with interest & Cost this 13th december 1838.

                              Thomas G. Gordon

[76]   Monday 17th December 1838

A. L. Heine }
    vs   } Assumpsit
Jacobi & Miedzielski }

We confess Judgment to plaintiff Five Hundred & seventy two dollars, with interest & Costs this 13th Decr 1838.

                              Colquit, Holt & Echols, def^{ts} att^{ys}

Amasa Walker }
    vs   } Assumpsit
Chisholm & Collins }

We Confess Judgment to the Plaintiff the Sum of Seven Hundred & forty two dollars & forty three cents, with Interest & Cost this 13th December 1838.

                              John Schley, def^{ts} att^y

Edward Kellogg & C⁰ }
    vs   } ~~Debt~~ Assumpsit
Bucklu & Short   }

We, the Jury, find for the Plaintiffs for the sum one thousand & eighty six dollars eighty one cents, with interest & Costs.

                          Jn⁰ McGough, form

Seaman & Ward   }
    vs   } assumpsit
G. H. & C. A. Peabody }

We Confess Judgment to the Plaintiff for the Sum of two hundred & Sixty five dollars & Sixty three cents, with interest & cost of suit.

                      Campbell, McDougald, & Watson, Def^{ts} Attorneys

Edward Kellogg }
    vs   } assumpsit
E. C. Bandy   }

I confess Judgment to the Plaintiff for the sum of one thousand & eighty six dollars eighty one cents, with interest & Costs. 13 December 1838

                      Campbell, McDougald, & Watson, Def^{ts} Att^{ys}

A. B. Davis   }
    vs   } assumpsit
John R. Lloyd & C⁰ }

We Confess Judgment to the Plaintiff for the Sum of One thousand & eighty five dollars & fifty seven cents, with interest & Costs. 13th December 1838.

                      Campbell, McDougald, & Watson, Def^{ts} Att^{ys}

[77]

A. L. Heine }
    vs   } assumpsit
E. Wheelock }

I confess Judgment to the Plaintiff for the sum of four hundred & fifty dollars, with interest & costs.

                       Campbell, McDougald, & Watson, Def[ts] Att[ys]

Thomas H. Hall }
    vs   } assumpsit
Joseph Davidson }

We, the Jury, find for the Plaintiff the sum of one hundred and fifty dollars, with interest & costs.

                       Jn° McGough, form

William T. Gould }
    vs   } assumpsit
William S. Hartsfield & C° }

We, the Jury, find for the Plaintiff the Sum of fourteen hundred & eighty four dollars & ninety cents, with interest & costs.

                       Jn° McGough, form

Doremus, Seydams, & Nixon }
    vs   } assumpsit
William S. Hartsfield & C° }

We, the Jury, find for the Plaintiff the sum of nine hundred & forty dollars & ninety six cents, with interest & costs.

                       Jn° McGough, form

Battle A. Sorsby }
    vs   } assumpsit
Micajah Bennett }

We, the Jury, find for the Plaintiff the Sum of one hundred & Seventy nine dollars & eighty two cents, with interest & costs.

                                          Jn° McGough, form

Battle A. Sorsby   }
    vs   } assumpsit
E. L. De Graffenried }

We, the Jury, find for the Plaintiff for the Sum of fifty eight dollars & fifty five cents, with interest & Cost.

                                          Jn° McGough, form

The State   }
    vs   } Simple Larceny
James Jernigan }

True Bill.   Mansfield Torrance, Foreman

The Court adjourned to meet again tomorrow morning at half past nine O'clock.

                                      Marshall J. Wellborn, J. S. C. C. C.

[78]   Superior Court October Term Adjourned term
                         Tuesday 18th December 1838

The Court met according to adjournment, present the Honorable Marshall J. Wellborn, Judge of the Superior Courts in the Chattahoochee Circuit.

The State of Georgia }
      vs   } Simple Larceny
John Fox   }
Western Harwell & }
Lorenzo Dow Glen }

1. John McGough
2. Umphrey Rowell
3. John Warren
4. Isaac H. Webb
5. Martin Brooks
6. Thomas V. Miller
7. Thomas Motley
8. Seaborn Eley
9. Francis Jepson
10. Bird B. Mitchell
11. Price Davis
12. Mathew H. Pool

We, the Jury, find the Prisoner, Lorenzo Dow Glen, guilty.

Jn° McGough, form

The State of Georgia }
    vs   } Simple Larceny
Lorenzo Dow Glenn }

Evidence

Hamilton Perry sworn. Mr Fox, Mr West Harvell, & Mr Glenn brought two horses to Witness. they gave one to Witness and gave one to Glenn. they told witness to take the one they gave him to Fayette County and sell him and bring back another. Witness took one and Glenn the other and went in different courses. One was a Bright Sorrel, the other a brown Sorrell of common size. was geldings worth about $100 each. The horses were brought to Witness on Saturday night about 11 O'clk about the second or third days of November last. Glenn had the bright Sorrell and Witness the dark Sorrell. Fox, West Harvell, & Glenn told witness to be at the place where the horses were brought, and they would meet him with the horses. the place designated was near Mrs Parks in this town. one of the horses was four years old and the other five years old. Witness knows the horses were stolen but did not know to whom they belonged. they were gone about twenty minutes after the horses and Mr Glenn said they would have been back sooner but there were some negroes shucking corn and he was afraid they would see him.

Cross Examination

Fox, Harvell, & Glenn brought the horses to Witness on Saturday night by previous arrangement made at Harvell's corner about

[79] two hours before they were brought. Witness took one horse and Glenn tok the ~~the~~ other. they required no certificate or instrument from him to return

the money for the sale of the horse. Glenn was on his horse and said he was going. Witness did not see him start. It was a moon light night and was raining. Witness got wet. Witness has lived in Harris County about five years. Had seen Glenn several times before. Witness got on his horse and went off leaving Glenn on his. Witness has been promised that if he would come out and swear to the truth and nothing but the truth against these fellows he should not be prosecuted. Witness made the disclosure to Dr Wilson & Mr Robinson before the promise was made to him not to prosecute him. The Bridle on the Horse given to Witness was an old snaffle bit Bridle without throat latch and a String tied to the end of the reins.

John Code Sworn. says on Saturday night about the time Terry's Horses were missing he and Higginson had a corn shucking near their Stable in the field where Terry's Horses were kept. Witness bridle was also missing. bridle was an old twisted bit snaffle and tied at the end of the Reins as well as he remembers. Witness knows that it was a moonlight night but does not remember that it rained.

Marks Higginson Sworn. Witness and Code had a corn shucking about the time Terry's were Missing in the field where the horses were kept. Witness drove the horses from the corn pile on the evening of the night upon which they were missing. it was a moon light night and commenced clouding up late in the night.

Wm Ross sworn. Saw Glenn at Mrs Evans's near the Bridge on Friday the Second day of November last. Glenn asked him if he did not want to take a ride that night. Witness replied that he did not. Witness asked Glenn whose horses he was going to take and he said he was going to take Terry's. Witness told him he had better let Terry's horses alone, for if Terry got on track of him he would pursue him to hell. He saw Glenn the next evening after eight O'clk. Glenn said every thing was Ready and asked witness if he would go. Witness said he would not. Cross Examined. It was about 8 or 9 O'clock in the morning when he saw Glen near the Bridge. Witness sent for Mr Bethune, Mrs Echols, and others to whom he divulged his knowledge of persons engaged in the business. He was told if he would tell the whole truth about it he would not be prosecuted.

Coln Seaborn Jones Sworn. Says that to the best of his recollection it rained on Saturday night the 3rd November last.

Robert Alexander Sworn. Says that it threatened rain in the fore part of Saturday night the 3rd November last and did rain in the latter part of it. Abraham Odom

[80] Tuesday 18th December 1838

Abraham Odom Sworn. That Glen went home with Witness on Friday night the second of November last & stayed all night. Witness rose on Saturday morning about five O'clock and Glen was there and went with him to the Justices court ground and remained with hm during the day till about sun set or a little after. Glenn & Aaron Turner then left ~~for Turner's Witnesses House~~ Witnesses House for Turner's House and he saw nothing of Glenn till next morning after breakfast. Witness lives about six or seven miles from Columbus. It rained on Saturday night in the latter part of it and misted in the early part of it. it rained at Intervals through Sunday. Glenn & Turner both married daughters of Witness. Turner lives about a mile and a half from Witness house. Witness thinks he saw avery Odom at the hanging of the Negro on Friday but did not see him on Saturday or Sunday.

☞ The ballance of the evidence on page 101.

James K. Daniel }
  vs   } Assumpsit
William B. Robinson & C°}

We, the Jury, find for the plaintiff Nine Hundred & fifty dollars, with interest & cost of Suit and three dollars for Cost of Protest.

          Jn° McGough, Fm

Simeon Peteet }
 vs   } Debt
Joseph Davidson }

I confess Judgment to the Plaintiff for Four Hundred & twenty five dollars, with Interest & costs of suit. Oct 15 1838

         D. Golightly, defs atty

Battle A. Sorsby }
    vs   } Debt
Arthur Johnson }

We, the Jury, find for the Plaintiff One Hundred & two dollars & Seventy five cents, with interest & Cost of Suit.

                                          Jnº McGough. Fm

Battle A. Sorsby }
    vs   } Debt
Charles F. Spiller }

We, the Jury, find for the plaintiff One Hundred & twenty three dollars & Eighty cents, with interest & Cost of Suit.

                                          Jnº McGough. Fm

[81]

Joseph B. Green & Cº }
    vs   } Assumpsit
John C. Corley   }

We, the Jury, find for the Plaintiff Eighteen Hundred & eight dollars and fifty five cents, with Interest from the fifteenth day of February Eighteen Hundred & thirty eight and costs of suit and three dollars Costs of Protest.

                                          Jnº McGough. Fm

The State   }
    vs   } Roberry
William Harwell }

        1. Thomas Preston, Junʳ   7. Thomas Motley
        2. John McGough   8. Francis Jepson
        3. Isaac H. Webb   9. Thomas V. Miller
        4. Umphrey Rowell   10. Pattrick H. Britton
        5. Zephaniah Parker   11. Robert Moore
        6. Seaborn Eley   12. Aaron Furgerson

We, the Jury, find the prisoner Guilty.

          Thomas Preston, Jun[r], forman

William Nelms }
  vs   } Assumpsit
James Rhind }

We find for the Plaintiff Thirteen hundred dollars, with interest & cost of suit.

          Jn° McGough, Fm

Spofford & Tileston }
  vs   } Assumpsit
W[m] & W. Toney }

We confess Judgment to the Plaintiffs for Three Hudred & forty seven dollars & forty seven cents, with interest & Costs of Suit.

          Colquit, Holt, & Echols, def[ts] att[ys]

John Jones   }
  vs   } Debt
Patrick J. Murray }

I confess judgment to the Plaintiff for One Hudred & fifty dollars, with interest & cost of Suit.

          D. Golightly, Def[s] Att[y]

Brewster, Solomon & C° }
  vs   } Assumpsit
B. A. Sorsby   }

We, the Jury, find for the Plaintiff Six Hundred & fifty two dollars & twelve Cents, with interest & Costs of Suit and Six dollars Cost of protest.

          Jn° McGough, Fm

[81]

Elliott W. Gregory } Assumpsit and verdict for the Plaintiff for
vs } ~~nineteen~~ Nine hundred and twenty one dollars,
Charles E. & Henry Mims } with interest & Cost

The Defendants, being dissatisfied with the verdict of the Jury rendered in the above cause and having paid all costs and demanded an appeal, brings George W. Martin and [blank] tenders them as their securities, and they, the said Charles E. Mims & Henry Mims, acknowledge themselves Jointly and severally bound to Elliott W. Gregory for the Payment of the eventual Condemnation money in said cause.

In Testimony whereof, they have hereunto set their hands and seals this twenty second day of December 1838.

Test. Gerard Burch, Clk   C. E. Mims
             H. Mims
             Ge° W. Martin

The Bank of Columbus }
  vs   } assumpsit
C. W. Buckley & C° }

We confess Judgment to the Plaintiff for the sum of Five hundred dollars, with interest & cost of suit & protest fee, reserving the right of Appeal.

             Colquitt, Holt, & Echols, Def^{ts} Att^{ys}

The Bank of Columbus }
  vs   } assumpsit
D. Hungerford & C° }

We ~~the~~ Confess Judgment to the Plaintiff for the sum of five hundred dollars, with interest & cost of suit & protest fee, reserving the right of Appeal.

             Colquitt, Holt, & Echols, Def^{ts} Att^{ys}

R. & G. Barker }
    vs   } Debt
John G. Mulford }

We, the Jury, find for the Plaintiff the Sum of Five thousand five hundred & fifteen dollars & fifteen cents, with interest & cost of Suit.

                        Jn° McGough, form

James H. Shorter }
    vs   } Assumpsit
Charles L. Bass }

I Confess Judgment to the Plff for the Sum of Seven hundred and Sixty six dollars & Sixty six cents, besides interest, cost of suit, & protest fee.

                        Thomas G. Gordon, Def[ts] Att[ys]

[82]

John Doe, on the Several demises }
of Allen Davis & Thomas Motley }
        vs   } Ejectment and verdict for the Plaintiff
Richard Roe, casual ejector &   } for the premises in dispute and twenty
Henry Mann, tenant in possession } four dollars mean profits

The Defendant, being dissatisfied with the verdict of the Jury in the above cause And having paid all cost and demanded an Appeal, brings Newitt L. Smith and tenders him as his Security. and they, the said Henry Mann, Defendant, and the said Newitt L. Smith, acknowledge themselves Jointly & Severally bound unto the said Thomas Motley & Allen Davis, Plaintiffs, for the payment of the eventual condemnation money in said cause.

In Witness whereof, we have hereunto Set their hands and seals this 27th day of December 1838.

Test. Gerard Burch, Clk   Henry Mann
                                           N. L. Smith

James H. Shorter }
    vs   } Assumpsit
Charles L. Bass }

I confess Judgment to the Plaintiff for one hundred and fifty dollars, besides interest & cost of suit & protest fee of three dollars, reserving the right of Appeal.

                                Thos G. Gordon, Def^{ts} Att^y

James H. Shorter   }
    vs   } Assumpsit
Timothy Collins, maker }
Underwood, Torrence &C^o & }
Benjamin P. Tarver, endorser }

We, the Jury, find for the Plaintiff five hundred dollars, besides interest and cost of suit.

                                Jno McGough, forman

James H. Shorter   }
    vs   } Assumpsit
Isaac Mitchell, pr & }
Battle A. Sorsby   }
endorser & Security}

We, the Jury, find for the Plaintiff eight hundred & forty nine dollars, besides interest & cost of suit.

                                Jno McGough, form

James H. Shorter }
    vs   } Assumpsit
Asa Bates   }

I confess Judgment for the Plaintiff eighteen hundred & Seventy five dollars, besides interest, costs of Suit, & protest fee.

                        Campbell, McDougald, & Watson, Def^{ts} Att^{ys}

James H. Shorter }
    vs   }
Wm W. Pool   }

We, the Jury, find for the Plaintiff Sixteen hundred and twenty dollars, besides interest, Costs of Suit, & three dollars Protest fee.

                                    Thos V. Miller, form

[83]   Tuesday 18th December 1838

Stewart & Fontaine }
    vs   } Debt
Jacob Funderburk }

Settled & cost paid.

Arthur B. Davis, Surviving Copartner }
of the firm Davis & Shorter   }
        vs   } Assumpsit
Philo D. Woodruff & James N. Bethune }

Dismissed at Plff^s cost.

Arthur B. Davis, Surviving Copartner }
of the firm Davis & Shorter   }
        vs   } Assumpsit
Philo D. Woodruff & James N. Bethune }

Dismissed at Plff^s cost.

Preston & Nelms   }
    vs   } Assumpsit
William B. Roberson & Co}
& Thomas C. Evans   }

Settled.

Hannah Hiatt }
    vs   { Trover &c
David Ritch }

Settled & cost paid to J. D. Bethune.

James H. Shorter }
    vs   } Asspt.
James H. Campbell, pr }
John D. Howell & }
Theobald Howard, endorsers }

We confess Judgment to the Plaintiff for the sum of thirteen hundred & fifty dollars, with interest & cost of suit.

            Campbell, McDougald, & Watson, Def^{ts} Att^{ys}

James H. Shorter, admtr. & }
Sophiah H. Shorter, admtrx. }
of Eli S. Shorter, dec^d }
    vs   } Asspt.
Daniel McDougald }

I Confess Judgment to the Plaintiff Six hundred & ninety dollars, with interest & Cost of Suit & three dollars for cost of Protest.

            Campbell, McDougald, & Watson, Def^{ts} Att^{ys}

James H. Shorter }
    vs   }
Thomas Hoxey }

We, the Jury, find for the Plaintiff twelve Hundred & fifty dollars, besides interest, costs of suit, & protest fee of three dollars.

            Jno McGough, form

[84]

James H. Shorter }
vs }
Thomas C. Evans }

We, the Jury, find for the Plaintiff twelve hundred and fifty dollars, besides interest, cost of suit, & protest fee.

Jn° McGough, form

James H. Shorter, admtr. & }
Sophiah H. Shorter, Admtrx. }
of Eli S. Shorter, dec^d }
vs } Asspt.
Thomas C. Evans }
Matt R. Evans & }
John H. Ware }

We, the Jury, find for the Plaintiff sixty three dollars & twenty five cents, besides interest & Cost of Suit.

Jn° McGough, form

James H. Shorter }
vs } assumpsit
Henry Mims }

I confess Judgment to the Plaintiff Seventeen hundred & fifty dollars, besides interest, costs of suit, & Protest fee.

Henry Mims

James H. Shorter }
vs } Assp^t
Calhoun & Bass, prin. & }
John L. Lewis, endorser & Security }

We, the Jury, find for the Plaintiff One thousand dollars, besides interest & Cost of Suit.

Thos V. Miller, form

James H. Shorter }
     vs   } Assumpt.
William P. Malone }

I confess Judgment to the Plaintiff thirty nine hundred dollars, besides interest, Cost of Suit, & protest fee.

W. P. Malone

James H. Shorter }
     vs   }
Kenith McKinzie }

I confess Judgment to the Plaintiff twelve hundred & fifty dollars, besides interest, Costs of Suit, & protest fee.

Kenith Mackenzie, Defendant

James H. Shorter }
     vs   } Assumpsit
Asa Bates & }
Thos C. Evans }

We, the Jury, find for the Plaintiff one hundred dollars, besides interest & cost of suit.

Jn° McGough, form

The Court adjourned to meet again tomorrow morning at nine O'clock.

Marshall J. Wellborn, J. S. C. C. C.

[unnumbered] Muscogee Superior Court October adjourned term
Wednesday 19th day of December 1838

The Court met according to adjournment, present the Honorable Marshall J. Wellborn, Judge of the Superior Courts of the Chattahoochee Circuit.

The State }
   vs } Simple Larceny
Maberry Howell }
Weston Harwell }
William Harwell } October adjourned term 1838
Avery Odom & }
John Fox }

I have Served Maberry Howell, Weston Harwell, William Hawell, & John Fox each with a Copy of this Bill of Indictment & list of Witnesses 18th December 1838.

       Alpha K. Ayer, Dep Shff

October adjourned term 1838.

Maberry Howell, Weston Harwell, William Hawell, & John Fox each arraigned & plead not Guilty.

       Henry L. Benning, Sol. Gen[l]

   Muscogee Superior Court Oct adjd term 1838

William H. Watkins, having commited a contempt of the Court in rushing from its presence in order to evade service upon the Jury & contrary to the order of the Court, it is ordered by the Court that he do pay a fine of Five dollars.

The State }
   vs } Misdemeanor
Magirt Ivey }

True Bill.   Mansfield Torrence, forman

The State }
   vs   } Furnishing a Slave with Spiritous liquor
Magirt Ivey }

True Bill.   Mansfield Torrence, form

The State }
   vs   } Furnishing a Slave with Spiritous Liquor
Magirt Ivey }

True Bill.   Mansfield Torrence, form

Smith & Wright }
    vs   } Assumpsit
Howard & Wittich }

[87]

Affa Maria Gray }
    vs   } Assumpsit
H. Mims & C° }

We, the Jury, find for the plaintiff Four Hundred dollars, with interest & Cost of Suit and three dollars for Cost of Protest.

                                  Jn° McGough, Fm

Rich^{ds}, Kingsland & C° }
    vs   } Assumpsit
Dana Hungerford & }
Edwd G. Rogers   }

We, the Jury, find for the plaintiff against Dana Hungerford Four Hundred & Seventeen dollars & forty cents, with interest & Costs of Suit and three dollars cost of protest.

                                  Jn° McGough, Fm

E. S. Greenwood & Cº }
     vs   } Debt
H. Mims & Cº   }

We, the jury, find for the plaintiff Two Hundred & four dollars & four cents, with interest & Cost of Suit.

                          Jnº McGough, Fm

Mary P. Grant, admrx & }
Thomas F. Foster, admr }
     vs   } Assumpsit
William P. Malone   }

We, the Jury, find for the plaintiff Eight Hundred dollars, with interest and Cost of suit.

                          Jnº McGough, Fm

J. W. & R. Leavitt }
     vs   } Assumpsit
Wm & W. Toney }

We, the Jury, find for the Plaintiffs Six Hundred & fifteen dollars & seventeen cents, with interest & Cost of Suit & three dollars for costs of Protest.

                          Jnº McGough, Fm

Insurance Bank of Columbus}
     vs   } Assumpsit
James C. Watson   }

I confess Judgment to the Plaintiff for Six Thousand two Hundred & fifty dollars, with Interest & Cost of Suit and three dollars for Cost of Protest.

                    Campbell, McDougald, & Watson, Defts Atty

[88]   Wednesday 19th December 1838

The Insurance Bank of Columbus }
        vs   } Assumpsit
James C. Watson   }

I confess Judgment to the Plaintiff for the Sum of Twenty Six Thousand dollars, with interest & Cost of Suit & three dollars for Cost of protest.

                       Campbell, McDougald, & Watson, Def[s] Att[y]

The State of Georgia }
       vs   } Robbery
William Harvil   }

Evidence 1st Witness. Hamilton Perry being sworn says he ate his supper & walked down to the Corner next the River in this town & County, turned the corner and came up to Western Harvil's grocery as he passed along by the [blank] William Havil came out of the grocery & joined him. there were several persons in the grocery gambling. thinks the boat hand came out of the house. won't be certain. he walked 5 or 6 steps in front of Witness & prisner walked on together about 30 steps & Harvil left Witness & Over took boat hand and knocked him down with a stick & took his pocket book. Witness asked prisner why he did it. prisoner said he had been owing him some time & he could not get it & would beat it out of the damned son of a bitch. prisner told him he had taken 10 dollars out of the pocket book & then threw it down in the face or on the boddy of the boat hand. Witness and prisner walked on about 100 yards towds the Columbus Exchange & prisner turned back & witness went on. don't know what time of night it was. thinks it was about 8 or 9 O'clk about the month of April 1837. Boat hand was a low, chunky, dark haired man, wearing a flat straw sailor hat and pea Jacket. hat was pitched over. when knocked down, lay motionless. this was done in Clumbus in this County.

                       Cross Ex

Witness says it was done the last day of March or first day of April 1837. When witness first saw boat hand, he was 6 or 8 feet above West Harvill's door walking up towds town. when witness fell in with Harvill, he did not know that he was pursuing the boat hand or intended to beat him. did not take him away from boat hand when Harvill struck. & had noting to do with him. never saw him before

[89] nor afterwards & don't know his name. Witness had been in Columbus 3 or 4 weeks. Witness ate his supper that evening at City Hall. didn't board there regularly. Witness knows it was the 1st of April because he was in town then. Harvill says he took ten dollars. Witness saw what he took to be money. witness went & viewed the boat hand. he was speechless. looked in his face. Harvill said he would beat it out of the damed son of a bitch. Concludes he was a boat hand from his dress. Can't recollect whether it was a moon shine night or not, but thinks it was a light night. Witness stayed sometime at Whiteside's, sometimes at Greaves', sometimes over the river. Witness saw the Paper in Prisner's hands. Prisoner said it was 10 dollars. thinks prisoner put it in his Pocket. don't recollect what day of the week it was. went over the river next day, next day after it happened. Witness went over the river & did not work on that day. does not know whether he put the money in his pocket or not but has reason to think so & his reason is that ~~when~~ men generally put money into their pockets when they have it. does not know whether it was money or not, but Harvill said it was. Witness says a big fat man was barr keeper at the City Hall when he eat there but does not know his name. Witness says Mr Ayer kept the City Hall at that time.

Alpha K. Ayer Sworn says that himself and Mr James kept the City Hall untill 29th March 1837. does not Recollect ever to have seen Mr Perry.

Thomas James Sworn says that a young man by the name of Williamson kept bar for him 29th March 1837.

X Ex. says that Williamson was a short, large, & stout but not high. not so tall as Co^l Holt. It was not generally known that Ayer had left James. after the seperation The Sign hung at the Tavern of Ayer & James some time after the separation.

Celia Stanley sworn says that prisner was at home that day and night and the next night he had been at home farming it and she had not missed him. Witness says that it was the last day of March and first day of April 1837, being Friday night & Saturday night. Witness remembered it from the fact that she was unwell & priner was with her to take care of her. witness says that prisner was busy writing and she was busy looking for papers that were mislaid and that prisner out sometime ~~in the~~ during the day but not during the night.

X Ex. Witness was verry bad off with a sore throat and was verry poorly but not confined to her bed. It was at Witness House that prisner was on the two nights above stated. Witness was poorly & thinks her throat was swelled about 10 days. Witness does not know how many days is in the month of March. Witness thinks prisner was generally at home on the 28th March. she says that prisoner was at home on the third day of April 1837 and it was on Sunday. thinks she was mistaken & it was monday instead of Sunday. Witness knows not where her brother, the prisner, was on the 5th day of April

[90] Wednesday 19th December 1838

but thinks he was at home. Witness says that the prisoner never was out after supper when she was unwell. Witness does not know where prisner was on the first of January, first of February, nor the first of March. Witness says that no person now lives with her. her aunt comes sometimes & sleeps with her & when she don't she's all alone. Witness says prisner left her house 3 or 4 months ago and lives by himself. Witness says that prisner was at Home on the 3 day of April 1837 in bed taking his rest. did not say he was unwell. Witness was sick most of the year 1837. she says that at one time she was sick 3 or 4 months along in August & September & October.

The State   }
    vs   } Simple Larceny
Maberry Howell }
Western Harwell}
William Harwell}
Avery Odom &   }
John Fox   }

   1. William Amos   7. Jesse J. Sutton
   2. George Greer   8. Isaac A. Brokaw
   3. Bunion Rhodes   9. ~~John~~ William McCurdy
   4. Madison Dancer   10. Archibald Campbell
   5. Devenport Ellis   11. Thomas W. Bowen
   6. Vernon D. Metcalf   12. William Reid

We, the Jury, find the defendant, Maberry Howell, guilty.

Wm Amos, Fm

John Vance }
vs } Bill in Equity
John Schley, administrator { Returnable to October term 1838
of Joseph T. Camp, dec^d }

On Motion, the defendant assenting thereto, ordered that a Copy of the above bill be established in lieu of the burnt Original.

Muscogee Sup^r Court – Oct Adj^d term 1838 – William W. Pool & Slayton Henly, having been summoned to attend the present term of the Court as Petit Jurors and having refused to appear, it is ordered by the Court that they each do pay a fine of Ten dollars.

[91]

The State }
vs } Simple Larceny
Maberry Howell }
Western Harwell }
William Harwell }
Avery Odom & }
John Fox }

1. John McGough
2. Matthew H. Pool
3. Thomas V. Miller
4. William Pride
5. John Patterson
6. John Bond
7. Henry B. Garrett
8. Joseph Moorefield
9. Matthew Hall
10. James Fleming
11. Hiram B. Plott
12. George W. Turentine

We, the Jury, find the Prisoner, Western Harvill, Guilty.

Jno McGough, F. M.

Muscogee Superior Court, Oc^t Adj^d Term 1838

Appeared in Open Court Hines Holt, Junr, administrator of William J. Beattie, deceased, who being sworn On oath, saith that he deponent has reason to believe and verily does believe that his intestate in his lifetime was possessed in his own right of notes, drafts, & receipts of which the above are in substance true Copies and that the same in the lifetime of the said Intestate were lost, and that copies thereof have not been established, and deponent further saith that he has reason to believe and does believe that the said notes, drafts, & receipts Still remain due and unpaid.

Sworn to & subscribed in Open Court 13th December 1838.

          Hines Holt, Junr

Muscogee Superior Court October adjourned term 1838.

It appearing to the Court upon the affidavit of Hines Holt, Junr, administrator of William J. Beattie, deceased, that the above are substantial copies of certain notes, drafts, & receipts held by the said William J. Beattie, deceased, in his lifetime and that the originals thereof have been lost and that the same remain due and unpaid.

It is on motion ordered that, unless good cause be shown to the the Contrary on or before the first day of next term of this Court, the said Copies be established and taken in lieu of the lost originals. and it further ordered that a copy of this rule be served upon each of the makers of the said notes, drafts, and receipts or published in one of the public Gazetts of the City of Columbus once a month for not less than three months previous to the next term of this Court.

[92]   Wednesday 19th December 1838

$1600 On or by the 1st day of April 1838, we promise to pay W. J. Beattie, or beared, Sixteen hundred dollars for value received.

Columbus 13th Febr^y 1837   A. J. Robertson
               D. McDougald

$600 On or by the 1st day of July 1837, I promise to pay W. J. Beattie, or bearer, Six Hundred dollars for Value Rec^d.

Columbus 20th June 1838   D. McDougald

$1300 By the 1st day of Jany 1838, I promise to pay N. P. Willard, or bearer, One Thousand three Hundred dollars for Value Received Novr 14th 1836.

         N. P. Willard

the above note Endorsed by John Westcott.

$200 One day after date, I promise to pay W. J. Beattie, or bearer, Two Hundred dollars for Value Received.

Columbus 1st Febr^y 1837   Luther Blake

$1000.00 One day after date, I promise to pay W. J. Beattie, or bearer, One Thousand dollars for Value Received.

Irwinton 10th Febr^y 1837   Seth Lord

$100.00 Due W. J. Beattie One Hundred dollars for cash loaned me.

New Orleans March 21st 1837   P. J. Murray

$500.00 I promise to pay Wm Elijah, or bearer, five Hundred dollars, being the ballance due for Negroes if I get them. Columbus Aug 16 1834

         Ben^j Hawkins

$30 Due W. J. Beattie Thirty dollars cash loaned me. New Orleans 19th March 1837

         R. H. Williams

$20 Due W. J. Beattie Twenty dollars cash loaned.

New Orleans 19 March 1837   W. Winstell

[unnumbered]

$125   Irwinton 10th Febry 1837

Capt J. Brown,

Sir, please pay W. J. Beattie One Hundred and twenty five dollars and place to account of

Seth Lord

$19.00 On or by the 25th december 1835, I promise to pay to the Sommerville land Company, or bearer, ninteen dollars for Value Recd. Irwinton May 20th 1834

Green Beauchamp
B. V. Iverson

$33.00 On or by the twenty fifth of December 1835, We promise to pay to the Sommerville Land Company, or bearer, thirty three dollars for Value Recd. Irwinton, Ala. Aug 12 1834

Blackwell & McKinzie

Recived. Irwinton, Ala. Feby 10th 1837 from W. J. Beattie the following notes of hand to collect & if not collected to be returned, Viz.

One note on John Morgan drawn on the 1st Febry 1837 due one day after date for five hundred & Sixty dollars. One note on Johnson Wellborn for five hundred & twenty Six dollars due 1st Jany 1837. One note drawn by James Seals due 1st Jany 1837 for One hundred & fifty one dollars. One note drawn by D. Whitehead for three hundred & ninety five dollars. One note drawn by William Wellborn due 1st Jany 1837 for Three Hundred Dollars. One do drawn by do due the 26 Febry 1836 for Eighty seven dollars. One do by do for One Hundred & forty dollars due 25th December 1836. One do by do due 1st Jany 1837 for Sixty Seven dollars. One do by do due 1st Jany 1837 Due 25 Decr 1836 for forty dollars.

Seth Lord

Chancey Pomroy }
    vs   } Bill for discovery, Relief, & Specific Performance
Burton Hepburn }

Ordered that the Copy presented, the def' assenting thereto, be established in lieu of the original.

~~Wm D. Hargraves & Wife~~ }
    ~~vs~~   } ~~Bill for discovery & account~~
~~Owen Thomas~~   } ~~To Oct term 1837~~

~~Owen Thomas~~   }
    ~~vs~~   } ~~Cross Bill for discovery, Relief, & Injunction &c~~
~~William D. Hargrave &~~ } ~~To Ap^l term 1839~~
~~Sophia W. Hargrave,~~ }
~~his Wife~~   }

[93]

The State   }
    vs   { Simple Larceny
Lorenzo Dow Glenn }

Oc^t Adj^d Term 1838. Prisoner arraigned & pleads not Guilty.

                               Henry L. Benning, So^l Genl C. C.

The State   }
    vs   } Simple Larceny
Thomas Howard {
Western Harwell }
& Avery Odom   }

Oc^t adj^d term 1838. The prisners, Thomas Howard & Western Harwell, are arraigned & plead not guilty.

                               Henry L. Benning, So^l Genl C. C.

Wm D. Hargraves & Wife }
  vs   } Bill for discovery & account
Owen Thomas   } To Oc^t term 1837

Owen Thomas   }
  vs   } Cross Bill for discovery, Relief, & Injunction &c
William D. Hargrave & } To Ap^l term 1839
Sophia W. Hargrave,   }
his Wife   }

It appearing to the Court that the above copys of Original Bills were burnt and that the parties assent to the establishment of the same. Ordered that the same be taken and established in lieu of the originals.

Henry Hall   }
  vs   } Judgments in Muscogee Sup^r Court
Paulin Miedzielski } at April Term 1838

           Principal debt $100.00
     Int to date of Judgment 15 May 1838   3.67
             Cost

It appearing to the Court that the Executions issued on the above stated judgments were burnt in the Clerk's office of this Court when it was consumed by fire on the night of the fourteenth of October last and there not being any credits on said fifa. It is therefore on motion of Plaintiff's attorney Ordered that other Ececutions do issue in the place and stead of the said burnt Originals.

[94]

The State   }
  vs   } Simple Larceny
Thomas Howard }
Western Harwell }
& Avery Odom   }

     1. Wm Amos, Fm   7. Isaac A. Brokaw
     2. George Greer   8. William McCurdy
     3. Bunion Rhodes   9. Archibald Campbell
     4. Devenport Ellis   10. Thomas W. Brown

  5. Vernon D. Metcalf   11. William Reid
  6. Jesse J. Sutton   12. Ben^j Wells

We, the Jurors, find the defendant, Thomas Howard, guilty.

               Wm Amos, Fm

The State   }
  vs   } Simple Larceny
Thomas Howard }
Western Harwell } Oct adj^d term 1838.
& Avery Odom   }

Nolle Proseque as to Western Harvell.

           Henry L. Benning, So^l Genl C. C.

The State   }
  vs   } Perjury
James R. Lyons } Oc^t adj^d term 1838

The defendant, James R. Lyons, is arraigned and pleads not guilty.

           Henry L. Benning, So^l Genl C. C.

The State   }
  vs   } Arson
Jacob Cunningham } October Adj^d Term 1838
& James R. Lyons   }

The defendant, James R. Lyons, is arraigned and pleads not guilty.

           Henry L. Benning, So^l Genl C. C.

Hill, Dawson & Co }
  vs   } Assumpsit
W. B. & B. Hasting }

Received of the defendant in this case fifty one dollars and Seventy ~~cents~~ seven cents in full of principal, interest, & cost.

Ge° H. Schley, Plff^s att^y

The Court adjourned to meet again tomorrow morning at half past nine O'clk.

Marshall J. Wellborn, J. S. C. C. C.

[95]   Muscogee Superior Court Oc^t Adj^d term 1838
Thursday 20 December 1838

The State   }
    vs   } Simple Larceny
Western Harwell }

Evidence

John Code sworn. Witness owned a boy by the name of Ben, yellow complexion, about five feet ten inches high, slim built, verry straight, smart and active, about twenty five years old, and worth fifteen hundred dollars. Witness gave the boy permission to go to the Races in this place commencing the Second tuesday in October last as well as he recollects. Witness never saw him after that time. this was in this County and this Town. It was on Saturday after the races commenced on Tuesday that Witness gave the boy permission to go there.

William Ross Sworn. On Sunday the day after the races Witness was at Western Harvell's Corner. saw this yellow boy there at the bar drinking. Mr Western Harwells & Maberry Howell Asked Witness if Avery Odom was in Town. Witness told them that he had gone out to his Father's. Western Harwells and Maberry Howell asked witness if he could take Harwell's poney and go out after him. Witness objected and said he could not go. Witness told them that would be in next day. it was agreed on to wait till next day. Mr Western Harwell told witness that the boy should stay there till next day, that he would care of him that night. did not then know Mr Code. Western Harwell & Maberry Howell said the boy belonged to Code. Witness thinks the boy was worth a Thousand or fifteen hundred dollars as he was a tailor. Western Harwell & Maberry Howell said that Mr Campbell had offered Fourteen Hundred dollars in Code's own notes payable in January for the boy. Mr Western Harwell and Maberry Howell told Witness that they and Avery Odom would have every thing fixed for Witness to take the negro over the River and that witness should not be seen in town, that there should be no evidence against him. this conversation took place on the Sunday after the the races commenced in this place in last October. Witness Stayed at Western Harwell's late that evening and the boy was in the bar room drinking liquor and intoxicated. Witness Slept at Mr Harwell's that night. It was about Sun rise next morning when Witness got up, saw the boy in the bar room again. Mr Code came down on monday morning in Seach of the boy.

[96] the boy was concealed in the Sellar when Code first made his appearance. the boy was Standing in the door and prisoner told the boy to go in the back room. And for fear Code might go in there to look for him, prisoner to Witness to tell the boy to go into the Cellar, which Witness done. Code spoke to Mr Lewis concerning the boy and offered him five dollars to apprehend him. when Lewis went to the cellar, the boy made his escape and went uptown. The Witness next saw the boy about twelve or one O'clock that day at a Warehouse below Western Harwell leaning against the tongue of a Waggon. Western Harwell, William Howell, and Maberry Howell was with him. the negro then ~~up~~ went up to Western Harwell's and got a drink. Western Harwell and Maberry Howell told the boy in his presence that he should have his regular Share of what he sold for, as much as either of them got. and they told the boy that he best not stay there, but to get out of the way so that Nat Roberson could not catch him. The next time he saw the boy was in the evening at the pump. the boy called out for Mr Western Harwell. Weston Harwell did not go, but told Witness to go and tell the boy to go under the Ware House into the Waggon and to change hats with the boy, which Witness did. that night being monday night. the boy went over the river and the next day Clothes were bought by Maberry Howell. Avery Odom gave Howell a twenty dollar Allabama Bill to buy them with. The Shoes which Witness has on was bought at Welles and the Shirt at Peabody's for the negro. on tuesday night about 7 O'clock, Witness, Mayberry Howell, Western Harwell, and Avery Odom all crossed the Bridge together and went into Gerard. At the branch near the Court in Gerard, the Company stoped. Weston Harwell told Avery Odom not to let Witness have any money because he might run off and not divide fair. Witness and Avery Odom then went to John Odom and Witness found the boy Ben in a negro house under the bed. two Saddles & Bridles were on the bed. A negro boy the name of Jim was in the cabbin where Witness found Code's boy.

Cross Examined.

It has been promised to Witness that, if he would come out and testify fully in this case, that he would not be prosecuted. this promise was made after he had made the disclosure. Witness was mistaken in saying that he slept at Western Harvell's on Sunday night. Witness slept at Harwell on Saturday night and at Mrs Evanses on Sunday night, before the Court house was burned on Monday morning. There was one waggon under the Ware house where the boy leaned against the tonge. Witness is a married man. his wife was at her mother's he thinks that night. he and his wife live Seperate. on monday morning, Witness took breakfast at Mrs Evans's or Harwell's. The last time Witness saw the negro on Sunday night was about 11 O'clock in Western Harwell's Grocery. the front door was Shut. that night Avery Odom & Witness went to Mrs Evanses and went to bed. did not go to bed as soon as they went there. cannot recollect what time he got up, but thinks he ate his breakfast there. recollects getting up and leaving Odom there in bed and did not get up till next morning to go to Harwell's. The thursday after the fire, Witness was between Mr Bushes and Abbeville. Witness Stayed at Western the latter part of monday night and got up there on tuesday

[97] on tuesday morning. Some times the Grocery at Harwell's belongs to ~~Harwell~~ Western Harwell, then to Mr Lewis, then to Mr Fox, and then to W. Harwell. Counsel has taken Witness at a nonplus. he don't properly know who it belongs to. Did you get up between ~~at~~ the time that you and Avery Odom went to bed at Mrs Evans's on Sunday night and the time you got up about sunrise and went to Harwell's ~~about sunrise~~ the next morning? No. Upon asked if he did not get up to go to the fire on that morning. Witness said he did and that he misunderstood the question. that he understood that he was asked if he got up to go to Harwell's before sunrise.

When John Code went down monday morning after the negro, Witness stepped up and took a drink of liquor and heard Code say to Lewis if he would tie the negro he would give him five dollars.

J. P. H. Campbell Sworn. Says that he thinks he offered Code fourteen hundred dollars for the negro boy Ben in a note indorsed by Code to him. don't recollect telling Western Harwell anything about it. Elbert Wells Sworn. Says that the Shoes Witness has on came out of his Shop. don't know whether they were Stolen from him or not. has not missed any. don't think he has sold the shoes to Ross. Witness thinks he has sold shoes to Maberry Howell. George W. Short Sworn. Says that John Odom has a negro named Jim and has had for four or five years. has seen Jim in Mr Odom's possession since Odom moved over the River. John Code reexamined. Says that Mr Campbell offered him fourteen hundred dollars in notes endorsed by him to Campbell for the negro Ben. did offer Lewis five dollars if he would tie the boy Ben and bring him to him. There were several persons about the Grocery. did not know Ross or any person present, except Lewis. Witness says that he did not recollect ever having told Western Harwell or any of the Company that he had been made that offer for the boy by Campbell.

Henry K. Hill Sworn. is a member of the Grand Jury. was present when William Ross gave in his Testimony on a Bill of Indictment against Lyons for burning the Court house. Ross testified that he saw Cunningham and saw two others, one of whom he thought was Lyons, the other he did not know. Witness says that Ross stated that he saw these persons near Mrs Evanses Corner on Sunday night on which the Court House was burned. it was pretty late in the night. don't remember the hour testified to by Ross. Ross said before the Grand Jury that he stayed at Mrs Evanses on Sunday night before the Court house was burned.

Stephen Lewis Sworn. Says the Grocery at Harwell's Corner is his and has been for two months. before that time, it was part owned by Maberry Howell. Witness had an interest in it. Witness now attends to it mostly. Witness thinks he was at the Grocery on Sunday morning and Sunday evening and possibly after night. knows Code's boy. did not see him there. Saw Ross there in the early part of the day. don't remember whether he was there in the evening. he might have been there and Witness not notice him. Cross Exam^d. Was there on monday morning. Saw Code's boy there early in the morning. Witness had been there and went home to breakfast before Code got there.

[98] did not see Ben there after monday morning. When Witness returned from Breakfast, Code came then and enquired after the Boy. Saw Ross there on monday morning. John Lewis Sworn. Says the yellow Boy Ben was at the Grocery on Sunday evening and asked Witness for liquor. the boy came back on monday morning and wanted more liquor. Witness refused both times to let the boy have it. William Ross got half pint liquor and carried it into the Cellar to the boy. Ross also carried provisions into the Cellar to the boy. Mr Code came down on monday morning and asked Witness if the negro had been there.

Witness told Code that the boy had gone off. Code told Witness that he would give him five dollars if he would catch him, tie him, and convey him to him. it was after Code had been there that Ross carried the liquor to the negro. it was late breakfast time when the liquor & provisions were carried into the Cellar. Witness told Western Harwell that he had seen Ross carry liquor and victuals to the negro boy. Witness and Harwell then went to take the negro. Witness had a rope and Harwell a pistol. the boy rushed out of the Cellar and ran into a black woman's house by the name of Violet. the boy then run into Mrs Webster's House. Witness and Harwell followed him there and he run down towards the river. Witness never saw the boy after that. William Ross came in that night with the negro's hat on and bought half pint of liquor and carried it to the negro back of Mrs Webster's house. When Ross returned, he threatened to whip the Witness. The negro came there on Sunday evening and asked for liquor. Witness refused to give it to him. the boy went away and Witness did not see him there any more that night.

Cross Exam^d. Witnesses Father had been there soon in the morning and had gone to Breakfast when Mr Code came there the first time. Witness does not know what time his Father came back from breakfast. he did not stay long at breakfast. Witness stayed at the Grocery till his Father came back. Witness Supposes it was one hour and a half or two hours sun when his Father returned from breakfast. Supposes his Father stayed half an hour or three quarters at breakfast. Witness went to get his breakfast when his Father returned from his Breakfast. Witness Stayed at Breakfast an hour or more. Mr Code came the first time when his father had gone to Breakfast. Witnesses Father had not walked over more that three Squares before Mr Code came. He did remain at the Grocery all the time his Father was gone. Witness went to watch William Ross carry the liquor to the negro and then informed Western Harwell of it and they then went after the negro. Witness left Maberry Howell in the Grocery in his absence. and his Father returned to the Grocery before witness got back. Don't know how long his father had been there when he got back. Witness thinks that he and Harwell were twenty or twenty five minutes after the negro. The pursuit after the negro by Witness and Harwell was after Code had been there making enquiry for him. When Witness returned from pursuing the negro, his Father was angry with him for leaving the Grocery. Witness explained to his Father that he and Harwell had been after the negro with rope and pistol. and his Father said no more. when Witness returned to the Shop, he went to get his breakfast and stayed an hour or more. William Ross was not in the Shop when Witness returned from pursuing the negro nor at the time he went to breakfast. Did not see Ross there after he went to breakfast till evening when Ross was there. Does not know whether Ross was there on tuesday or not. did not notice. did not see Ross there for several days afterwards. Did not hear of Rosses going to Macon to the Races. Saw Avery Odom at the Grocery on Sunday morning. does not

[99] remember to have seen him on Monday. Ross was there about an hour after dinner on monday. does not recollect to have seen him there on tuesday, but he might have been there. Does not recollect to have seen him for several days after that. Witness was at Grocery when Code first came and was there when he left. did not See Code any time. has seen Mr Code today.

William Ross reexamined. Says that if he has said if he was in the street he would be afraid that the friends of defendants would kill him.

Stephen Lewis Reexamined. Witness first went to the fire before day, then went to his Grocery very early. Stayed at his Shop till he went to his breakfast which was about a hour by sun or the usual time. from his breakfast, he went to the place where the negro was killed and he thinks he got his dinner before he returned to his grocery. Can't say whether he saw William Ross at the grocery that evening or not. can't say that he saw him in the morning before he went to his breakfast. Witnesses Son did not tell him in the morning before he went to breakfast or on that day at all that Code had been there after the negro. Mr Code came there on some morning, he does not recollect which, and asked his son about the negro and afterwards asked Witness about him. Witness told Mr Code that his negro had been there. Witness saw the negro there in the morning. Witnesses Son Said that Code had offered him five dollars to catch the negro. his son told him that he and Harwell had tried to catch him. Witnesses son told him that they had run the negro out of the Cellar through the yard and into a negro woman's house on Harwell's lot. Son told Witness that before Mr Code asked him about the negro, but will not be positive about it, does not think he told Code that his son and Harwell had run the negro. never spoke to Mr Code concerning the negro after that. Can't say whether he saw Mr Ross on tuesday or not. Can't say that he saw Ross for several days afterwards. Can't say that he heard that Ross left town on tuesday evening. Went out to see the negroes who were killed on the morning that it was done. does not know what day it was that Code spoke to him or his son about the negro.

John Code reexamined. Says that he enquired of young Lewis on monday morning about the negro. that he does not recellect to have enquired of the elder Lewis concerning the boy. Witness says that he asked Western Harwell on tuesday morning if he had Seen the negro. Harwell said that he had not on that day. Witness does not recollect that Harwell told him he had seen the negro on the day before. Don't recollect that he said any thing to Harwell about the negro on monday. John Lewis came up to Witness house in the afternoon of tuesday & told him that he had tried to catch the negro. Witness thinks, that H but is not certain, that Harwell told him on monday morning at the time Witness enquired of young Lewis about the negro, that he Harwell had seen the negro that morning.

William S. Chipley }
     vs   } Debt
Timothy Collins }

Settled.

[100]

Anne Reid   }
    vs   } Assumpsit and verdict for the Plaintiff for Two
Elijah Corley   } thousand dollars, with interest & cost of Suit
Benjamin Howard }
& Eli B. W. Spivey }

The defendants, being dissatisfied with the verdict rendered by the Jury in the abouve caus. And having paid all cost and demanded an Appeal, brings William P. Malone and tenders him as Security and they, the said Elijah Corley, Benjamin Howard, & Eli B. W. Spivey, acknowledge themselves and William P. Malone acknowledge themselves jointly & Severally bound unto the Plaintiff for the payment of the eventual condemnation money in said cause.

In Testimoney whereof, they have hereunto Set their hands and seals this 28th day of December 1838.

Test. Gerard Burch, Clk   Elijah Corley
                                                 Benjamin Howard
                                                 Eli B. W. Spivey
                                                 W[m] P. Malone

Robert McQueen }
    vs   } Debt
Joshua R. McCook}

Settled.

Norborn B. Powell}
    vs   } Assumpsit
Burton Hepburn }

Settled.

Maitland, Kenedy & C° }
    vs   } Assumpsit
Edward Cary   }
& John Day   }

Settled.

John H. Howard }
    vs   } Assumpsit
Wᵐ S. Chipley   }
J. B. Webb &   }
John W. Campbell}

Settled.

Bogert & Hawthorn}
    vs   } Assumpsit
Burton Hepburn }

Setthed & Cost paid.

Bogert & Hawthorn vs David Hudson. asspt. Settled & cost paid.

The Court adjourned to meet again to morrow morning at half past nine O'clock.

                            Marshall J. Wellborn, J. S. C. C. C.

[101]   October adjourned term Friday 21 December 1838

The Court met according to adjournment, present the Honorable Marshall J. Wellborn, Judge of the Superior Courts of the Chattahoochee Circuit.

Elliott W. Gregory }
     vs   } Assumpsit and verdict for the Plaintiff for nine
Charles E. &   } hundred and twenty one dollars & Sixty one cents
Henry Mims   } with interest & cost of suit

The State vs John Fox, Western Harwell, & Lorenzo Dow Glen.

Evidence as to Glen continued from page 80.

Aaron Turner Sworn. Says that Glen went home with him on Saturday evening about sun set, or a little after, the third of november last from Abraham Odom's House and went to be at his house about nine O'clock and got up there next morning. Witness & Glen went to Abraham Odom's on Sunday morning after breakfast. Cross Exam^d. Witness & Glen went to bed two or three hours after they left Abraham Odom's house. Witness Slept pretty soundly. Witness says that Dow Glen told him that he heard man say that two horses were to be stolen on the night of the day on which the negro was hung and that the witness has so stated in company. Glen told witness that a man whose name witness does not recollect told him that two horses were to be stolen that night. Witness does not recollect saying or telling any person that Glen would go to bed at house and get up and go without his knowing it and go to Odom's. Witness does not remember that Glen has done so. Dow Glen lives in Stewart County near the Muscogee line and the river Road is the most direct to his house.

Pinkney Hazleton Sworn. Says that he has heard Aaron Turner say Joking about Dow Glen that he Glen would lie down at his house and get up at Odom's.

Elias B. Crane }
     vs   } assumpsit
Martin Brooks }

I confess Judgment to the Plaintiff for the Sum of five hundred Dollars, with interest & cost of suit.

                        Campbell, McDougald, & Watson, Def^s at^{ys}

Elias B. Crane }
    vs   } assumpsit
James H. Campbell }

I confess Judgment to the Plaintiff for the Sum of five hundred dollars, with interest & cost of suit.

                                J. H. Campbell

[102]   In the Superior Court of Law for the County of Muscogee the same being a Court of Record having a Clerk and a Seal

The Petition of James Blair, an alien friend and free white person desirous of becoming a citizen of the United States, Respectfully Sheweth that he was born in the Town Land of Straid nanannah near the Town of Carrick furgus in the County of the town of Carrick Furgus in the Parish of Ballybinny in the Kingdom of Ireland a part of the Brittish Dominions, that he is twenty six years of age, and by profession a Merchant, that he is the Subject of William the fourth, King of Great Brittain and Ireland, that he migrated from his native place & Sailed from Bellfast some time in the month of November 1829, that he arrived in the City of Charleston, South Carolina on the tenth day of January 1830, that is his intention to Settle in the County of Muscogee and State of Georgia, that it is bona fide his intentions to become a citizen of the United States, being Seriously attached to the Constitution, principals, and well being of the Same, that he hereby renounces forever all allegiance and fidelity to all and every foreign Prince, potentate, State, or Sovreignty whatever and particularly to William the fourth, King of Great Brittain and Ireland, whose Subject he now is.

Sworn to & Subscribed in Open Court this
18th day of April 1836.   James Blair
Alfred Iverson, J. S. C. C. C.

We, the undersigned citizens of the United States, do hereby Certify that we have been for Some time past acquainted with James Blair, the within declarent, during all of which time he has conducted himself as a moral upright man and that we believe that it is bonafide his intention to become a Citizen of the Untied

States and that he is Sincerely attached to the Constitution and principles thereof.

   Signed   J. H. Campbell
          John Fontaine

  Muscogee Superior Court October adjourned term 1838

Personally appeared in Open Court James Blair, who, after being duly Sworn, deposeth & Saith that the within declaration of intention is a Copy in Substance of the original of file in the Clerk's Office of the Superior Court of Said County and which was destroyed by the late Conflagration of the Clerk's Office.

Sworn to and Subscribed in Open Court
this 21st day of December 1838   James Blair
Marshall J. Wellborn, J. S. c. c. c.

On motion it is ordered that the within & foregoing Copy of Declaration & Oath of intention be established in lieu of the lost original. ~~the~~

The Petition of James Blair respectfully sheweth that, on the Eighteenth day of April 1836, he filed his declaration and Oath of intention to become a Citizen of the United States in the Clerk's Office of the Superior Court of said County of Muscogee and State of Georgia and

[103]   October Adj^d Term Friday 21st Decr 1838

more than two years having Elapsed since the filing such declaration of intention, he therefore prays that he may be permitted to take the Oath of Allegiance prescribed by the act of Congress and admitted to all the rights, privileges, and immunities of a Naturalized Citizen.

I, James Blair, do Solemnly & sincerely swear that I will support and defend the Constitution of the United States and that I do solemnly and entirely abjure all allegiance & fidelity to every foreign Prince, Potentate, State, or Sovereignty whatever and particularly to Victoria Alexandria, the first Queen of Great Brittain & Ireland, whereof I was before a subject. so help me god.

Sworn to and Subscribed in Open Court this 21st day of Decr 1838.

Marshall J. Wellborn, J. S. C. C. C.   James Blair

In the Superior Court of Law for the County of Muscogee
the same being a Court of Record having a Clerk and a Seal

The Petition of William Blair, an alien friend and free white person desirous of becoming a citizen of the United States, Respectfully Sheweth that he was born in the Town Lands of Straid nanannah near the Town of Carrick furgus in the County of the town of Carrick Furgus in the Parish of Ballybinny in the Kingdom of Ireland a part of the Brittish Dominions, that he is thirty four years of age, and by profession a Merchant, that he is the Subject of William the fourth, King of Great Brittain and Ireland, that he migrated from his native place and sailed from the town of Belfast in Ireland on the Seventh day of April eighteen hundred and thirty Six and landed in the City of New York on the thirteenth day of May eighteen hundred and thirty Six, that it is his intention to Settle in the County of Muscogee and State of Georgia, that it is bonafide his intention to become a citizen of the United States, that he hereby renounces forever all allegiance and fidelity to all and any foreign prince, Potentate, State, or Sovereign whatever and particularly to William the fourth, King of Great Brittain and Ireland, whose Subject he now is, and that he is sincerely attached to the Constitution & principles of the United States and the well being and good order of the same, and that he will the Same Support and defend.

William Blair

Superior Court April Term 1836

Personally appeared in open Court William Blair, who, after being duly sworn, deposeth and saith that the facts stated in the foregoing declaration of intention are true and that it is bonafide his intention to become a citizen of the

[104] United States, being sincerely attached to the principles, constitution, well being, and happiness of the same, the he hereby forever renounces all allegiance to all and every foreign prince, potentate, state, or sovereignty whatever, particularly to William the fourth, King of Great Brittain and Ireland, whereof he is now a Subject, and that he will support and defend the constitution of the United States.

Sworn to & Subscribed before me this 18th day of April 1836.

Alfred Iverson, J. S. C. C. C. William Blair

Muscogee adjourned Term 1838

Personally appeared in Open Court William Blair, who, after being duly sworn, deposeth and Saith that the within is a Copy of Substance of his declaration of intention filed by him in the Clerk's Office of the Superior Court of said County and therein recorded and which was destroyed by the late conflagration of said Clerk's Office.

Sworn to & Subscribed before me this 21st day of December 1838.

Marshall J. Wellborn, J. S. C. C. C. William Blair

On motion, it is ordered that the within and foregoing Copy declaration and oath of intention be established in lieu of the lost original.

We, the undersigned Citizens of the United States, do hereby Certify that we have been for Some time acquainted with William Blair, the within declarant, and that during all that time he has behaved as an orderly and upright citizen and we have no doubt but that it is bonafide his intention to become a citizen of the United States and that he is attached to the principles and form of the Government thereof.

J. H. Campbell
Jn° Fontaine

The petition of William Blair respectfully Sheweth that, on the eighteenth day of April eighteen hundred and thirty six, he filed his declaration and Oath of intention in the Clerk's Office of the Superior Court of said County of Muscogee State of Georgia to become a naturalized citizen of the United States. And more than two years having elapsed since the fileing of the same, he therefore prays that he may be permitted to take the Oath of allegiance prescribed by the act of Congress and admitted to all the rights of Citizenship.

William Blair

On motion, it is ordered that the Oath of Allegiance be administered to the said William Blair and that he be thenceforward admitted to all the rights, previledges, and immunities of an American Citizen.

I, William Blair, do Solemnly and Sincerely Swear that I will Support and defend the Constitution of the United States. And that I do absolutely and entirely

[105] entirely renounce and abjure all allegiance and fidelity to every foreign prince, Potentate, State, and Sovereignty whatever and particularly to Victoria Alexandria, the first Queen of Great Brittain and Ireland, whereof he was before a Subject. So help me God.

Sworn to & Subscribed in Open Court this 20th day of December 1838.

Marshall J. Wellborn, J. S. C. C. C.   William Blair

Battle A. Sorsby }
   vs   } Debt in Muscogee Superior Court
Joseph Davidson } Judgment, Ca sa, & Bond

It appearing to the court that the Original petition, process, and entries thereon, Judgment, Ca sa, & Bond, & entries thereon in the above case were destroyed by the late fire. And it further appearing that the foregoing are in Substance copies of the same. On Motion, ordered that the same be and are hereby established in lieu of the said lost Originals, with leave to proceed as on Originals.

            Marshall J. Wellborn, J. S. C. C. C.

Edwin L. De Graffinried, for }
the use of Battle A. Sorsby }
   vs   } Assumpsit in Muscogee Superior Court
Joseph Davidson   } April Term 1837

I appearing to the Court that the Original petition, process service, and Judgment, and entries thereon in the above case were destroyed by the late fire. And it appearing further that the papers filed in the above case are Copies of the same.

On motion, ordered that the same be and are hereby established in lieu of the Originals so destroyed and that the Clerk do issue fire facias upon application.

Marshall J. Wellborn, J. S. C. C. C.

Henry Hall }
    vs } Mortgage Fi fa
Ephraim Wheelock & }
Nathan P. Willard }

The Sheriff having money in his hands received on the above fi fa. Ordered that he shew Cause why he should not pay over the same.

I acknowledge Service of the above Rule ni Si 3 Jany 1839.

Joseph D. Bethune, Shff

The Sheriff having Shewn no Sufficient Cause upon the above Rule. Ordered that he pay over the Sum of nine hundred dollars, deducting therefrom his Costs to the above fi fa.

[106]

The State of Georgia }
    vs } Indictment for Simple Larceny and verdict
John Fox } of Guilty as to John Fox
Western Harwell & }
Lorenzo Dow Glen }

Whereupon it is considered and adjudged by the Court that the said John Fox be remanded to Jail and there safely kept untill he shall be demanded by a Guard to be sent for the purpose from the penitentiary of this State. that he be then & there delivered to said Guard and be by them removed and conveyed together with a Copy of the record of his conviction & Sentence to the said Penitentiary where he be kept in confinement from the twenty fourth day of December Eighteen hundred and thirty eight and fully to be completed and ended.

[107] [blank page]

[108]

Muscogee Superior Court Oct Adj^d Term 1838

Perry Browning, having attended the present Superior Court of the Court in the capacity & office of Bailiff to the Petit Jury for and during the Term of Ten days. It is ordered by the Court that the County Treasurer do pay him for his service as aforesaid the sum of Ten Dollars out of the County funds.

The Court adjourned to meet again tomorrow morning at half past nine O'clock.

Marshall J. Wellborn, J. S. C. C. C.

[109] October adjourned Term Saturday 22nd December 1838

The Court met according to adjournment, present the Honorable Marshall J. Wellborn, Judge of the Superior Courts of the Chattahoochee Circuit.

The State }
   vs }
Edward Boynton } October adjourned term 1838

The defendant, Edward Boynton, arraigned and pleads not Guilty.

Henry L. Benning, Sol. Genl

Stevens Thomas }
   vs } Assumpsit returned to April term 1838
James S. Calhoun}
& John Crowell }

The death of Plaintiff having been Suggested at the last term of this Court and a Scire Facias having been issued returnable to the present term requiring defendants to appear & Shew cause why Penina Thomas, Executrix of the last will and testament of said Stevens Thomas, deceased, should not be made party Plaintiffs in said case and the defendants having failed to shew cause to the Contrary. It is ordered by the Court that the said Penina Thomas, Executrix as aforesaid, be made party Plaintiff in said case and that the cause proceed.

Stevens Thomas }
    vs   } Assumpsit
John J. Willson }

It appearing to the Court that at the last term of this Court being the appearance term of the case above Stated the death of the Plaintiff, Stevens Thomas, was Suggested. And it further appearing that a Scire facias was issued returnable to the present term requiring the said defendant to shew cause why Penina Thomas, Executrix of the last will & Testament of said Stevens Thomas, deceased, Should not be made party Plaintiff in said case and no Sufficient cause having been Shewn. It is ordered that said Penina Thomas, Executrix as aforesaid, be made party Plaintiff and that the cause proceed.

Stevens Thomas }
    vs   } Assumpsit
John J. Boswell }

I appearing to the Court that at at the last term of this Court being the appearance term of said case the death of the Plaintiff, the said Stevens Thomas, was Suggested. And it further appearing to the Court that a Scire facias was issued returnable to the present term requiring

[110] the said defendant to shew cause why Penina Thomas, Executrix of the last will & Testament of said Stevens Thomas, deceased, should not be made party Plaintiff in said case and no Sufficient cause being shewn to the contrary. It is ordered that said Penina Thomas, Executrix as aforesaid, be made party Plaintiff and that the cause proceed.

M. W. Perry }
    vs   } Muscogee Superior Court October adjourned term 1838
A. K. Ayer } Rule ni si to foreclose Mortgage

It appearing to the Court upon the petition of Michael W. Perry that Alpha K. Ayer did on the seventh day of March in the year eighteen hundred and thirty seven execute and deliver to George W. E. Bedell his certain Deed of Mortgage, Witnessing that the said Alpha K. Ayer had thereupon, to wit, on the seventeenth day of February in the year aforesaid, made, executed, and delivered to the said George W. E. his four certain promissory notes, all of the day and date last aforesaid. Whereby, by the first of which said notes, he the said Alpha K., eighty two days after the date thereof, promised to pay the said George W. E., or order, at the Columbus Bank, Three thousand dollars for value received. And by the second of which notes, he the said Alpha K. promised by the twelve day of January next (thereafter) to pay as aforesaid the other sum of three thousand dollars for value received. And by the third of said notes, he the said Alpha K. promised by the twelfth day of December Eighteen hundred and thirty eight to pay the said George W. E., or order, at either of the Banks in Columbus, the other sum of three thousand dollars for value received. And by the fourth and last of said notes, he the said Alpha K. promised by the twelfth day of May in the year eighteen hundred and thirty nine to pay the said George W. E., or order, at either of the Banks in Columbus the other sum of three thousand dollars for value received. And further reciting in the said Deed of Mortgage that for and in Consideration of five dollars to the said Alpha K. in hand paid by the said George W. E. as well as for the better securing the payment of the said promissory notes, he the said Alpha K. on the date of the said Deed Mortgage bargained, sold, granted, & confirmed and did by the same bargain, sell, grant, and confirm unto the said George W. E., his heirs, and assigns all that tract or parcel of land lying, situate, and being in the City of Columbus & County of Muscogee known as the North half of the Wooden building in said City of Columbus, usually called the City Hall, the same being located on lot number one hundred and sixty six by the original plan of Survey of said City, containing forty nine feet three inches and one third of an inch front on Broad Street and one hundred and forty seven feet ten inches front on St. Clair Street, except the priviledge of two feet on the Eastern end was reserved as a passway into the lot running south through said Lot. And also a Certain other lot or parcel of Land in said City, it being part of lot number one hundred and Sixty five, Commencing at the Corner of number one hundred and Sixty Six on St. Clair Street and running thence along said Street ninety two feet to a line between Templeton Reid's and said lot, thence south through said Lot the whole length of said lot, Thence west through said Lot to number One hundred and sixty six

[111] Sixty six, and thence North to the beginning point. And also that the said Alpha K. did by the said Deed of Mortgage sell and convey to the said George W. E. certain personal property therein specified. To have and to hold the said real and personal property to the said George W. E., his heirs, and assigns forever, except upon the condition that the same was to be void provided that the said Alpha K. paid the several promissory notes specified as they became due. And it further appearing to the Court that the said George W. E. Bedell

did afterwards, to wit, on the twenty seventh day of March in the year eighteen hundred and thirty seven, tranfer and assign the said Deed of Mortgage and the notes therein Specified to one Abraham Levison for value received. And that the said Abraham Levison did afterwards, to wit, on the fourth day of December in the year eighteen hundred and thirty eight, transfer the said Deed of Mortgage with the last two mentioned ~~notes~~ promissory notes remaining due and unpaid to the said Michael W. Perry.

And it further appearing to the court that the third note mentioned in the said Deed of Mortgage, to wit, the Note for the sum of three thousand dollars falling due on the twelfth day of December in the year eighteen hundred and thirty eight, with the interest thereon remain due and unpaid.

Whereupon it is on motion of Counsel for the said Michael W. Perry Ordered that the said Alpha K. Ayer do pay into this Court on or before the first of the next term thereof the said sum of three thousand dollars with the interest which may be due thereon or that the Equity of redemption in and to the provisions Specified in the said Deed of Mortgage be forever barred & foreclosed. And it is further ordered that a copy of this Rule be served upon the said Alpha K. Ayer in terms of the Law in such case made and provided.

On motion Ordered unanimously by the Bar that the Clerk have leave to bring up the appearance Dockett during the recess and that the same be considered as defaulted without calling the Same, with leave to plead in all cases on or before the first day of the next term of this Court.

Benjamin P. Tarver }			The Same }		
vs	}	assumpsit	vs	}	assumpsit
Elijah Corley	}		The Same }		

Personally came before me, Marshall J. Wellborn, presiding Judge of the Superior Courts of the Chattahoochee Circuit, Ge° H. Schley who, being duly sworn, deposeth that the Declarations filed in the above stated cases were at the time he filed them Copies in substance of the Originals ~~when he filed them~~ ones destroyed by fire in the burning of the Clerk's Office to the best of his knowledge and belief. And further states that the Copies produced by Coln. R. J. Crews do not remind him that there has been any change in the party Plaintiff, although there is a difference in the ones he desires to establish & those he desires in the possession of the Def[t]

[112] and he believes it is not only possible but highly probable that if a mistake exists from this Circumstance, Viz, That at or about the time that the originals ones were filed he also handed in five cases in which Arthur B. Davis was the Plaintiff and in which ten copies were necessary and that it is his opinion that in the Confusion of business and combination in Plff^s & Attorneys the mistake if any was made, and further, if he mistakes not, Mr Burch was in the Habit of signing blanks to be made out by amanuenses the copies being Signed by him and made out by some one else.

Ge° H. Schley

Marshall J. Wellborn, J. S. C. C. C. On motion of Plaintiff's Counsel, ordered by the Court that the Copies Stated above and here in Court be and the same are hereby established in lieu of the Originals so lost & destroyed.

Thomas Moore	}		Thomas Moore	}	
vs	}	Fi Fa	vs	}	Fi fa
John H. Watson	}		Nathaniel W. Howell	}	

The Original Fi fas above Stated having been returned to the Clerk's Office wholly unsatisfied and destroyed by fire, it is ordered that the Clerk do issue alias fi fas in lieu thereof.

The State of Georgia	}	
vs	}	Indictment for an assault and Battery and plea of
Bird F. Roberson	}	Guilty. Muscogee Superior Court Octr adj^d term 1838

Whereupon it is considered and adjudged by the Court that the said Bird F. Roberson do pay a fine of thirty dollars and pay the Cost of said Indictment.

Thomas A. Brannon	}	
vs	}	Debt, Judgment, & Fi fa
Thomas C. McKeen	}	In Muscogee Superior Court

It appearing to the Court that the Original petition & process & Service of the above case was destroyed as also the Judgment and Fi fa founded on the Same by the late fire, and further that the foregoing here filed in Office are in Substance Copies of the same. On motion Ordered that they be and are hereby established in lieu thereof and the Clerk do issue an alias Fifa on said Judgment.

Whereas many papers belonging to the Court have been destroyed by the fire by which the Court House and Clerk's Office were consumed. On motion Ordered that upon application in Chambers in vacation, Copies of Such papers which were of file in the Clerk's Office or belonging to the Court may be established in lieu of the destroyed Originals upon Such proof and in the same manner as if the said application were made in term time and the established cases be entered on the respective Docketts of the Court accordingly. it is further Ordered, the Sheriff consenting, that all money Rules against

[113]   October Adjourned Term Saturday 22nd December 1838

the Sheriff Shall upon application be determined at Chambers and the orders upon the same be entered as of this term.

It appearing to the Court that the Original Declarations in the following named Cases were destroyed by fire when the Clerk's Office of this Court was burnt on the night of the fourteenth day of October last and that Copies in substance thereof are now presented to Court by Phillip T. Schley as Attorney for the Plaintiffs. It is therefore ordered by the Court that said Copies be and they are hereby established in Stead & place of the said burnt Originals, viz.

Doremus, Saydams, & Nixon vs William S. Hartsfield & C°. Assumpsit

William T. Gould vs The Same. Assumpsit

Arthur B. Davis vs John R. Lloyd & C°. Assumpsit

Battle A. Sorsby vs Micajah Bennett. Assumpsit

Edward Kellogg vs Ephraim C. Bandy. Assumpsit

The Same vs Hiram Fuller. Assumpsit

The Same vs Isaac Mitchell. Assumpsit

The Same vs Carnes & Tatum. Assumpsit

Seaman & Ward vs G. H. & C. A. Peabody. Assumpsit

Amasa Walker & C° vs Chisholm & Collins. Assumpsit

Thomas H. Hall vs Joseph Davidson. Assumpsit

William Atkinson vs Thomas C. McKeen. Assumpsit

Adolphus L. Heine vs Jacobi & Miedzilski. Assumpsit

The Same vs Ephraim Wheelock. Assumpsit

Brown Brothers & C° vs Kagan, Colquitt, & Grant. Assumpsit

[114] Brown Brothers & C° vs Hampton S. Smith. Assumpsit

Battle A. Sorsby vs Samuel E. Peacock. Assumpsit

Battle A. Sorsby vs William S. Holstead. Assumpsit

The Same vs Asa Bates. Assumpsit

The Same vs Ge° W. Way. Assumpsit

The Same vs Jonathan P. Jackson. Assumpsit

The Same vs Lemuel Jepson. Assumpsit

Ann H. Brooking & Wm P. Haynes, as Admtrx. & Admtr. of Francis Brooking, dec^d vs Robert E. Broadnax. Case for Trover &c

Hamilton & Cole, for the use &c vs Howard & Wittick. Assumpsit

Richard S. Williams vs John B. Peabody. Assumpsit

Edward Kellogg & C° vs Buckler & Short. Assumpsit

The Same vs Dana Hungerford & C°. Assumpsit

Wetherell, Fowl & C° vs Chisholm & Collins. Assumpsit

Thos H. Hall vs Wm Pride, Bird F. Roberson, & Wm C. Holland. Assumpsit

Edward Kellogg & C° vs Moore & Tarver. Assumpsit

Randolphs & Underhill vs Moore & Tarver. Assumpsit

Eli Wainwright vs The Same. Assumpsit

$1000. Two years after date, I promise to pay to Stephen G. Wells, or bearer, One thousand Dollars, for value received the 16th day of May 1833.

Calvin Stratten

[115]   October adjourned Term Saturday 22 December 1838

$750. Twelve months after date, I promise to pay Stephen G. Wells, or bearer Seven hundred and fifty dollars, for value received this 16th day of May 1833.

Calvin Stratton

[The clerk wrote the following notation vertically across the foregoing note.]

Received on the within Note two hundred dollars June 17th 1834.

Georgia   }
Muscogee County } Personally Came before me, George Chatfield, a Justice of the Peace in & for said County, Stephen G. Wells, who being duly Sworn, deposeth & Saith that the two original notes, of which the above & foregoing are in Substance Copies, to the best of his knowledge and belief have been lost, mislaid, or destroyed So that he cannot find them and that the foregoing are in substance Copies of the same to the best of his knowledge, recollection, & belief.

Sworn to & Subscribed before me this 24th day of December 1838.

George Chatfield, J. P.   S. G. Wells

Georgia   }
Muscogee County } To the Honorable Superio Court of Said County

The petition of Stephen G. Wells Respectfully Sheweth that he was the lawful owner and holder of the original notes of which the foregoing are Copies in Substance And that when he made application to take the benefit of the act for the relief of Honest Debtors he brought the same into Court and delivered the

Said notes over but that they are lost or destroyed. Wherefore he prays that a rule ni si may be had to establish said copies in lieu of Said originals.

       Thomas & Shivers, Attorneys for Petitioner

It appearing to the Court ~~that~~ by the affidavit of Stephen G. Wells that the foregoing are in Substance Copies of the original notes lost or destroyed and that the said original notes have been lost, mislaid, or destroyed. On motion ordered that the Said Calvin Stratton, the maker of Said notes, do Shew Cause (if any he has) why the said Copies be not established in lieu of said original notes at the next term of this Court and that a Copy of this Rule be personally Served on the Said Calvin Stratton if to be found in this State. And if he cannot be found then that the same be served by publication in some public Gazette in the State for the Space of three months.

Insurance Bank vs Alfred Iverson. Asspt. Dismissed, entered page 40.

Smith & Wright vs Howard & Wittich. Asspt. Dismissed.

[116] Muscogee Superior Court April term 1838 Rule Ni Si to foreclose Mortgage

It appearing to the Court upon the petition of James C. Leonard & William Ellis that, on the nineteenth day of June eighteen hundred and thirty seven, Benjamin F. Ellis then & there made, executed, & delivered to the said James C. Leonard and William Ellis his certain Mortgage Deed to Secure & Save harmless the said James C. Leonard and William Ellis as endorsers & Securities on the following notes, to wit. One note dated on the [blank] day of [blank] in the year eighteen hundred and thirty six payable to one Jesse Umphries, or bearer, due on the twenty fifth day of December eighteen hundred and thirty Seven for the sum of nineteen hundred and fifty six dollars & Sixty Six cents

And the Said James C. Leonard & William Ellis became and Subscribed their names as Securities for the Said Benjamin F. Ellis on the following notes, to wit. One made and executed on the Sixteenth day of January 1837 payable to William H. Torrence & John Brown, Executors of George A. Brown, dec^d, or bearer, for the Sum of fourteen thousand one hundred and fifty eight dollars due and payable on or before the first day of January next thereafter. Also the said James C. Leonard and one Francis Leonard became & entered and Subscribed themselves as securities to and for the Said Benjamin F. Ellis and Joseph L.

Ellis in & upon five promissory notes of hand all bearing date on the third day of May eighteen hundred and thirty seven and due and payable on the 25th day of December 1837, payable to Robert Southugs, or bearer. three of said promissory notes being for the Sum of twelve hundred and eighty nine dollars each, two others of said promissory notes being one for the sum of nine hundred and fifty dollars and the other for the sum of nine hundred & thirty five due and payable as above, the whole making the aggregated amount of five thousand seven hundred and fifty two dollars. And also to Secure a debt due from the said Benjamin F. Ellis & Joseph F. Ellis to James C. Leonard amounting to the Sum of four thousand one hundred & Seven dollars & Seven cents payable on or before the first day of January 1838, notes for said Sum bearing date on the 8th day of May 1837. And also to Secure to the Said James C. Leonard the further sum of eleven hundred & Sixty dollars due and payable on the 18th day of January 1836 notes for this amount bearing date on the 10th day of January 1835. And also to secure to the said James C. Leonard, as administrator on the estate of William Smith, deceased, the sum of three thousand four hundred and forty two dollars, note for the same bearing date on the 16th day of August 1835. And for the better Securing the payment of the said Several Sums of money and to save the said James C. Leonard & William Ellis harmless, the said Benjamin F. Ellis did, on the day & year first aforesaid, make, execute, and deliver to the said James C. Leonard his certain Mortgage Deed enbracing amongst other things the following described tracts of Land, to wit, lot number eighty two, eighty nine, and one hundred & Sixteen, and seven & one half acres more or less, and also together with the then present crops growing thereon. And the said petitioners further sheweth that they have become liable and have taken up

[117] October Adjourned term 1838 Saturday 23rd December 1838

said notes and in which they were so bound & liable as aforesaid. And the said petitioners further representing that the Set time for the payment of the money aforesaid and for the foreclosure of the said Mortgage having expired and the said claims still remaining unpaid. It is therefore ordered that the said Defendant, Benjamin F. Ellis, pay into this Court on or before the first day of the next term the full amount of principal, interest, and cost due upon said claims or that the equity of redemption in and to the said Mortgaged premises be forever barred and foreclosed and that a copy of this Rule be served upon the defendant in terms of the law.

A true Statement from the minutes of the Superior Court of said County 16th day of April 1838.

Muscogee Superior Court Oct adjourned term 1838

Personally appeared in open Court James H. Campbell, who after being duly Sworn, deposeth and Saith that the within is a Copy of Substance of the Original Rule Ni Si for foreclosure of Mortgae which was destroyed in the late destruction of the Clerk's Office by fire.

Sworn to & Subscribed in Open Court this 18th day of December 1839.

Marshall J. Wellborn, J. S. C. C. C   J. H. Campbell

It appearing to the court that the original Rule Ni Si for the foreclosure of Mortgage given by Benjamin F. Ellis to James C. Leonard & William Ellis was destroyed by fire in the late Conflagration of the Clerk's Office. It is therefore ordered on motion ordered that the within Copy Rule Ni Si be established in lieu of the lost Original.

Muscogee Superior Court October Adjourned term 1838
To the Honorable Superior Court of the County of Muscogee

The petition of Calvin W. How & Fisher How, Merchants & partners trading under the firm of Calvin How & Cº, Sheweth that Robert P. Guyard, on the twelfth day of November in the year eighteen hundred and thirty six, made & executed to one William A. Garland his certain Deed of Mortgage for four certain lots or parcels of Land Situate, lying, & being in the City of Columbus & County of Muscogee aforesaid & known & distinguished in the plan of said City as numbers One hundred and fifty six, One hundred & fifty seven, One hundred & fifty eight, and the North third part of lot one hundred & fifty five. which said Mortgage was executed by the said Guyard to the said Garland for the better securing the payment of five certain acceptances by the said Gayard of drafts drawn by John Dillingham in favour of said Garland on said Guyard

[118] which said drafts bear date the tenth day of November in the year eighteen hundred and thirty six and are payable as follows, to wit. one at fifteen months after date for four thousand dollars. One at two years after date for four thousand dollars. One at three years after date for four thousand dollars. One at three years and six months after date for One thousand dollars. And one at

four years after date for two thousand dollars. And your petitioners further shew that, on the thirty first day of January in the year eighteen hundred and thirty eight, the said William A. Garland signed, set over, & transferred to your petitioners the said Mortgage together with the said Drafts and acceptances. which said Mortgage and assignment are now to the Court shewn. And your petitioners further shew that the said Robert P. Guyard has wholly failed to the amounts due on the two drafts and acceptances first above stated. They therefore pray this Honorable Court to grant them a Rule Ni Si for the foreclosure of said Mortgage for the amount due thereon as authorised and required by the Statutes in such cases made & provided.

T. F. Foster
D. Golightly, Attorn[s] for Petitioners

The foregoing Petition having been heard and considered, it is ordered and adjudged by the Court that the Mortgagor, Robert P. Guyard, do pay into this court, on or before the first day of the next term, the principal now due on said Mortgage and the interest thereon, together with the costs of this Rule. An in default of such Judgment the equity of redemption in and to Said Mortgaged premises be forever barred and foreclosed.

And it is further ordered that a Copy of this Rule be published in one of the public Gazettes of this State once a month for four months or served on the Mortgagor personally at least three months previous to the next term of the Court.

City of New York L. L.

Be it Remembered that John Merz, late of Germany, appeared in the Marine Court of the City of New York, held in the City Hall of the said City, on the second day of November in the year of our Lord one thousand eight hundred & thirty five (the said Court being a Court of Record, having Common Law Jurisdiction and a Clerk & Seal) and declared on Oath in open Court that it was bona fide his intention to become a Citizen of the United States and to renounce forever all allegiance and fidelity to any foreign Prince, Potentate, State, or Sovereignty whatsoever and particularly to the Grand Duke of Baden. In Testimony whereof, the Seal of the said Marine Court of the City of New York is hereunto affixed this 2nd day of November in the year of our Lord One thousand eight hundred and thirty five and of our Independence the Sixtieth.

John Barberie, Clk

The Petition of John Merz Respectfully Sheweth that he is an Alien friend and that on the second day of November eighteen hundred and thirty five before the Marine Court of the City of New York he filed his declaration and Oath of intention to

[118] Muscogee Superior Court October Adj^d term Saturday 22nd Decem 1838

become a Citizen of the United States and more than two years having elapsed since the filing of the same, he therefore prays that he may be permitted to take and Subscribe the Oath of Allegiance and be thence admitted to all the rights of an American Citizen.

John Merz

On motion, it is ordered that the Oath of Allegiance be administered to the said John Merz and that he be thence admitted to all the rights, priviledges, and immunities of an American Citizen.

I, John Merz, do Solemnly and Sincerely Swear that I will Support and defend the Constitution of the United States. And that I hereby renounce forever all allegiance and fidelity to all and every foreign Prince, Potentate, State, or Sovereignty whatever and particularly to the Grand Duke of Baden whereof I was before a Subject. So help me God.

Sworn to & Subscribed in Open Court this 24th day of December 1838, the Same being a Court of Record, having a Clerk and Seal.

Marshall J. Wellborn, J. S. C. C. C.   John Merz

John P. Trice }
     vs } Assumpsit and verdict for the Plainff for the sum
James C. Watson } of One hundred ~~dollars~~ and twelve dollars
James Abbercrombie } with cost of suit
Felix Gibson }
Charles Abbercrombie }
Anderson Abbercrombie }
& John Martin }

The defendants, being dissatisfied with the verdict of the Jury rendered in the above cause and having paid all cost, demands an Appeal and brings Alfred Iverson, their attorney at Law, and tenders him as their Security, and they the Said defendants by their Attorney aforesaid, Alfred Iverson, and [blank] acknowledge themselves Jointly & severally bound to John P. Trice for the payment of the eventual condemnation money in said cause. In Testimony whereof, they have hereunto set their hands and Seals this 24th day of December 1838.

Test. Gerard Burch, Clk   Alfred Iverson
                                               Att^y at Law for Def^{ts}
                                               Mansfield Torrance

James C. Leonard }
& William Ellis }
     vs } Rule absolute for the foreclosure of
Benjamin F. Ellis } a Mortgage. Octr Adj^d term 1838

It appearing to the Court that a Rule Ni si was taken at the last term of this Court calling upon the defendant to pay into this Court on or before the first day of the present term the principal, interest, and Cost due on the above Mortgage. And Service of the above Rule ni si having been perfected and the said defendant

[120] having failed to make such payment. And it further appearing to the Court that there is now due on said Mortgage the sum of seven thousand seven hundred and fifty three dollars and thirty seven cents Principal & interest. Whereupon it is ordered, considered, and adjudged by the Court that the Plaintiffs do recover of the defendant to be levied upon the said Mortgage premises the said sum of seven thousand seven hundred and fifty three dollars

& thirty seven cents and the further sum of [blank] for their Cost in this behalf laid out and expended and that the equity of redemption in and to the said Mortgaged premises be and the same is hereby and forever henceforth barred and foreclosed.

Henry Bird }
  vs   } October term 1838. Assumpsit for Rent
Ge° W. Way }

The declaration in the above Stated case having been filed in the ~~abov~~ Clerk's Office of this Court, with the process attached, & Service having been perfected in time, and the Said declaration having been destroyed by fire. It is ordered that the Copy herewith presented be established in lieu of the Original.

James H. Shorter, Administrator &   }
Sophiah H. Shorter, Administrix of the }
estate of Eli S. Shorter, dec^d, Respondants }
    vs   }
Calhoun & Bass, Appellants   }

Muscogee Superior Court October adjourned term 1838

David Golightly in open Court being duly Sworn & Saith that the Original declaration, process, Sheriff's return, & the finding of the Jury in the above Stated case has been lost by fire, and that the Bond given by the Appellants in Said Case to insure the payment of the eventual condemnation money has also been lost in like manner. And that the Copies of the Same papers above Stated Shewn to the Court are true Copies in Substance of the said originals.

Sworn to in open Court 14th December 1838.

Gerard Burch, Clk   D. Golightly

Whereupon, it is ordered by the Court that said Copies be established in lieu of Said Originals.

      Muscogee Superior Court Octr adj^d term 1838

David Golightly in open Court, duly sworn, makes Oath that the original Bond for the payment of the eventual condemnation money mentioned in the within case was duly executed within four days after the adjournment of the said Superior Court for the Spring term 1838 and that the Original note described in the Copy

[121]   Superior Court October Adjourned term 1838

Copy of the said original declaration has been lost by fire, and that the Copy appended to said declaration is a true Copy in Substance of the Said original note.

Therefore, it is ordered by the Court that said Copy note be established in lieu of the original.

Muscogee Superior Court October adj^d term 1838

We, the Grand Jurors Selected and Sworn for the present term of said Court, in closing our labour deem it a duty to make Some presentments of General Character.

In common with every good Citizen, we have become alarmed at the great increase of Crime in the County and hold it to be the duty of every friend of Social order to aid in bringing the offenders to Justice. And while we are active in Small offences to prosecute them, We should be carefull that large ones Should not escape, the public net Should be so constructed as to catch the large fish as well as the minnows. We consider the Stealing of a pony an offence of much less magnitude than extensive Banking or Mercantile frauds, and we believe that is owing to a want of moral courage that in the community that so many of the latter Class go unpunished. Men appear to be afraid of striking at vice in high places. Persons who [blank] dashing equipages and dress finely commit crimes with impunity, which would send a man with his elbows out to the Penitentiary. This Should not be so. It is in vain to crowd your Books with penal Statutes, unless those Statutes are enforced. A Community should have no Simpathy for offenders. Individual feeling should be Sacreficed for the public good, nor should offenders against the laws escape in consequence of the wealth and Standing of themselves or their friends and relatives. Crime should be prosecuted wherever it is found, and we are happy to see a disposition on the part of the people to set about this work in good earnest.

And it is not by prosecutions alone that crime is to be put down. we must frowm down all unpunished offences when we have in our own knowledge such evidence of their guilt as would satisfy us as Jurors in finding them guilty. Let every man in the Country refuse to associate with the violaters of the law, and it would do more for the promotion of good order and morality than all the penal Statutes from the days of Alfred to the present time. No community since the days of Lycugus was ever made moral by Legislation. We are convinced that the laws now of force when correctly & promptly administered are competently to secure us in life and property. There is another evil which we deem a very great & we believe a growing one, the frequent elevation to the first Officers in the State of men notorious for their want of moral worth. Members of the Church, Members of Temperant Societies, Members of Antigambling associations votes for gamblers and libertines

[122] for executive and Judicial Offices, and then complain that the laws are not enforced, as if they expected offenders would prosecute or punish one another. So long as this evil exist, we may expect to see violations of the law, the people who are the fountain of all honour can and should remedy this evil.

There is also another evil to which we beg leave to call to the attention of the Community. we allude to the election of Subordinate Magistrates and peace Officers. there is too little attention paid to this matter by the orderly and business part of the Citizens. the consequence is that we seldom See these Offices filled with those who are qualified for the post and in some districts owing to this Apathy the elections are made by the idle and profligate who take care to place in Office Such persons as will either aid them in the Commission of Crime or Screen them after it is committed. Without intending to arraign the motives of those members of the present Legislature who voted against the Bill to organize a Supreme Court, we must regret its failure. Independent of the constitutional obligations to organize the Court, we think Justice and policy require it. Strangers in passing through the united States are often astonished at the diversity of laws in the different States, all having the same central Government. This is not Strange, as every State is a separate & Sovereign Community. But here within our own limits, we have the Same diversity. What is law within one Circuit is not law in another, and what is law to day is not law tomorrow in the same circuit. This Should be remidied.

We likewise present as a greviance the too great number of our Legislature and hope that our delegates in the contemplated convention to revise the Constitution will use their exertions to lessen the number and render more equal the representation. Individuals and property and not teritory Should form the Basis of Representation.

We present William H. Lewis, Nicholas Lewis, and R. J. Wade for the Offence of an Affray in the Streets of Columbus in November last. Witnesses Emanuel Ezekiel.

We present R. J. Wade for carrying an unlawfull weapon, to wit, a Bowie Knife, in November last. Witness William S. Chipley.

A true Bill having been found against Jacob Cunningham for burning the Court House and Clerk's Office of this County, we recommend to the Inferior Court and the City Counsel of Columbus to offer a Suitable reward for the apprehension and delivery of said Jacob Cunningham to the Jailor of this County.

We cannot close our presentments without warmly commending the promptness, zeal, and orderly conduct of those of our fellow Citizens who aided the Officers of Justice in arresting a portion of that gang of desperadoes who have so long infested our Community and brought disgrace on our County. And the thanks of every good Citizen is due to the Sheriff, his deputy, and the Marshall of the City of Columbus for their unremiting efforts in bringing those violators of the Law to condign punishment.

Though opposed to the practice of thanking public servants for doing ~~not~~ what they are not only paid for, but Sworn to do, we take pleasure in returning our thanks to his Honor Judge Wellborn for his Strict attention to business during the [blur] present term, more business having been transacted than we ever knew in the same time.

We likewise present our thanks to the Solicitor General for his attention to business

[123] October Adj^d term 1838 (Saturday 22 December}

and for his Courtesy to this body.

We request that these presentments be published in each of the City papers.

1. Mansfield Torrence foreman	12. Hiram Fuller
2. Thomas Hoxey	13. John Johnson
3. Anderson Hunt	14. Jeremiah McCoy
4. William S. Chipley	15. Augustus Hayward
5. William P. Malone	16. William Clark
6. Henry K. Hill	17. Emanuel Ezekiel
7. William L. Jeter	18. Frederick Toby
8. George A. Norris	19. Henry Mims
9. John D. Jordan	20. George Smith
10. James M. Russel	21. Theophelus Bryan
11. Jonathan P. Jackson	22. Willis P. Baker

On motion of Henry L. Benning, Sol^r General, ordered that the above presentments of a public nature be published in the Several newspapers of the City.

North Hampton County S. S.

Report of Henry Charles Adolphus Habermann, an Alien friend and free white person, desiring to become a Citizen of the United States, made to the Prothonotary of the Court of Common Pleas of Northampton County, Pennsylvania the twenty eighth day of May in the year of our Lord one thousand eight hundred and thirty five.

Name	Birthplace	Age	Nation & Allegiance	Place whence migrated
Henry Charles Adolphus Habermann	Town of Niese	24 years	Lippe Detmold Prince of Lippe Detmold	he migrated from the place of his nativity

Arrived in the United States on the 24th of May 1833 at New York. Place of intended Settlement Easton, Northampton County, Pennsylvania.

In the Court of Common Pleas of Northampton County
Northampton County S. S.

I, Henry Charles Adolphus Habermann, do declare on Oath that it Bona fide my intention to become a Citizen of the United States and to renounce for ever all allegiance and fidelity to any foreign Prince, Potentate, State, or Sovereignty whatever and particularly to the Prince of Lippe Detmold of whom I am now a subject.

Henry Charles Adolphus Habermann

[124] Sworn to in open Coourt the 28th day of May A. D. 1835.

Wm L. Sebring, Prot.

I Certify that the foregoing is a true Copy of the original filed of Record in my office. Given under my hand and the Seal of said Court at Easton the 28th day of May A. D. 1835.

Wm L. Sebring, Prot. of the Court
of Com. Pleas of N. C.

Muscogee Superior Court October adjourned term 1838

The petition of Henry Charles Adolphus Habermann, an Alien friend and free white person, Respectfully Sheweth that, on the 28th day of May 1835, he filed his declaration and Oath of intention to become a Citizen of the United States in the Office of the Prothonotary of the Court of the Common Pleas for the County of Northampton in the State of Pennsylvania and was then & there before said Court duly and regularly qualified to the same as by a transcript from the Records and under the Seal of said Court hereunto annexed will more fully and at large shew. And more than two years have elapsed since the filing of the same, he prays that he may be permitted to take and Subscribe the Oath of Allegiance prescribed by the act of Congress. And thence admitted to all the rights of Citizenship.

H. C. A. Habermann

On motion, it is ordered by the Court that the said Henry Charles Adolphus Habermann be admitted to Swear and Subscribe to the Oath of Allegiance prescribed by the act of Congress and be thence forward admitted to all the rights of an American Citizen.

I, Henry Charles Adolphus Habermann, do Solemnly and Sincerely Swear that I will Support and defend the Constitution of the United States and that I do absolutely and entirely renounce and abjure all allegiance and fidelity to any foreign prince, Potentate, State, or Sovereignty whatever, and particularly to Lippe Detmold Prince of Lippe Detmold whereof I was before a Subject. So help me God.

H. Habermann

Sworn to & Subscribed in Open Court this 20th day of Dec 1838.

Marshall J. Wellborn, J. S. c. c. c.

James H. Shorter }
    vs   }
Thomas Hoxey }

We, the Jury, find for the Plaintiff seven thousand five hundred dollars, besides interest, cost of suit, & protest fee.

Jn° McGough, forman

The Court adjourned to meet again monday morning at half past nine O'clock.

Marshall J. Wellborn, J. S. C. C. C.

[125] Muscogee Superior Court October Adjourned Term
Monday 24th day of December 1838

The Court met again according to adjournment, present the Honorable Marshall J. Wellborn, Judge of the Superior Courts in the Chattanoochee Circuit.

James H. Shorter }
    vs   }
Wm B. Roberson & C°}

We, the Jury, find for the Plaintiff eighteen hundred and Seventy five dollars, besides interest & Cost of Suit & protest fee.

John McGough, form

James H. Shorter }
    vs   } Assumpsit
Wm B. Roberson }

We, the Jury, find for the Plaintiff twelve hundred and fifty dollars, besides interest, costs of Suit, & protest fee.

                                            Jn° McGough, form

James H. Shorter }
    vs   } Assumpsit
John T. Walker }

We, the Jury, find for the Plaintiff six hundred and twenty five dollars, besides interest & Costs of Suit.

                                            Jn° McGough, form

James H. Shorter   }
    vs   } Asspt
Battle A. Sorsby, pr   }
Read & Talbot, endorsers & Securities }

We, the Jury, find for the Plaintiff six hundred and twenty five dollars, besides interest & Costs of Suit.

                                            Jn° McGough, form

James H. Shorter }
   vs   }
T. & M. Evans   }

We, the Jury, find for the Plaintiff Seven thousand five hundred dollars, besides interest & Costs of Suit & Protest fee.

                                            Jn° McGough, F. M.

James H. Shorter }
   vs   } Assumpsit
Moore & Tarver }

We, the Jury, find for the Plaintiff fourteen hundred & forty Dollars, besides interest & Costs of suit & three dollars protest fee.

        Jn° McGough, F. M.

Dana Hungerford, for the use &c }
   vs   } Assumpsit
John A. Urquhart   }

We, the Jury, find for the Plaintiff thirty four hundred and thirty four dollars, besides interest & Costs of suit & protest fee.

        John McGough, F. M.

[126]

James H. Shorter   }
   vs   } Assumpsit
Timothy Collins, Prin   }
T. & M. Evans, endorsers & securities }

We, the Jury, find for the Plaintiff Twelve hundred and fifty dollars, besides interest & costs of suit.

        Jn° McGough, F. M.

James H. Shorter }
   vs   } Assumpsit
James S. Calhoun}

We Confess Judgment to the Plaintiff for twenty five hundred dollars, besides interest & cost of suit & protest fee.

        Tho[s] G. Gordon, Def[ts] Att[ys]

James H. Shorter }
   vs   } Assumpsit
Thomas G. Gordon }

I Confess Judgment to the Plaintiff for twenty four hundred dollars, besides interest & cost of suit & Protest fee.

        Tho[s] G. Gordon

James H. Shorter, Admtr. }
Sophia H. Shorter, Admtrx &c }
   vs   } Assumpsit
Micajah W. Thweatt & }
Thacker B. Howard   }

We, the Jury, find for the Plaintiffs four hundred & twenty dollars, besides interest & Costs of suit.

        Tho[s] V. Miller, Form

James H. Shorter }
  vs   } Assumpsit
Richard Hooper }

We Confess Judgment to the Plaintiff in the sum of Sixteen hundred and fifty dollars, besides interest, costs of suit, & protest fee.

        Thomas & Shivers, Def[ts] Att[ys]

James H. Shorter }
  vs   } Assumpsit
James Rankin }

I Confess Judgment to the Plaintiff for Twelve hundred and fifty dollars, besides interest, costs of suit, & protest fee.

        Garrett, Hallenbeck, Def[ts] At[ys]

James H. Shorter }
  vs   } Assumpsit
Edward Cary }

I confess Judgment to the Plaintiff for seven thousand five hundred dollars, besides interest, costs of suit, & protest fee.

Edwd Cary

Dana Hungerford, for the }
use of James H. Shorter }
     vs } Assumpsit
Lucian A. Bowdre }

I Confess Judgment to the Plaintiff thirty four hundred & thirty four dollars, besides interest & costs of suit & three dollars protest fee.

L. A. Bowdre

[127]   Muscogee Superior Court October Adjourned Term 1838

James H. Shorter }
     vs } Assumpsit
John Warren }

I Confess Judgment to the Plaintiff Seventeen hundred and fifty dollars, besides interest & cost of suit & protest fee.

Jn° Warren

James H. Shorter }
     vs } Assumpsit
William P. Malone }

I Confess Judgment to the Plaintiff for seventeen hundred & fifty dollars, besides interest & costs of suit & protest fee.

W. P. Malone

James H. Shorter }
     vs } Assumpsit
Dana Hungerford }

I Confess Judgment to the Plaintiff for Eighteen hundred & twenty five dollars, besides interest & costs of suit.

Dana Hungerford

James H. Shorter }
    vs   } Assumpsit
John D. Jordan }

We, the Jury, find for the Plaintiff thirty nine hundred hundred dollars, besides interest, costs of suit, & protest fee.

Thos V. Miller, F. M.

James H. Shorter }
    vs   } Assumpsit
James S. Calhoun }

I Confess Judgment to the Plaintiff for fourteen hundred & forty dollars, besides interest & costs of suit & protest fee, reserving right of Appeal.

Thos G. Gordon, def^{ts} Att^{ys}

James H. Shorter   }
    vs   } Assumpsit
Peter V. Guerry, Senr }
Richd Jones   }
Seymour R. Bonner }
Joseph B. Green   }

We, the Jury, find for the Plaintiff one thousand dollars, besides interest & costs of suit.

Thos V. Miller. Form

James H. Shorter }
    vs   } Assumpsit
T. & M. Evans }

We, the Jury, find for the Plaintiff Eighteen hundred & Seventy five dollars, besides interest, costs of suit, & three dollars protest fee.

Thos V. Miller, Form

James H. Shorter, Admtr. & }
Sophia H. Shorter, Admtrx. }
of Eli S. Shorter, dec^d }
  vs   } Assumpsit
Daniel McDougald }

I confess Judgment to the Plaintiff for the sum of Six hundred & five dollars & forty three cents, with interest & costs of suit and three dollars for cost of protest.

Campbell, McDougald, Watson, Def^{ts} Att^y

[128]

James H. Shorter }
  vs   } Assumpsit
John B. Peabody }

I Confess Judgment to the Plantiff Eight hundred and sixty five dollars & forty cents, besides interes, costs of suit, & protest fee.

Jno B. Peabody

Smith & Wright }
  vs   } Assumpsit
Howard & Wittich }

Dismissed.

The Insurance Bank of Columbus }
  vs   } Assumpsit
Alfred Iverson   }

We, the Jury, find for the Plaintiff Six thousand dollars, with interest & cost of suit and three dollars Protest fee.

         Jnº McGough, F. M.

The Insurance Bank of Columbus }
   vs   } Assumpsit
John W. Campbell   }

I Confess Judgment to the Plaintiff for the sum of two thousand dollars, with interest & cost of suit and three dollars protest fee.

         J. W. Campbell

Hall & Moses   }
   vs   } Assumpsit for Rent
Dennis Sullivan }
John H. Watson }
Theobald Howard }
James H. Campbell }
Walter T. Colquitt }
& Martin Brooks }

We Confess Judgment to the Plantiffs for the sum of Three hundred and Seventy five dollars, with interest & Costs of suit & three dollars for cost of protest.

      Campbell, McDougald, & Watson, Def[s] Att[ys]

John Locke   }
   vs   } Assumpsit
Seymour R. Bonner }

We, the Jury, find for the plaintiff Seven hundred & Eighty Two dollars, with interest & Cost of suit.

         Jnº McGough, F. M.

Richard Kingsland & Cº }
   vs   } Assumpsit
Battle A. Sorsby   }

I Confess Judgment to the Plaintiffs for fourteen fourteen hundred & thirty one dollars & sixty Cents & costs of suit and nine dollars for costs of protest.

Thomas & Shivers, Def^{ts} Att^{ys}

The Insurance Bank of Columbus }
      vs   } Assumpsit
James C. Watson   }

I Confess Judgment to the Plaintiff for the sum of Six thousand dollars, with interest & cost of suit & three dollars for cost of Protest.

Campbell, McDougald, & Watson, Def^{ts} Att^{ys}

[129]   Monday 24th December 1838

Insurance Bank of Columbus}
      vs   } Assumpsit
James S. Calhoun &   }
Charles L. Bass   }

I Confess Judgment to the Plaintiff for the sum of nine thousand dollars, with interest & cost of suit & three dollars cost of protest.

Thos G. Gordon, Def^{ts} Att^y

Tavner W. Fortson, Admtr. &c }
for the use of George Carter   }
      vs   } Assumpsit
Wm W. Pool   }
Wm T. Lively &   }
Tavner W. Fortson, partners &c }

We, the Jury, find for the Plaintiff against Wm W. Pool & Tavner W. Fortson Three hundred and five dollars, with interest & cost of suit.

Jno McGough, F. M.

The Insurance Bank of Columbus }
        vs   } Assumpsit
Benjamin V. Iverson   }

I Confess Judgment to the Plaintiff for the sum of Six thousand two hundred & fifty dollars, with interest & cost of suit and three dollars cost of protest fee.

                      Jacob M. Guerry, Def^{ts} Att^y

John Locke   }
     vs   } Assumpsit
Wm B. Robinson & Co}

We, the Jury, find for the Plaintiff ~~the sum of~~ Nine hundred & thirty Eight dollars and forty cents, with interest & cost of suit.

                      Jno McGough, F. M.

Insurance Bank of Columbus}
     vs   } Assumpsit
Edward Cary   }

I Confess Judgment to the Plaintiff for the sum of Nine thousand dollars, with interest & Cost of suit and three dollars for cost of protest.

                      Seaborn Jones, Def^t Att^{ys}

Insurance Bank of Columbus}
     vs   } Assumpsit
Thomas C. Evans &   }
Matthew R. Evans   }

I Confess Judgment to the Plaintiff for the sum of Nine thousand dollars, with interest & costs of suit and three dollars for cost of Protest.

                      Seaborn Jones, Def^t Att^{ys}

John Locke }
  vs   } Assumpsit
William Rogers }
John H. Ware & }
Walter T. Colquitt }

We Confess Judgment to the Plaintiff for fifteen hundred dollars, with interest & Cost of Suit.

            Colquitt, Holt, & Echols, Def[ts] Att[ys]

[130]

Cebra & Cumming }
  vs   } Assumpsit
Ragan, Colquitt, & Grant }

I confess Judgment to the Plaintiff for the sum of three hundred & twelve dollars and forty four cents, with interest & cost of suit. Also nine dollars & thirty seven cents for the difference of exchange between Columbus in the State of Georgia and the City of New York at the time the note declared on became payable and three dollars for cost of Protest.

            Colquitt, Holt, & Echols, Def[ts] Att[ys]

Rose, McKnight & C[o] }
  vs   } Assumpsit & Bail
John G. Mulford }

I confess Judgment to the Plaintiff for the sum of twelve hundred and Seventy three dollars and Seventy cents, with interest and Cost of suit and three dollars for cost of protest.

            J. N. & J. M. Bethune, Def[ts] Att[ys]

Bogert & Kneeland }
  vs   } Assumpsit
Seaborn Jones, endorser }

I confess Judgment to the Plaintiff for the sum of twenty seven hundred ~~Six~~ & twenty six dollars & ninety cents, with interest & cost of suit and the further sum sum of one hundred & ninety dollars & eighty eight cents for the difference of Exchange between Columbus in the State of Georgia and the City of New York at the time the note sued on became payable & three dollars for cost of protest.

$$\text{Seaborn Jones, Def}^t$$

J. W. & R. Leavitt }
  vs   } assumpit
Read & Talbott }

We, the Jury, find for the Plaintiffs Six hundred & thirteen dollars & twenty cents, with interest & cost of suit and three dollars for cost of Protest.

$$\text{Jn}^o\text{ McGough, form}$$

J. W. & R. Leavitt }
  vs   } asspt
Battle A. Sorsby }

I confess Judgment to the Plaintiff for Six hundred & fifteen dollars & Seventeen cents, with interest & costs of suit & three dollars for Cost of protest.

$$\text{Thomas & Shivers, Def}^{ts}\text{ Att}^{ys}$$

J. W. & R. Leavitt }
  vs   } asspt
Battle A. Sorsby }

I confess Judgment to the Plaintiffs for Six hundred & thirteen dollars & twenty cents, with interest & cost of Suit & three dollars for cost of protest.

$$\text{Thomas & Shivers, Def}^{ts}\text{ Att}^{ys}$$

[131]   Monday 24ᵗʰ December 1838

Spofford & Tileston }
    vs   } Asspt
H. Mims & Cº   }

We confess Judgment to the Plaintiffs for four hundred & five dollars & eighty one cents, with interest & Cost.

                                J. N. & J. M. Bethune, Defᵗˢ Attʸˢ

The Insurance Bank of Columbus}
    vs   } Asspt
Thomas C. Evans &   }
Matthew R. Evans   }

We Confess Judgment to the Plaintiff for three thousand five hundred dollars, with interest & Cost of suit & three dollars for Cost of protest.

                                Thoˢ G. Gordon, defᵗˢ attʸ

The Bank of the State of Georgia }
    vs   } Asspt
Isaac Mitchell   }

I confess Judgment to the Plaintiff for four hundred & thirty eight dollars, with interest & Cost of suit & three dollars for cost of protest.

                                J. N. & J. M. Bethune, Defᵗˢ Attʸˢ

The Insurance Bank of Columbus}
    vs   } Assumpt
Burton Hepburn   }

We, the Jury, finf for the Plaintiff the Sum of Six thousand two hundred & fifty dollars, with interest & Costs of Suit & three dollars for cost of protest.

                                Jnº McGough, form

The Insurance Bank of Columbus }
   vs   } Asspt
John J. Boswell   }

We, the Jury, find for the Plaintiff the Sum of Six thousand two hundred & fifty dollars, with interest & Cost of suit & three dollars for Cost of Protest.

         Jnº McGough, form

The Insurance Bank of Columbus }
   vs   } assumpt
J. B. Webb   }

I confess Judgment to the Plaintiff for two thousand dollars, with interest & cost of suit & three dollars for cost of Protest.

      Campbell, McDougald, & Watson, Def[ts] Att[ys]

J. B. Green & Cº }
  vs   } Asspt
Noel Mathews }

We, the Jury, find for the Plaintiffs the sum of eighteen hundred & eight dollars & fifty five cents, with interest from 15th Feb 1838 & Cost of Suit & three dollars cost of protest.

         Jnº McGough, form

[132]

S. Grosvener & Cº }
  vs   } assumpsit
Mims & Fuller }

We, the Jury, find for the Plaintiffs Sixteen hundred & Seventy dollars & Sixty one cents, with interest & Cost of suit & three dollars for costs of Protest.

         Jnº McGough, form

Thompson T. Adams }
     vs   } assumpsit
Wm B. Roberson & Co }

We, the Jury, find for the Plaintiff the sum of two hundred & fifty seven dollars & Seventy nine cents, with interest & Cost of Suit & three dollars for cost of protest.

                                    Jn° McGough, form

John B. Baird   }
     vs   } Assumpsit
Edwin L. De Graffenried }

We, the Jury, find for the Plaintiff thirteen hundred and eleven dollars and twenty cents, with interest & cost of suit and three dollars cost of protest.

                                    Jn° McGough, F. M.

Insurance Bank of Columbus {
     vs   } Assumpsit
Burton Hepburn   }

We, the Jury, find for the Plaintiff nine thousand dollars, with interest & cost of suit and three dollars for cost of Protest.

                                    Jn° McGough, F. M.

Insurance Bank of Columbus {
     vs   } Assumpsit
Burton Hepburn   }

We, the Jury, find for the plaintiff Six thousand dollars, with interest & cost of suit and three dollars for cost of protest.

                                    Jn° McGough, F. M.

Hays Bowdre }
    vs } Case
James H. Shorter & }
Sophia H. Shorter }
Admtr. & Admtrx. }
of Eli S. Shorter }

We, the Jury, find for the Plaintiff the sum of Twenty five hundred dollars, with interest & Cost of suit and three dollars for cost of protest, to levied & made of the goods & chattels, lands, tenements, & effects of Eli S. Shorter, dec^d in the hands of the said defendants to be administered if to be found, but if not to be found then to levied & made of the individual property of the said defendants.

                                Jn° McGough, F. M.

Ezekiel B. Stoddard }
    vs } Assumpsit
Robinson & Williams }

We, the Jury, find for the Plaintiff one hundred and sixty two dollars & eighty five cents, with interest & cost of suit and three dollars for cost of Protest.

                                Jn° McGough, F. M.

[133]   Monday ~~Saturday~~ 24th December 1838

James K. Daniel }
    vs } Asspt
Thomas C. Evans }

We, the Jury, find for the Plaintiff nine hundred and fifty dollars, with interest & cost of suit and three dollars for cost of Protest.

                                Jn° McGough, F. M.

James K. Daniel }
    vs } Assumpsit}
Bernard Matthewson }

We, the Jury, find for the Plaintiff two hundred dollars, with interest & cost of suit and three dollars for cost of Protest.

Jn° McGough, F. M.

Rose, McKnight & C° }
      vs   } Assumpsit
Bernard Matthewson }

We, the Jury, find for the Plaintiff five hundred and Eighty dollars and ninety three Cents, with interest & cost of suit.

Wm Amos, F. M.

Edward W. Right }
      vs   } Debt
Edward Delony }

We, the Jury, find for the Plaintiff Sixty dollars & Six cents principal & four dollars interest & cost of suit.

Jn° McGough, F. M.

James H. Shorter, Adm. Admtr. & }
Sophia H. Shorter, Admtrx. of the }
Estate of Eli S. Shorter, deceased } And verdict for the Plaintiff three
      vs   } thousand dollars, besides interest
Calhoun & Bass } & costs of Suit

The defendants, being dissatisfied with the verdict of the Jury rendered in the above cause and paid all cost & demanded an appeal, brings (by their Attorney Thomas G. Gordon) Mathew R. Evans and tenders him as their Security and they, the Said Calhoun & Bass, by their Attorney Thomas G. Gordon, & Mathew R. Evans acknowledge themselves Jointly & Severally bound to said James H. Shorter, Administrator, & Sophia H. Shorter, Administratrix, of the estate of said Eli S. Shorter, deceased, the Plaintiffs, for the payment of the eventual condemnation money in Said Cause.

In Testimony whereof, they have hereunto set their hands and seals this [blank] day of May 1838.

          Calhoun & Bass
         By their Attorney Thomas G. Gordon
Test. Gerard Burch, Clk   Matt R. Evans

[134]

The State   }
  vs   } True Bill for Simple Larceny
Maberry Howell }
Western Harwell }
& Avery Odom }

It appearing to the Court that Avery Odom, one of the defendants in the above Stated case, has given a Bond in the sum of One thousand dollars with condition to appear in this Court and answer for the said Offence and that he has been Called by the Sheriff three times and has failed to appear. It is Ordered that the said Bond be forfeited by the Solicitor General according to Law and that the Clerk issue a Scire facias against the said defendant and his Securities in the manner prescribed by Law.

Insurance Bank of Columbus}
   vs   } Judgment April term 1838
John H. Love   }

The execution issued in this Case having been returned Nulla Bona and the same consumed by fire by the burning of the Clerk's Office. Ordered that the Clerk issue an alias fifa.

Seaton Grantland } Rule Absolute
  vs   } Fi fa from Muscogee Superior Court returnable
Stephen M. Ingersoll} to the April term 1837 thereof

It appearing to the Court that Asa Bates, Sheriff of Muscogee County, had failed to make the money on the above Stated Fi fa. It is therefore ordered by the Court that the rule ni si taken in the said Fi fa be and the same is hereby made absolute and that the Said Asa Bates do pay over to the plaintiff's Attorney the principal & interest of the above Stated fi fa in thirty days and in default thereof that the Clerk of this Court do issue on the application of said attorney an attachment against Said Asa Bates as for a contempt and that said Asa Bates be incarserated within the four walls of the Jail of said County untill Said principal & interest is paid to said Attorney.

The State }
    vs } assault & Battery
George Ward }

George Ward, having been bound for his appearance at October term 1838 for the above offence and the Grand Jury having discharged and no Bill prefered against him. It is ordered by the Court that the said George Ward & Garland B. Terry, his Security, be henceforth discharged from their attendance in this Court.

Edward W. Wright }
    vs } Assumpsit October Term 1837
Van L. McKeen, maker & }
Thomas C. McKeen, endorser }

It appearing to the Court that the original petition, process, & Bail bond, as well as the entries

[135]   October adjourned term Monday 24th December 1838

entries thereon and the orders passed in relation thereto were destroyed by the late fire. and it appearing further that those filed in Office in the above case are in Substance Copies of the same. On Motion, ordered that they be & are hereby established in lieu of the Originals So lost and that the same proceedings be had thereon that could have been had upon the Originals.

Lucy Elizabeth Dillingham & }
Geo W. Dillingham, by his }
Guardian Lucy Dillingham }
    vs } Bill for discovery, relief, account &c
John Dillingham, Administrator of }
George W. Dillingham, deceased }

It appearing to the Court that the Bill above Stated was returned to October term Eighteen hundred and thirty six of this Court and that the same was regularly

Served within the time prescribed by law. and it further appearing to the Court that the answer of the Defendant was filed in the Clerk's Office on the fourteenth day of December Eighteen hundred and thirty Seven, to which answers eight exceptions (which are now of file in the Clerk's Office) were taken and argued at April term last of this Court, which exceptions were argued and decided on, but in consequence of the destruction of the Records of said Court the decision thereon cannot be ascertained. And it further appearing to the Court that at April term aforesaid the intermarriage of the said Complainant, Lucy Elizabeth Dillingham, with William D. Cairns and the appointment of William D. Cairns as Guardian of the Complainant, George W. Dillingham, in lieu of the said Lucy E. Dillingham whose Guardianship ceased by reason of her said intermarriage were suggested of Record. And orders passed by the Court that the said William D. Cairns be made party Complainant with his said wife, the said Lucy Elizabeth, formerly Lucy Elizabeth Dillingham. And that the said Bill was ordered to proceed in the Joint names of the said William D. Cairns & Lucy Elizabeth Cairnes, his wife, and the said George W. Dillingham by his said Guardian, William D. Cairns. And the said orders of the Court heretofore passed having been destroyed by the buring of the Records of the Court. It is therefore ordered that the said Several orders be reaffirmed and held & considered good and valid, and that said cause proceed in conformity therewith. And it is further ordered that said exceptions be reargued at Chambers on thursday after the fourth monday in January next, and that the decision then made thereon Shall be the Judgment of the Court as though pronounced at this term.

Muscogee Superior Court April term 1837

It appearing to the Court upon the petition of Harvy Hall that Ephraim Wheelock and Nathan P. Willard did, on the twentieth day of May A. D. 1835, execute their promissory note to him, the said Harvy Hall, for the sum of twenty nine hundred & fifty dollars payable to him, the said Hall, or order, at

[unnumbered] the Union Bank of Florida twelve months after date, and that for the better Securing the payment thereof and of the Said Harvy Hall as first indorser upon said promissory note did execute, on the first day of August in the year 1835, a Mortgage Deed embracing among other things five town lots in the town of Columbus, to wit, number Seventy two & Seventy six, two hundred & Seventy nine, two hundred and eighty one, and two hundred and eighty two. And the said petition further representing that the set time for the payment of the money aforesaid and foreclosure of the said Mortgage having expired, and the note remaining Still unpaid & Judgment having been rendered against them and against the Said Harvy Hall as first indorser. It is therefore ordered by the Court that the said defendants, Ephraim Wheelock and Nathan P. Willard pay into this Court, on or before the first day of its next term, the amount of principal, interest, and cost due upon said note and Judgments or that the Equity of Redemption in and to the aforesaid lots in the town of Columbus be forever barred and foreclosed, and that a Copy of this Rule be served upon the defendants in terms of the law or published in one of the Gazetts of Columbus once a month for four months.

A true extract from the minutes of the Superior Court of said County this 14th day of June 1837.

    (Signed)   Gerard Burch, Clk

Harvy Hall   }
    vs   } Rule absolute for fore Closure
Ephraim Wheelock & } October Term 1837
Nathan P. Willard   }

A Rule Ni si having been Granted at the last Term of this Court calling upon the defendants to pay into Court at the present term the principal, interest, and Cost due on the above Mortgage. And service of the said Rule having been perfected and the said defendants having failed to make Such payment.

Whereupon, it is considered, ordered, and adjudged that the said Plaintiff recover of the said defendants, to be levied upon the Said Mortgaged premises the sum of twenty nine hundred and fiftty dollars, with interest thereon from the twentieth day of May 1836 and the further sum of [blank] for Costs expended. And the equity of Redemption in and to the said Mortgaged premises be and the same is hereby henceforth for ever barred and foreclosed.

Georgia   }
Muscogee County } To the Honorable the Superior Court of Said County

The petition of Robert Watson Respecrfully Sheweth that, on the tenth day of May in the year of our Lord eighteen hundred and thirty eight, that Lemuel Jepson, of Said County, executed to your petitioner his deed of Mortgage in and to a lot of Land in the City of Columbus & Said County known and distinguished in the plan of said City as lot number three hundred and thirty two, which said Mortgage was executed to Secure the payment of two Certain promissory notes by the Said Lemuel Jepson and delivered to your petitioner and bearing even date with said deed of Mortgage. And by one of which he promised, on or before the twenty fifth day of

[137]   October adjourned term Monday 24th December 1838

December then next, to pay your petitioner, or bearer, Seven hundred dollars, for value received from him, with interest from date. And by the other of said notes the said Lemuel promised, on or before the twenty fifth day of December then next, to pay your petitioner, or bearer, Eight hundred and fifty dollars, for value received, with interest from date. And your petitioner Sheweth that said promissory notes are due & unpaid and prays that this Court will grant to him a Rule Ni si directing the said Lemuel Jepson to pay into this Court, on or before the first day of the next term thereof, the principal, interest, and costs due on said Mortgage and the Said notes & that in default thereof the Equity of Redemption in and to the said Mortgaged premises be forever barred and foreclosed.

It appearing to the Court that Lemuel Jepson, of Said County, did, on the tenth day of May Eighteen hundred and thirty eight, execute and deliver to Robert Watson his certain deed of Mortgage in and to a certain Lot of Land in the City of Columbus & said county, which said lot is known & distinguished in the plan of said City by lot number three hundred and thirty two. And that said Mortgage was executed for the better securing the payment of two certain promissory notes by the said Lemuel made and delivered to the said Robert and bearing even date with the said Mortgage, by one of which he promised, on or before the twenty fifth day of December then next, to pay the said Robert Watson, or bearer, Seven hundred dollars, for value received of him, with interest from date. And by the other of said notes he promised, on or before the twenty fifth day of December next, to pay the said Robert Watson, or bearer, eight hundred & fifty dollars, for value received, with interest from date. And that the said promissory notes are now due and unsatisfied. It is, on motion of Counsel for the Plaintiff, ordered that the said Lemuel pay into this Court, on or before the first day of the next term thereof, the principal, interest, and cost due on said notes and Mortgage. And in default thereof the equity of Redemption of the said Lemuel in & to the said Mortgaged premises be thence forward and forever barred & foreclosed, and that a Copy of this Rule be Served on the defendant in terms of the Law.

James Rhind }
    vs   } Ca Sa
Paul H. Tiller }

Whereas Paul H. Tiller was arrested in the above Case and William B. Brown became his bail for his appearance at this Term of said Court to take the benefit of the act for the Relief of honest debtors and the said Paul H. Tiller having failed to appear, on motion ordered that Judgment be entered up on said bond against the Principal & his bail aforesaid, to be discharged upon the payment of the debt & cost.

[138]

Thomas B. Greenwood }
    vs   } Assumpsit
James Boykin, Admtr. &c }

It appearing to the Court that Original declaration in the above case was destroyed by fire at the buring of the Court House & Clerk's Office and that the Copy herewith filed is a copy in Substance. it is on motion Ordered that the said Copy be established in lieu of said Original.

George Hargraves }
    vs   } Fi Fa. On foreclosure of a Mortgage issuing from the
George W. Ross } Inferior Court of Muscogee County

And now at this Term comes Calhoun & Bass by their Attorney and suggest to the Court that the Mortgage upon which the above fi fa was founded was made to defraud the other Creditors of the said George W. Ross and particularly the said Calhoun & Bass whose debt was then in suit and of this they put themselves upon the Country.

                      Seaborn Jones Att^y
                      for Calhoun & Bass
                      J. N. & J. M. Bethune, Att^o for Hargraves

Theobald Howard }
      vs   } Mortgage Fi fa
John R. Lloyd & Co }

and now at this term comes James C. Watson and Ed Hill by his guardian James W. Harris by their Attorneys and suggest to the Court that said Execution in favour of Theobald Howard was issued upon a Mortgage which was made and executed to defraud the other Creditors of John R. Lloyd & Co and particularly the said James C. Watson and Ed^d Hill and of this they put themselves upon the Country &c.

                        James N. Bethune, Att^y
                        for Watson & Hill
                        And Theobald Howard doth the like &c
                        Iverson & Guerry, Plff Att^{ys}

S. R. Bonner vs Paul H. Tiller. Fi fa   A. McDougald vs Paul H. Tiller. Fi fa
James Woodard vs Paul H. Tiller. Fi fa   John Logan vs Paul H. Tiller. Fi fa
Wiley Williams vs Paul H. Tiller. Fi fa

It appearing to the Court that Joseph D. Bethune, Sheriff of said County, has in his hands the sum of Five hundred and Eighty five dollars, money raised out of the defendant in the above case. It is therefore on motion Ordered that he pay out the same to said fi fas according to their priority of date and to those of the same date Prorate.

John G. Dunlap   }
      vs   } Assumpsit, Judgment, Verdict, & Ca sa
Stephen M. Ingersoll }

It appearing to the Court that the following is a Copy in Substance of the Original above stated Ca sa and that the said Original has been destroyed. It is ordered that

[139] the said Copy be established in place of said lost Original.

October Adj^d Term 1838

Insurance Bank of Columbus vs James B. Butts. Fis fa Princ. $4000.
Insurance Bank of Columbus vs Columbus Mills   "   " 2500.

Ordered that Copies of the above lost Originals be established in lieu of said lost Originals.

Jacob Fogle vs Lucian A. Bowdre. Debt

Jacob Fogle vs Lucian A. Bowdre. Assumpsit

Lewis J. Davies bs Isaac Mitchell. Assumpsit

Jacob Fogle vs Ephraim Mandell. Assumpsit & Bail

J. S. Smith & C° vs Elisha S. Norton. Debt

Alfred F. Brannon, who sues for the use of Elias B. Crane vs Charles E. Mims. Debt

Fewtrall Hall vs Daniel Loftin. Assumpsit

Joseph S. Smith vs Elisha S. Norton. Debt

Walter T. Colquitt vs William McGee. Assumpsit

Eaton Flewellen vs John R. Lloyd. Assumpsit

Charles Nelson vs William B. Robinson & C°. Assumpsit

Ephraim Brown vs Joseph Davidson. Assumpsit

Bennett Bunn vs Theophilus Bryan, Admtr. of Thomas Bryant, dec^d. Debt

H. Mims & C°, who sue for the use of the Union Bank of Florida } vs James H. Jones, Junr & Robert W. Carnes. Assumpsit }

Samuel Bernard vs Theophilus Bryan, Admtr. of Thomas Bryan } Dec^d } Debt

[140]

McKee & Prickett vs John Hardie, maker, & John Windham, } Henry L. Lestarget, Horton W. Hamner, endorsers } Assumpsit

Hampton S. Smith }   Fellows, Wadsworth & C° }
   vs   } Debt   vs   }
Elijah Corley   }   G. H. & C. A. Peabody   }

D. Hungerford & C° vs Menoah D. Robinson. Debt

Cary & Day, for the use of Edward Cary vs Albert G. Beckham. Debt

W^m & W. Toney vs Menoah D. Robinson & Thomas J. Hand. Debt

A. & S. & S. Thorpe vs Jacobi & Heine. Assumpsit

It appearing to the Court upon sufficient evidence that the original declarations and processes in the above stated cases have been destroyed by fire and that Copies of the same in substance have been filed with the Clerk. It is ordered that said Copies be established and stand in lieu of said Originals.

Carpenter, Griffin & C° vs John G. Mulford. Debt

George Howard & Claiborn Howard vs Benjamin Howard. Assumpsit

Benjⁿ H. Brinkley vs Michael N. Clarke. Debt

Grigsby E. Thomas vs Peter M. Thomas. Assumpsit

Booraem & C° vs William S. Hartsfield & C°. Debt

Nancy Dewell vs James Holland. Assumpsit

Hyatt, McBurney & C° vs William S. Hartsfield & C°. Debt

Perkins, Hopkins, & White vs Randol Tillery, maker, & Thos A. Brannon, Security. assumpt

George Howard vs Benjamin Howard. Debt

Booraem & C° vs Clark, Tarver & C°. Debt

[141]   October Adj^d Term Monday 24th December 1838

Hill, Dawson & C° }
     vs   } Debt
James T. McNorton }

Booraem & C° vs Benjamin F. Malone. Assumpsit

Mathew Roberson vs Charles A. Peabody, maker, & Ge° Smith, endorser. asspt

A. G. Marshall, endorser vs B. T. Robinson (maker) & Richard Johnson Wade, endorser. Asspt

Hiram Fuller vs Moore & Tarver & Milton J. Tarver (makers) & Allen & Norton, endorsers. asspt

Booraem & C° vs Wm H. Harper. Debt

J. & M. Townsend vs Code & Quinn. Debt

Hill, Dawson & C° vs Noah Pitman. Debt

Baldwin, Phelps & C° vs Clark, Tarver & C°. Debt

Booraem & C° vs Ja^s H. Jones (maker) & B. F. Malone, endorser. assumpt

William Owens vs William Kopman. Attachment

Hill, Dawson & C° vs E. G. A. Moss. Debt

R. & G. Barker vs John Dillingham & C°. Debt

A. G. Marshall vs Robert Watson. Case

John Simmons vs Jacob Funderburk. Debt

It appearing to the Court that the Petitions, Processes, and entries thereon filed in Office in the foregoing cases returnable to October Term 1838 are Copies in Substance of the Originals which were destroyed by the late fire. On motion ordered that the same be and are hereby established in lieu of the same.

[142]

John U. Brown vs Luther Blake. Assumpsit

Wm S. Hartsfield vs W. S. Holstead. Debt

C. Alling & Co vs Code & Quinn. Debt

William Tyack vs C. E. Mims & Co. Debt

W. E. & J. T. Craft vs Noel Matthews. Assumpsit

E. & F. Bradley vs John J. Smith. Debt

George Granberry vs Ben^j Howard, Elijah Corley, & Thomas Davis. Debt

E. & C. Robbins & Co vs Pool & McCrary. Debt

Henry L. Mason vs H. Mims & Co. Debt

E. & F. Bradley vs B. V. Lucas & John H. Lucas. Debt

E. & C. Robbins & Co vs T. T. Gammage & Co. Debt

Richard Yarborough vs Wm Sullivan. Debt

W. E. & J. T. Craft vs Henry G. Robinson, Menoah D. Robinson, & David R. Myers. Asspt

Hall & Moses vs John H. Watson. Debt

Alfred Wellborn vs Ragan, Colquitt, & Grant, Principals, & Wiley B. Ector, security. Debt

Peter McLaren vs Thos J. Templeton & Bernard Matthewson. Debt & Bail

Nelson & Carlton vs Thomas Davis. Assumpsit

E. & F. Bradley vs J. W. Hand, principal, & Joseph Coleman, security. Assumpsit

Nelson & Carlton vs A. Gilbert. Assumpsit

Joseph L. Burges vs Starr & Reese. Assumpsit

[143]   October Adj^d Term 1838 Monday 24th Decr 1838

Ja^s Boykin, Admtr. of Jno Owens, dec^d vs Wm B. Robinson & Co & Thos C. Evans. Debt

Ann Owens vs Wm B. Robinson & Co & Thos C. Evans. Debt

John Howland & Son vs Wm S. Hartsfield & Co. Debt

Wiley E. Jones vs E. Ezekiel, H. B. Horton, & B. M. Gray. Assumpsit

John U. Brown vs J. S. Smith, R. W. Morris, & F. A. Fairchilds. Assumpsit

It appearing to the Court that the Petitions, Processes, and entries thereon filed in Office in the foregoing cases returnable to October Term 1838 are Copys in substance of the Originals which were burnt & destroyed by the late fire. On motion ordered that the Same be and are hereby established in lieu of the same.

Nicholas Howard vs Slaton Henly. Fi fa

George W. E. Bedell vs Templeton Reid. Fi fa

Hill & Dawson vs Seaborn Eley. Fi fa

George W. E. Bedell vs Joseph Davidson. Fi fa

Ayer & Hogg vs Seaborn J. Herron. Fi fa

It appearing to the Court that the above Stated Fi fas were returned to the Clerk's Office unsatisfied and that the Same Fi fas have been destroyed by fire. It is ordered that the Clerk issue alias Fi fas.

Lucy Elizabeth Dillingham }
& George W. Dillingham }
by his Guardian }
Lucy Elizabeth Dillingham }
     vs } Bill for discovery, relief, partition, account, &c
Daniel K. Dodge }
Columbus C. Mills }
Luther Blake }
Fielding Scoggins }
Norborne B. Powell }
Burton Hepburn }
James C. Watson }
& John Dillingham, Admtr. }
of George W. Dillingham }
deceased }

It appearing to the Court the Bill above stated was filed returnable to the April term Eighteen hundred and thirty seven of this Court

[144] and that all Said defendants were regularly served personally, except Daniel K. Dodge and Fielding Scoggins, upon whom service of said bill was perfected by publication in a public Gazette of this City, and an order granted requiring them to answer said Bill by the next term. And it further appearing to the Court that at April term Eighteen hundred and thirty eight of said Court the intermarriage of Complainant, Lucy Elizabeth Dillingham, with William D. Cairns and the appointment of William D. Cairnes as Guardian of said Complainant, George W. Dillingham, in lieu of the Said Lucy E. Dillingham, whose Guardianship had ceased by virtue of Said intermarriage, was suggested of record. and orders granted by the Court that the Said William D. Cairnes be made party Complainant with his wife, the said Lucy Elizabeth, formerly Lucy Elizabeth Dillingham. and that the Said bill proceed in the Joint names of the Said William D. Cairns & Lucy Elizabeth Cairnes, his wife, and the Said George W. Dillingham by his said Guardian, William D. Cairns. and a further order having been granted by the Court at April term last aforesaid requiring the defendants to answer Said Bill within three months, which anwers have not been filed. It is therefore ordered by the Court that the orders of the Court heretofore passed, except the last, be reaffirmed and held and considered good and valid and that said Cause proceed in conformity therewith. And it is further

ordered that Said defendants do file their Answers to said Bill in the Clerk's Office within two months from this time.

Henry King }
    vs   } Rule Nisi to foreclose a Mortgage
Francis Jepson }

It appearing to the Court, upon the petition of Henry King, that Francis Jepson did, on the thirty day of October Eighteen hundred & thirty six, execute to the petitioner his deed of Mortgage in & to all that lot or parcell of land situate in the City of Columbus known & distinguished in the plan of said City by Number One Hundred & fifty three, containing half an Acre, which said mortgage was executed for the purpose of securing the payment of a certain promissory note bearing even date with the said Mortgage & made & delivered to the said petitioner by the Said Francis Jepson, Whereby he promised to pay the Said Henry King, or bearer, thirteen Hundred Dollars on or before the twenty fifth of December Eighteen Hundred & thirty seven, for Value Received, if not punctually paid to draw Interest from date, and the said sum of money is now due & the Said Mortgage wholly unsatisfied. it is on Motion of J. N. & J. M. Bethune, counsil for Plaintiff, ordered that the said Francis Jepson pay into this Court the Principal, Interest, & Cost due on said Mortgage on or before the first day of the next term thereof and that in default thereof the Equity of Redemption of the said Francis Jepson in & to the said Mortgaged

[145]   Oct Adj^d Term Monday 24 Decr 1838

be thenceforn forever bared & foreclosed & that a copy of this rule be served on the defendant in terms of the Law in such case made & provided.

George Hargraves }
    vs   } Rule Niso for Foreclosure of Mortgage
George W. Ross }

It appearing to the Court upon the petition of George Hargraves that George W. Ross, of the County of Muscogee, did, on the thirty first day of March Eighteen hundred & thirty eight, execute & deliver to the said George Hargraves his certain deed of Mortgage to all those tracts or lots of land situate, lying, & being in the City of Columbus and in that portion of said City Know and distinguished in the plan of said City as the part reserved to & for the use of the County of

Muscogee for County purposes ten acres and which said portion was afterwards was Sold and disposed of by the County of Muscogee according to an act of the General Assembly of the State of Georgia, which tracts or lots of Land are known and distinguished in said portion of said City as numbers as nine & ten, lying between Jackson & Troup Streets & bounded on the north by Washington Street, and said lots containing one half acre each, which said Mortgage deed was executed for the better securing the payment of a Certain promissory note executed by the said George W. Ross and one John A. Urquhart to the said George Hargraves, bearing the fifteenth day of February Eighteen hundred & thirty seven, whereby they promised, on or before the first day of January then next, to pay the said George Hargraves, or order, five thousand Six hundred & twenty & twenty five dollars, for value received. & it further appearing from said Petition that the said sum of money in said promissory note is due & unpaid. It is on motion of Counsel for said George Hargraves ordered that the said George W. Ross do pay into this Court, on or before the first day of the next term thereof, the principal, interest, & cost due on said Mortgage, and that in default thereof the equity of redemption in & to the said Mortgaged premises be thenceforward & forever barred & foreclosed. And that a Copy of this Rule be served on the said George W. Ross in terms of the Law in such case made & provided.

[146]

Burton Hepburn vs Jonathan P. Jackson. Assumpsit

Montclaiborne Andrews, Admtr. of Josephine Andrews, dec[d] }
vs Clapp & Chandler & ~~George W. B. Towns~~   } Assumpsit

George W. B. Towns vs Luther Blake   } Assumpsit

Theobald Howard vs Rainy C. Ragland } Assumpsit

Burton Hepburn vs John C. Jacobi, Thomas C. Evans, }
Joseph D. Bethune, James C. Calhoun   } Assumpsit
Elisha S. Norton, and Luther Blake   }

Burton Hepburn vs Starr & Reese   } Assumpsit

Burton Hepburn vs George C. Sherwood, Peter McLain }
William Wade, & Frederick Toby   } Assumpsit

Burton Hepburn vs Adolphus L. Heine } Assumpsit

Burton Hepburn vs John B. Peabody }
~~and John T. Blount~~ } Assumpsit

John T. Blount }
    vs } Assumpsit
Manoah D. Robinson }

Burton Hepburn vs John J. Wilson } Assumpsit

Patrick Monroe vs Allen Caldwell } Assumpsit on appeal

Obadiah P. Cheatham vs James S. Calhoun, } Assumpsit
Charles L. Bass, & Bird Grace } on Appeal

Green B. Ball vs James S. Calhoun, }
Charles L. Bass, Bird Grace } Assumpsit on Appeal

It appearing to the Court that the Original declarations in the foregoing cases have been destroyed and that the accompanying Copies are Correct & true. it is ordered that the said Copies be established in Lieu of the said destroyed originals.

[147]   Oct Adj^d term 1838 December 24 1838

Robert C. Wetmore }
    vs }
Hezekiah Hawly & }
Thomas H. Smith, Security }
on Ca Sa Bond }

It appearing to the Court that the Ca sa and Ca Sa Bond in this case have been destroyed by fire and that Copies of the same have been filed in this Office with the Clerk, together with Copies of the entries thereon. it is therefore ordered that said Copies be considered and taken and be established in lieu of said Originals.

Georgia }
Muscogee County } Superior Court Oct adj^d term 1838

To the Honorable the Superior Court of said County

The Petition of James L. Brander, Hamilton Murray, & Charles H. Gallaghar, Merchants & partners trading under the firm of Brander, Murray, & Gallaghar, sheweth that, on the first day of December Eighteen Hundred & thirty seven, William P. Malone executed to your petitioners a certain deed of Mortgage, bearing date the day & year aforesaid, to a Certain Lot of Land known as Lot N° One Hundred & Seventy nine in the City of Columbus in said County for the better Securing to your petitioners the payment of Ten promissory notes, bearing date on the day and year aforesaid, each for the Sum of Five Hundred & twenty five $^{31¼}/_{100}$ dollars, with the Current rate of exchange on New York, five of which said notes were made by said Malone and payable to the order of R. Hooper at the Bank of Columbus and payable at Six, nine, twelve, Fifteen, & Eighteen Months respectively after the date thereof and Indorsed in Blank by said Hooper to your petitioners. and the other five of which said promissory notes were drawn payable at six, nine, twelve, Fifteen, & eighteen months respectively by said Hooper to the order of said Malone at the bank of Columbus and indorsed in Blank by said Malone to your petitioners. and your petitioners shew that default has been made in the payment of the two notes given by said Malone and falling due at six & twelve months after the date thereof respectively and in the payment of the three notes given by said Hooper and payable at six, nine, & twelve months after the date thereof respectively. Your petitioners therefore pray this honorable Court to grant them a Rule Nisi for the fore

[148] closure of said Mortgage for the amounts of said notes, which have become due and Remain unpaid according to the provision of the Statutes of the State prescribing the mode of foreclosing Mortgages.

T. F. Foster, Att^y for Petitioners

The foregoing petition having been heard & considered, it is ordered by the Court that the Mortgager, William P. Malone, do pay into the Clerk's office of this Court, on or before the first day of the next term, the principal & interest due on said Mortgage and the Costs of this Rule and that in default of such payment the equity of Redemption in and to said Mortgaged premises be forever barred & foreclosed. And it is further Ordered that a Copy of this Rule be served on the Mortgajor personally or published in one of the public gazetts as required by the statutes in such cases made & provided.

The State }
vs } Cheating & Swindling
John L. Lewis } October adjourned term 1838

Whereas it appears to the Court that the defendant has appeared in Open Court and that ~~and~~ there was then & there a Jury empanneled to try Said case and he having demanded a trial. It is therefore on motion ordered by the Court that the said defendant be tried at the next Succeding Term of this Court, provided that at next term there Shall be a Jury then & there empanneled and qualified to try the defendant. And if the said defendant shall not be tried at Such term, he Shall be absolutely discharged and acquitted of the Offence charged in said Indictment. December 24th 1838

Colquitt, Holt, & Echols
Campbell, McDougald, & Watson
Defts Attys

The State }
vs } Simple Larceny
Hamilton Perry }

It appearing to the Court that the defendant is committed to the common Jail of said County on the above Charge and that he has not been indicted and that the Grand Jury is discharged. It is ordered that the Sheriff release and discharge him from said Jail without recognizance and that the Said defendant go without a day.

[149] October adjd Term Monday 24th December 1838

S. R. Bonner vs Paul H. Tiller. Fi fa

A. McDougald vs Paul H. Tiller. Fi fa

It appearing to the Court that the Original Fifas in the above Stated cases were returned to the Clerk's Offices with the entry of Nulla Bona thereon and that the same were destroyed by the late conflagration of the Clerk's Office. It is on motion ordered that the Clerk do issue Alias Fifas in each of said cases.

Robert C. Wetmore }
      vs   } to enter up Judgment on Ca Sa Bond
Hezekiah Hawley & }
Thomas H. Smith }
Security on Ca sa bond }

It appearing to the Court that the defendant, Hezekiah Hawley, was arrested on the fifth day of July in the year Eighteen hundred and thirty Eight by Joseph D. Bethune, Sheriff of said County, by virtue of a ca sa issued from the Superior Court of said County in favour of the Plaintiff against him and gave bond with the said Thomas H. Smith as his security in Terms of an act entitled an act For the relief of honest debtors passed in the year eighteen hundred and twenty three. And it appearing to the Court further that the said Hawley has filed failed to appear at this term of this Court, or to file his schedule, or to give notice to the Plaintiff in terms of said Statute. It is therefore Ordered by the Court that the Plaintiff have leave to enter up Judgment upon said bond in terms of said act against said Hawley and his said security, Thomas H. Smith.

Georgia }
Muscogee County } This Indenture, made this twenty eighth day of April in the year of our Lord one thousand eight hundred and thirty seven, between James H. Iverson, Attorney in fact for Lucian A. Bowdre, of the County aforesaid, of the one part, and Wood, Miers, & Iverson, of the Territory of Florida, Commission Merchants at Appallachacola, of the other part. Witnesseth that the said firm of Wood, Miers, & Iverson at the Special instance & request of said Lucian A. Bowdre and under a letter of Credit given to the Said Wood, Miers, & Iverson by the firm of Bowdre & Richards did at divers times for the benefit of Lucian A. Bowdre of the firm of Bowdre & Richards draw drafts upon the Said Bowdre & Richards to the amount of fifteen thousand nine hundred and nine Dollars, to wit, one from the Farmers Bank of Chattahoochee for five thousand and sixty one dollars due the thirteenth and sixteenth of April.

[150] One other from the same Bank for One thousand dollars due the Seventh & tenth of May, also one for twenty five hundred dollars. One from the Columbus Bank for One thousand and five hundred dollars due the twenty fifth

and eigth of April. One other from the same for eleven hundred dollars due the thirtieth and Second. One other for four thousand Seven hundred and forty eight due the first & third of April, making in all the Sum of fifteen thousand nine hundred & nine dollars aforesaid, with also a balance of eleven hundred & nineteen dollars and eighty one cents due the Said Wood, Miers, & Iverson by Bowdre & Richards for Commissions. Now for and in Consideration of the liabillity of the Said Wood, Miers, & Iverson to pay said drafts and to Secure them and to Save them harmless against all injuries that accrue to them by virtue of Said liabillity as well as for the better securing the said balance of eleven hundred and nineteen dollars and eighty one cents due by the Said Lucian A. Bowdre of the firm Bowdre & Richards to the Said Wood, Miers, & Iverson the aforesaid James H. Iverson, attorney in fact for Lucian A. Bowdre, of the firm Bowdre & Richards, by virtue of the Authority in him vested, hath granted, bargained, and Sold and doth by these presents grant, bargain, & Sell unto the said Wood, Miers, & Iverson, their heirs, & assigns the following property lying and being in the town of Columbus, to wit, Lots number three hundred and ten (310), three hundred & nine (309), three hundred & eight (308), three hundred & Seven (307), half of three hundred & Six (306), half of three hundred & five (305), and four hundred & eighteen, also the said Bowdre's interest in the following described lots, that is to say, part of Lots number fifty five & fifty six in the plan of the town of Columbus written in the following meetes and bounds, begining at the North east corner of said lot number fifty six, runing thence South down Broad Street Sixty feet to an Alley, thence along the said Alley due West ninety two feet, thence due South twenty eight feet eight inches to the lot formerly owned and Occupied by Golstein & Heine, thence due West fifty four feet six inches to the lot owned by Mrs Elizabeth A. Billups, thence due North to the North east corner of Mrs Billups lot, thence due West to front Street, thence due North up said Street to Randolph Street, thence due east along the Said Street two hundred and ninety five feet eight inches to the begining, with also the following negroes, to wit, Joe a fellow thirty eight years of age, Mack a fellow twenty four years of age, Hal a fellow twenty four years of age, Bill a fellow twenty five years of age, William a fellow twenty two years, Stephen a fellow twenty five years of age, James a Boy eight years of age, and also Rosanna Womon twenty four years old & her two children. To Have and to hold said bargained premises and property to the said Wood, Miers, & Iverson, their heirs, and assigns to them & their own proper use, benefit, & behoof forever. and the Said James H. Iverson, Attorney in fact as aforesaid, by virtue of Said power in him vested, the Said bargained premises & property unto the said Wood, Miers, & Iverson will warrant & forever defend against the claim of Lucian A. Bowdre and his heirs & against the claim of all other persons whatever. Provided Nevertheless that if the said Lucian A. Bowdre or the firm of

[151] October adj^d Term 1838

Bowdre & Richards, their heirs, executors, or administrators Shall well & truely pay or cause to be paid within the Space of twelve months the aforesaid drafts or Sum of money or Secure the Said Wood, Miers, & Iverson against all liabillity as aforesaid then & forever thenceforth, as well this present Indenture and the right thereby conveyed Shall determine and be void to all intents & purposes.

In Testimony whereof, the said James H. Iverson, as Attorney in fact of Lucian A. Bowdre, hath hereunto set his hand and Seal the day and year above written.

Signed, Sealed, and delivered in the presence of Alfred Iverson, J. S. C. C. C.

(interlineation made before Signed.)

         James H. Iverson
         Attorney in fact for
         Lucian A. Bowdre

Georgia   }
Muscogee County } For value received, we do hereby assign, transfer, & relinquish to the President, directors, and Company of the Southern Life Insurance & trust Company all the right, title, and interest which we have and hold to the within Deed of Mortgage and the property therein conveyed & described, Subject to the conditions and limitations therein described, with full and ample right, power, and authority to foreclose the Same agreeable to law. In Witness whereof, we have hereunto set our hands & Seals of our firm this the 4th day of May 1837.

Signed, Sealed, and delivered in the }
presence of A. Iverson, J. S. C. C. C. } Wood, Miers, & Iverson

Jn° Crowell (Recorded 5th May 1837.)

State of Georgia }
Muscogee County } I, Gerard Burch, Clerk of the Superior Court of Said County, do hereby Certify that the above and foregoing Copy Mortgage and transfer are correct Copy of the records now in my Office.

Given under my hand this 15th day of November 1838.

> Gerard Burch, Clk

State of Georgia } To the Honorable Superior Court to be holden on the
Muscogee County } third monday in April 1839

The Petition of the President, directors, and Company of the Southern Life Insurance & Trust Company of Florida respectfully sheweth unto this Honorable Court that they were in possession by regular transfer of a certain Mortgage Deed of conveyance made and entered into between James H. Iverson, as Attorney for Lucian A. Bowdre, Mortgajor, on the one part, and the firm of Wood, Myers, & Iverson, Mortgagee, on the other part, dated on the twenty eighth day of April in the year of Our Lord one thousand eight hundred & thirty seven, which Mortgage deed was transfered to your petitioners on the fourth day May eighteen hundred and thirty seven. Since which last mentioned

[152] date, the Said Mortgage deed by accident has burned up and destroyed and your petitioners aver that the Copy hereto attached is a Copy in Substance of the Said Mortgage deed & transfer so burned up & destroyed. Your petitioners therefore pray this Honorable Court to Grant unto them a rule ni si calling on the Said Lucian A. Bowdre, the Mortgagor, to Shew Cause, if any he has. why the Copy hereunto attached Should not be established in lieu of the original So burned and destroyed and your petitioners will ever pray.

> Jnº Schley, for life Trust Cº

State of Georgia }
Muscogee County } Personally appeared before Michael N. Clark, a Justice of the peace in and for said County, George Field, who being duly sworn, saith that he is cashier of the Southern Life Insurance and trust Company of Florida and that said Company was in possession by regular transfer of an original Mortgage deed made by James H. Iverson, attorney in fact for Lucian A. Bowdre on the twenty eighth day of April in the year of our Lord Eighteen Hundred & thirty seven to Wood, Myers, & Iverson, which was tranfered by

them to the Southern Life Insurance & trust company on the fourth day of May eighteen Hundred & thirty seven, a copy of which mortgage deed & transfer hereunto attached is a Copy in substance of the one which was burned and destroyed by the great fire at apalachicola, Florida in the Summer of Eighteen Hundred & thirty seven and that the original of which the one attached hereto is a Copy in Substance & was burned in said fire at said time and place.

Sworn to and Subscribed before me this 1st day of May Eighteen hundred and thirty eight.

      Signed George Field, Cashier, S. Life In. & Trust Comp.

(Signed) Michael N. Clarke, J. P.

At April Term 1838 of the Superior Court of Muscogee County

It appearing to the Court, by the Testimony of George Field, that he is the Cashier of the Southern Life Insurance and Trust Company of Florida and that said Company was in possession of an Original Mortgage deed made by James H. Iverson, attorney in fact for Lucian A. Bowdre to Wood, Miers, & Iverson on the twenty eighth day of April in the year of our Lord eighteen hundred and thirty seven, which was transfered to Said Company on the fourth day of May eighteen hundred & thirty seven, and that said Mortgage deed & transfer was burned up & destroyed, and that the Copy hereunto attached a copy in Substance of said Mortgage deed and transfer so burned and destroyed. On motion ordered by the Court that the said Lucian A. Bowdre do shew cause at the next term of said Superior Court why the Copy hereunto attached should not be established in lieu of the Original Mortgage Deed & transfer so burned

[153]   October adj^d Term Monday 24th December 1838

and destroyed.

State of Georgia }
Muscogee County } Personally appeared in Open Court John Schley, Attorney at Law for the Southern life & trust Insurance Company & trust Company of the Territory of Florida, and being duly Sworn, deposeth and Saith that the within is a Copy in substance of the petition, Affidavit, order &c which was presented and passed at the last April term of the said Superior Court and which were burned in the Clerk's Office So far as the facts therein contained is

derived from his own knowledge, and so far as the facts are derived from the knowledge of others he believes to be true.

Jn° Schley, Atty for
S. Life Ins. & trust Compy.

Sworn to in Open Court this 13th December 1838.
Gerard Burch, Clk

October adjourned term 1838

It appearing to the Court that the above and foregoing petition, affidavit, & Rule ni si, &c to establish a lost Mortgage Deed thereunto Attached was burned in the Clerk's Office of Muscogee County and that the foregoing is a copy in Substance of the same. On Motion, Ordered by the Court that the above and foregoing be and the same is hereby established in lieu of the Original so burned.

October adjourned term 1838

It appearing to the Court from the petition of the Southern Life Insurance & trust Company of Florida and from the affidavit of George Field, Cashier of said Company, that said Company was in possession by transfer of a Certain Original Mortgage Deed made by Lucian A. Bowdre by his attorney in fact, James H. Iverson, to Wood, Miers, and Iverson, dated on the twenty eighth day of April eighteen hundred and thirty seven. And that the Copy hereunto attached is a true Copy of the same, which Original was burned and destroyed by accident in the great Fire at Appallachicola some time since. and that a Rule ni si was granted by the Superior Court at the last April Term calling on the Said Lucian A. Bowdre to Shew cause, if any he had, at this term of the Court why the Said Copy hereunto attached Should not be established in lieu of the Original so burned & destroyed. and that said Rule ni si was served personally on the said Lucian A. Bowdre on the Sixteenth day of June eighteen hundred and thirty eight according to law. and the said Lucian A. Bowdre having failed to shew any cause why the Copy hereunto attached should not be established in lieu of the original so burned and destroyed. On Motion Ordered by the Court that the said Copy hereunto attached be and the Same is hereby established in lieu of the said Original So burned and destroyed, with the same powers, liabillities, and legal effect as the said original had or could have were it now in existance.

[154]   Muscogee Superior Court October adjourned Term 1838

Rule Ni si To Foreclose Mortgage Deed

It appearing to the Court, upon the Petition of the Southern Life Insurance and Trust Company of the Territory of Florida, that Lucian A. Bowdre, by his Attorney in fact, James H. Iverson, on the twenty eighth day of April in the year of our Lord one thousand eight hundred and thirty seven, made his certain Mortgage Deed to the firm of Wood, Myers, & Iverson, merchants at Apalachicola, of the Territory of Florida, at the special interest & request of the said Lucian A. Bowdre, to secure & save harmless the said firm of Wood, Myers, & Iverson for the Payment of Certain drafts drawn at divers times by the said firm of Wood, Myers, & Iverson at the special instance & request & for the benefit of the said Lucian A. Bowdre upon the firm of Bowdre & Richardss as follows, to wit. one from the Farmers Bank of Chattahoochee for Five thousand and Sixty one dollars due the thirteenth & sixteenth of April in the year first aforesaid, one other from the same Bank for One thousand dollars due the seventh & tenth of May in the same year aforesaid, also one of twenty five hundred dollars, one from the Columbus Bank for One thousand five hundred dollars due the twenty fifth & eighth of April in the year first aforesaid, one other from the same Bank for Eleven hundred dollars due the thirtieth of April & second of May of the year first aforesaid, one other for four thousand [blot] hundred and forty eight dollars due the first & third of April of the year first aforesaid, making in all the sum of fifteen thousand nine hundred & nine dollars principal. And also to Secure the said firm of Wood, Myers, & Iverson the Sum of eleven hundred & nineteen dollars & eighty one cents due by the said Bowdre & Richards to said firm of Wood, Miers, & Iverson for Commissions. and in consideration of the liabillities of the Said Wood, Miers, & Iverson the above Stated on Said drafts as drawers of the Same and for the better Securing the said amount of eleven hundred & nineteen dollars & eighty one cents due by said Bowdre & Richards to said Wood, Miers, & Iverson for Commissions aforesaid the following property was Mortgaged in and by virtue of said Mortgaged Deed, to wit, Town lots situate, lying, & being in the town of Columbus known as number three hundred and ten (310), three hundred and nine (309), three hundred & eight (308), three hundred & Seven (307), half of three hundred and Six (306), half of three hundred & five (305), and four hundred & eighteen (418), also the Said Bowdre's interest in following described town lots, that is to say, part of lots number fifty five and fifty six in the plan of the town of Columbus written in the following meetes & bounds, begining at the north east corner of said lot number fifty six, running thence South down Broad Street Sixty feet to an alley, thence along the said Alley West ninety two feet, thence due South twenty eight feet eight inches to the lot formerly owned and Occupied by Goldstein & Heine, thence due West fifty four feet six inches to the lot owned and Occupied by Mrs Elizabeth A. Billups, thence due North to the north east corner of Mrs Billups's lot, thence due west to Front Street, thence due north up said Street to Randolph Street, thence due east along said Street two hundred and ninety five feet eight inches to the begining. And together with [blot] the following negroes, to wit, Joe a fellow thirty eight years of age,

[155] October Adjourned Term 1838 Monday 24th Dec^r

Mark a fellow twenty four years of age, Hal a fellow twenty four years of age, Bill a fellow twenty five years of age, William a fellow twenty two years of age, Stephen a fellow twenty five years of age, James a boy eight years of age, and also Rosannah a woman twenty four years of age, and her two children. And that the said Mortgage Deed was regularly transfered by the said Wood, Myers, & Iverson on the fourth day of May in the year first aforesaid to said Southern Life Insurance and Trust Company for a valuable consideration. and that the said Lucian A. Bowdre and the said firm of Bowdre & Richards failed to pay up the amount due on said drafts when the same became due and payable, and also the said sum of eleven hundred and nineteen dollars and Eighty one cents due to said Wood, Myers, & Iverson by the said Bowdre & Richards for commissions according to the requisitions of said Mortgage deed. and the said Wood, Myers, & Iverson, in consequence of this liability on said drafts as drawers of the same, have been compelled to pay off and discharge the said drafts. On motion of John Schley, Attorney for the Southern Life Insurance & Trust Company, ordered by the Court that the said Lucian A. Bowdre pay into Court the amount of Principal and interest due on said Mortgage Deed, together with the Costs for foreclosing the Same on or before the first day of the next Term of the Superior Court. & in default thereof the Equity of Redemption in & to said Mortgage property above described shall cease determine and be forever barred and foreclosed. And it is further Ordered that this Rule be published in one of the Public Gazetts of the Town of Columbus once a Month for four months or served on the said Lucian A. Bowdre or his special agent or

Attorney at least three months before the first day of the next Term of the Superior Court aforesaid.

It appearing to the Court that Charles F. Spillers has served as bailiff for five days at this Court, it is ordered that he be Paid out of the County funds One dollar per day for the said five days.

State of Georgia   } To the Honorable the Superior Court
Muscogee County } in and for said County

The petition of Ben[j] P. Tarver respectfully sheweth unto the Court that heretofore, to wit, on the fourth day of November in the year of our Lord one thousand Eight Hundred and thirty six, John R. Lloyd made, executed, and delivered to James S. Moore and Milton J. Tarver his certain Mortgage deed for all that tract, Lot, or parcel of Land situate, lying, and being in the town of Columbus, being all that part of the Lot in said town known as Lot N° fifty nine, begining on the east side of Broad Street at the South west corner of the house (then lately occupied by D[r] Sanky), thence running due east One hundred & forty seven feet ten inches, thence due

[156] north to the northern line of the Lot, thence due West along said line untill it intersects that part of said lot then held and owned by Bonner & Jones as a Confectionary, thence due South along their line to the north east corner of the house first aforesaid, thence due west to Broad Street, including the house first aforesaid and all the ground upon which it stands or it covers, with the use of a five foot ally by the consent of the tenants adjoining. that said Mortgage deed was executed and delivered to the said James S. Moore & Milton J. Tarver to secure the payment punctually of six certain promissory notes made by the said John R. Lloyd payable to one Jacobus T. S. Collins, or order, each for the sum of four hundred & forty one dollars & sixty six Cents, and each bearing date on the first day of October in the year Eighteen Hundred & thirty six. two of which said notes became due and payable within one year from the date thereof and two of which said notes became due and payable within two years from the date thereof and the two last of said notes are to become due and payable within three years from the date thereof. and that, in default thereof such payment, the Mortgage deed should remain in full force and virtue. and your petitioner further sheweth that heretofore, to wit, on the twenty eighth day of February in the year of our Lord one thousand eight hundred and thirty eight, the said James S. Moore & Milton J. Tarver, for a valuable Consideration,

transfered and assigned each of the aforesaid promissory notes, together with said Mortgage deed, to your petitioner and that there is now due and payable on said ~~deed~~ notes & Mortgage the sum of One thousand seven hundred and sixty six dollars and sixty four cents principal, with interest thereon from the time the same became due, according to the tenor and effect thereof, no part whereof has been paid. Wherefore your petitioner prays that a rule nisi may be granted to him for the foreclosure of said Mortgage in terms of the Statute in such case made and provided. October Adj^d Term 1838

Campbell, McDougald, & Watson
Attorneys for Petitioner

Georgia }
Muscogee County } Application having been made for the foreclosure of the Mortgage specified in the above petition. On Motion of Campbell, McDougald, & Watson, attorneys for petitioner, Ordered by the Court that the said John R. Lloyd, the Mortgagor, do pay into the Clerk's Office of the Superior Court of said County the whole amount of principal & Interest due on said Mortgage on or before the first day of the next term of this Court and that in default thereof the Equity of Redemption in & to the said Mortgaged premises be from thenceforth forever barred & foreclosed. And it is further ordered that a Copy of the Rule Ni Si be served personally on the said John R. Lloyd as required by the Statute in Such case made & provided or published once a month for four months in one of the public gazetts of Columbus before the next term of this honorable Court. Oc^t Adj^d term 1838

[157]   Monday 24th December 1838

The Insurance Bank of Columbus} Assumpsit and verdict for the Plaintiff
              vs   } for Twenty Six Thousand dollars, with
Burton Hepburn   } interest & cost of suit & protest fee

The Defendant, being dissatisfied with the verdict of the Jury rendered in the above cause and having paid all cost and demanded an Appeal, brings James C. Watson and tenders him as his security, and they, the said Burton Hepburn and James C. Watson, acknowledge themselves Jointly and severally bound to the Plaintiff for the Payment of the eventual Condemnation money in said cause.

In Testimony whereof, they have hereunto set their hands and seals this 2nd day of January 1839.

Test. Gerard Burch, Clk   B. Hepburn
                                  J. C. Watson

The Insurance Bank of Columbus } Assumpsit and confession of Judgment to
             vs   } the Plaintiff for Twenty six thousand
James C. Watson   } dollars, with interest & Cost of suit

The Defendant, being dissatisfied with the Verdict of the Jury rendered in the above cause and having paid all cost and demanded an Appeal, brings Burton Hepburn and tenders him as his security, and they, the said ~~Burton Hepburn and~~ James C. Watson and Burton Hepburn, acknowledge themselves Jointly and sevearally bound unto the Plaintiff for the Payment of the eventual Condemnation money in said cause.

In Testimony whereof, they have hereunto set their hands and seals this 2nd day of January 1839. (Erasure made before signing.) (interlineation made before signing.)

Test. Gerard Burch, Clk   J. C. Watson
                                  B. Hepburn

Insurance Bank of Columbus } Assumpsit and Verdict for the Plaintiff for
           vs   } Six Thousand Dollars, with interest & Cost
Alfred Iverson   } of Suit

The Defendant, being dissatisfied with the Verdict of the Jury rendered in the above cause, and having paid all cost and demanded an appeal, brings Benjamin V. Iverson and tenders him as his security, and they, the said Alfred Iverson and Benjamin V. Iverson, acknowledge themselves Jointly and severally bound unto the Plaintiff for the Payment of the eventual Condemnation money in said cause.

In Testimony whereof, they have hereunto set their hands and seals this 2nd day of January 1839.

                                  Alfred Iverson
                                  Benjamin V. Iverson

[158]

State of Georgia } To the Honorable the Superior Court
Muscogee County } in & for said County

The petition of Benjamin P. Tarver respectfully sheweth that heretofore, to wit, on the tenth day of January Eighteen Hundred & thirty eight, one Theobald Howard & one John R. Lloyd made, executed, and delivered to James S. Moore & Milton J. Tarver their Certain Mortgage Deed for all that lot or parcel of land Situate, lying, & being in the County & State aforesaid & City of Columbus known and distinguished in the plan of survey of said City as lot number Eighty, Containing one half acre, more or less, and that said Mortgage Deed was made, executed, & delivered as aforesaid, for the better securing the payment of two certain promissory notes, one bearing date on the twenty second day of November in the year eighteen hundred and thirty six for twelve hundred & fifty Dollars, with interest from the date thereof, and due fifteen months after the date thereof, payable at the Bank of Columbus, made & signed by the said Theobald Howard, & payable to the order of the said John R. Lloyd, & by him indorsed. the other of said notes, bearing date on the eighteenth day of November in the year Eighteen hundred and thirty seven, for the sum of Three thousand seven hundred & fifty nine dollars & sixty eight cents, and due one day after the date (thereof) made & signed by the said Howard & Lloyd, and payable to Moore & Tarver, or order, and that there is now due & unpaid on said Mortgage as principal the sum of five thousand and nine dollars & sixty eight cents, besides interest thereon from the time said sum became due, and that no part of said sum has been Paid and that in default of the payment of said sum of money said Mortgage Deed should be in full force & virtue. And your petitioner further sheweth that after the making of said Mortgage & notes and before the payment thereof, to wit, on the twenty eighth day of February in the year Eighteen hundred and thirty eight, the said James S. Moore, for a valuable consideration, transfered & assigned to your petitioner said notes & Mortgage, in consideration of all which, your petitioner prays that a rule ni si may be granted unto him for the foreclosure of said Mortgage in terms of the Statute in such case made and provided. Wherefore, On motion of Campbell, McDougald, & Watson, Attorneys for Petitioner, it is ordered by the Court that the said John R. Lloyd & Theobald Howard, the Mortgajors, do pay into the Clerk's Office of the Superior Court the whole amount of Principal, interest, & cost due on said Mortgage on or before the first day of the next Term of this Court. And that in default thereof the Equity of Redemption in & to said

Mortgaged premises be from thenceforth forever barred and foreclosed. And it is further ordered that a true Copy in substance of this Rule Ni si be served upon the said John R. Lloyd & Theobald Howard in Terms of the Statute in such case made & provided or published once a month for four months at least before the next Term of this Honorable Court. October Adjourned Term 1838

The Court adjourned to meet again on Saturday next at ten O'clock.

Marshall J. Wellborn, J. S. C. C. C.

[159]   October adj^d term Saturday 29th December 1838

The Court met again According to adjournment, present his Honor Judge Wellborn.

State of Georgia   }
Muscogee County   }   To the Honorable the Superior Court of said County

The Petition of Benjamin P. Tarver Respectfully Sheweth that heretofore, to wit, on the twenty Seventh day of November in the year of our Lord one thousand eight hundred and thirty Seven, James S. Moore & Milton J. Tarver, both of the County & State first aforesaid, made, executed, and delivered to your petitioner their Certain Mortgage Deed to & for the hereinafter mentioned real estate, to wit, all that tract, lot, or parcel of land, situate, lying, and being in the County & State aforesaid and City of Columbus, known and distinguished in the plan of said City as lot number seventy nine (N° 79), the same being the South east Corner of Thomas & Front Streets, Containg one half acre each, more or less, also all that tract, lot, or parcel of land situate, lying, and being in the County & State first aforesaid & City of Columbus, usually known as the McIntosh Row on broad Street in said City, extending from the South corner of said Row up Broad Street to Lloyd's tenements, thence East in a straight line through to Oglethorp Street, including So much of the lot North of said Line as will make up the full front of a half acre lot on Oglethorp Street, thence due West to the begining corner, excepting nevertheless all that part or portion thereof whereon the new Theater is now there located, together with all and Singular the buildings, improvements, rights, members, & appurtenances whatsoever thereto belonging or in any wise appurtaining. which said Mortgage Deed was made, executed, & delivered to your petitioner for the better Securing the payment of four Several certain promissory notes made, executed, & delivered by the said James S. Moore & Milton J. Tarver, each bearing date on the sixth day of December in the year of our Lord one thousand eight hundred & thirty four, each for the sum of two thousand four hundred & thirty one dollars & twenty five cents, making in the aggregate the sum of nine thousand Seven hundred & twenty five dollars, which said Several promissory notes were due & payable on the Sixth day of December in the year of our Lord one thousand eight hundred and thirty six, and which Said notes are all now due and unpaid. and also to Secure and Save harmless and keep indemnified your petitioner as endorser upon a certain promissory note made, executed, and delivered to the Said James S. Moore and Milton J. Tarver and endorsed by your petitioner for the accomodation of the Said makers, to wit, one promissory note dated on the sixth day of May in the year eighteen hundred & thirty seven for the sum of eight thousand five hundred dollars due & payable on the sixth day of July in the year last afore Said. also one note bearing date the thirtieth day of April in the year eighteen hundred & thirty six, for the Sum of twelve hundred & thirty nine dollars & eighty nine cents, due & payable on the nineteenth day of April in the year Eighteen hundred & thirty seven. also one note bearing date on the twenty ninth day of July in the year eighteen hundred & thirty six for the Sum of two thousand four hundred & thirty five dollars & one cents, due & payable on the Sixth

[160] day of June in the year eighteen hundred and thirty seven, also one note dated on the twenty fifth day of September in the year eighteen hundred & thirty seven for the sum of four Hundred and fifty dollars, due and payable on the twenty fourth day of November in the year last aforesaid, also one note for the sum of three thousand eight hundred and fifty dollars, bearing date on the same day & year of the note last aforesaid and due and payable as last aforesaid, also one note or Draft bearing date on the second day of August in the year last aforesaid for the sum of two thousand dollars, due and payable on the second day of November in the same year, also one note or draft for the sum of three thousand Dollars dated, due, & payable as the one last aforesaid, also one other note or draft bearing date on the twenty third day of February in the year last aforesaid for the sum of Two thousand dollars, due and payable on the twenty fourth day of May in the same year. And your petitioner further sheweth that he became, was, & now is endorser upon each and every of the aforesaid promissory notes or drafts solely for the accommodation of the said James S. Moore & Milton J. Tarver and that there is now due and unpaid upon the whole of said promissory notes as Principal the sum of thirty three thousand one hundred & eighty nine dollars & ninety cents. and also the sum of four thousand

one dollar and sixteen cents interest thereon up to this date and that your petitioner is now liable & responsible as endorser for the whole amount of Principal & interest due on said notes or drafts. In consideration of all which, your petitioner prays that a rule ni si may be granted unto him in Terms of the Statute Calling upon the said James S. Moore and Milton J. Tarver to shew cause, if any they have, on or before the first day of the next Term of this Court, why the Equity of Redemption in & to the before described premises should not be forever barred & foreclosed. Wherefore, on motion of Campbell, McDougald, & Watson, Attorney for Petitioner, it is ordered by the Court that the said James S. Moore & Milton J. Tarver do pay into the Clerk's Office of the Superior Court of said County, on or before the first day of the next Term of said Court, the whole amount of Principal & interest due on said mortgage, together with the cost of this application, and that in default thereof the Equity of redemption in & to said Mortgaged premises be from thenceforth forever barred and foreclosed. And it is further ordered that the said James S. Moore & Milton J. Tarver be each served personally with a Copy of this Rule Ni si at least three months before the first day of the next Term of this Honorable Court.

October Adjourned Term 1838   Campbell, McDougald, & Watson
                                                             Att^y Pro Petitioner

William M. Roberts vs John B. Hoffman. Debt & Bail

Daniel Johnson vs Caswell Johnson. Debt & Bail

Bogert & Forbes vs Mathew M. Hitchcock. Debt

William H. Lewis vs Asa Bates, Prinp^l &   }
Joseph Smith, Richard W. Morris,   } Assumpsit
Frederick A. Fairchild, Indorsers   }

carried to the next page (161)   Georgia

[161]   October Adjourned Term 1838 Monday 24th Decr 1838

James H. Shorter, Admtr. & }
Sophia H. Shorter, Admtrx. } Assumpsit & Verdict for the Plaintiff
of Eli S. Shorter, Dec^d } for Nine hundred & sixty dollars
        vs   } with interest and cost of suit
Solomon Averitt   }

The Defendant, being dissatisfied with the Verdict of the Jury rendered in the above cause and having paid all cost and demanded an appeal, brings James Sarsnet and tenders him as his security, and they, the said Solomon Averitt and James Sarsnett, acknowledge themselves Jointly & severally bound unto the Plaintiffs for the payment of the eventual condemnation money in said cause.

In Testimony whereof, they have hereunto set their hands and seals this second day of December 1839.

Test. Gerard Burch, Clk   Solomon Averitt
                                            James Sarsnett

(From page 160)

Georgia }
Muscogee County } Personally appeared John S. Lewis, one of the Attorneys of the Plaintiffs in the above Stated cases, who being duly sworn in Open Court, Saith that the original declarations in the above mentioned cases were to the best of his recollection filed to the April term last past of this Court, that the same were destroyed by the late buring of the Clerk's Office in the City of Columbus, that the Copies herewith filed, the processes, and the entries of the Sheriff thereon are to the best of the recollection, information, & belief of the deponent Copies of the Said Originals as they existed in the Clerk's Office at the time of the destruction thereof by fire.

Sworn to & Subscribed in Open Court
this 24th day of December 1838.   Jn° S. Lewis
Gerard Burch, Clk

It appearing to the Court by the foregoing affidavit that the Original declarations, together with the process & entries thereon, were destroyed at the late burning of the Clerk's Office in this City and that Said cases were regularly called at the last term of this Court. It is on motion Ordered that the Copies herewith filed be established, held, & taken in lieu of the Originals and that the said cases be restored to the dockett in the same situation in which they Stood at the time of their destruction.

[162]

Grand Jurors drawn to Serve at April term 1839

1. John H. Ware
2. Ephraim C. Bandy
3. William H. Harper
4. George Hargraves, Junr
5. Moses Butt
6. Thomas McGinty
7. James M. Chambers
8. Samuel Boykin
9. Samuel W. Flournoy
10. George B. Nuckols
11. William S. Chipley
12. Garland B. Terry
13. John L. Harp
14. Edward T. Taylor
15. Edward Delony
16. Henry L. Densler
17. Darius Cox
18. William Kirk
19. Philo D. Woodruff
20. Wm H. Watkins
21. Richard T. Sanky
22. Hampton S. Smith
23. George W. E. Bedell
24. John J. Boswell
25. Rhodam A. Green
26. Hiram Young
27. James S. ~~Shivers~~ Calhoun
28. Thomas J. Shivers
29. Martin Brooks
30. William E. Bacon
31. Marcus Cook
32. Aaron Odom
33. William F. Luckie
34. Samuel R. Andrews
35. James Kirlin
36. Nathaniel M. C. Thorton

Second Pannel drawn to serve as Grand Jurors at April term 1839

1. Eli B. W. Spivey
2. James Shaw
3. Edward W. Starr
4. John Johnson
5. Thomas Davis
6. Henry K. Hill
7. James Boykin
8. Jacob J. Moses
9. Henry C. Phelps
10. Prior Dozier
11. James Hickey
12. John T. Howard
13. James M. Landrum
14. Benjamin F. Colemon
19. William H. Alston
20. Robert A. Ware
21. William Clark (8th dist)
22. John S. Duncan
23. Elisha Reid
24. Joseph M. Terry
25. Henry Favors
26. Mathew Roberson
27. E. S. Greenwood
28. Alexander Liggon
29. John Fontaine
30. Albert G. Beckham
31. James Pattillo
32. Josiah Grimes

15. Jonathan A. Hudson
16. N. M. C. Roberson
17. Jacob M. Johnson
18. William K. Schley

33. John D. Jordan
34. William Y. Barden
35. Madison Sapp
36.

[163] October adjourned term Monday 24th December 1838

Names of persons drawn to Serve as petit Jurors at April Term 1839, the first pannel.

1. James Kent
2. Frederick W. Chandler
3. William Pickett
4. Edmund Simkin
5. Zachariah Watkins
6. James Cooke
7. A. J. Biggers
8. B. Massy
9. Timothy Collins
10. Jossas Hay
11. John W. Morgan
12. James Wadsworth
13. Lewis Anthony
14. Jeremiah Parker
15. Benjamin Jepson
16. John Dillingham
17. Emanuel Brittain
18. Joseph Hammock
19. William J. Rylander
20. Samuel Hemphill
21. Richard Greer
22. Thomas Nix
23. E. J. Kellum
24. John W. Thompson

25. Thomas H. Kendall
26. H. F. Biggers
27. William Guerry
28. William McGee
29. W. M. Morgan
30. C. A. Smith
31. James Berry
32. J. C. W. Rogers
33. D. Adkinson
34. George W. Brown
35. Francis N. Ruse
36. William Traywick
37. Henry Hurst
38. J. H. Herndon
39. Wm Snow
40. John L. Walton
41. David Wall
42. Henry Owen
43. William Scurlock
44. John Pollock
45. R. C. Patterson
46. T. C. McLary
47. Chesley Moore
48. John Lytle

Petit Jurors drawn to serve on the Second pannel at April term 1839.

49. James Kirkpatrick
50. Rany C. Ragland

59. Blalock Bullock
60. Daniel Crawford

51. Nathan Haynes
52. John Odom
53. C. Howard
54. Jerre Thurmond
55. James Flemming
56. Thomas J. Clark
57. James L. Wacker
58. John H. Jenkins

61. Bewford W. Sanders
62. Joseph E. Webster
63. Henry C. Anderson
64. D. H. Williams
65. Farris Wray
66. Richard P. Spencer
67. Samuel W. Butts
68. Howell Delany

[164]

69. H. H. McDaniel
70. Richard Allsop
71. Burrell Lee
72. John Nickolson
73. Jacob Morris
74. Jacob Williams
75. Vincent P. Roquemore
76. James J. Rorie
78. James Harris
79. William Hammond
80. John F. Lasseter
81. Augustus G. Laurence
82. Hillery Gray
83. James S. Fetner

84. Green E. Lamb
85. Dempsey Odum
86. Richard Gray
87. Joseph Phillups
88. William Haynes
89. Samuel Beck
90. N. S. Vanzant
91. James Wilkerson
92. Patrick Crogan
93. Jerre Dunn
94. James M. Hopkins
95. John Murphy
96. John Parmer
97. William Porter

Third Pannel of the Petit Jury to Serve at April term 1839.

97. ~~Th~~
98. Thomas A. Brown
99. Charles H. Hight
100. B. J. Biggers
101. V. D. Metcalf
102. William Weathers
103. Jerre Cartledge
104. John L. Becase
105. Little Berry Harris
106. A. Arney
107. Jonathan Burton

121. D. McNeal
122. John Womack
123. D. Maddin
124. James Monk
125. John C. Dennard
126. John K. Jones
127. J. C. Porter
128. Cullen Clark
129. Thomas B. Atkins
130. William C. Moore
131. John Flin

108. N. P. Foster	132. Henry King
109. Alfred Weatherford	133. Bartlett Lee
110. Benjamin Walker	134. William J. Eagan
111. Green B. Stephens	135. Madison Dancer
112. John McDuffy	136.
113. George Campbell	137.
114. E. Evans	138.
115. Jacob Lamb	139.
116. James Peal	140.
117. Leroy Prescot	141.
118. David Lockhart	142.
119. Richard Manly	143.
120. G. W. Powell	144.

[165] October adjourned Term 1838 Saturday 29th December 1838

The Court met according to adjournment. Present the Honorable Marshall J. Wellborn, Judge of the Superior Courts C. C. C.

Hervy Hall }
    vs } Mortgage, Rule for foreclosuer & Mortgage Fi fa
Ephraim Wheelock & }
Nathaniel P. Willard }

Ordered that the Copies presented be established in lieu of the Burnt Originals.

A. L. Heine }
    vs } Fi fa
Edward J. Hardin }

It appearing to the Court that the original fi fa was destroyed by the late Conflagration of the Clerk's Office. It is therefore on motion ordered that the Clerk do issue an alias fi fa in said case.

The Same }
    vs } Fi fa
James H. Jones, J^r }

It appearing to the Court that the Original fi fa was destroyed by the late conflagration of the Clerk's Office. It is therefore on motion ordered that the Clerk do issue alias fi fa.

Joseph B. Green & C° }
   vs   } Ca Sa & Bond
William McGee }

It appearing to the Court that the above Stated Ca sa & Bond were destroyed by the buring of the Clerk's Office & that a Copy in Substance of each is herewith established to the Court, it is ordered that said Copies be established in lieu of said lost Originals.

Joseph B. Green & C° }
   vs   } Ca Sa & Bond
William McGee }

It is on motion of Counsil for Plaintiffs ordered that they have leave to enter up Judgment on said bond for the amount of the Principal, interest, & Cost due on said ca sa.

It Appearing to the Court that the Original declarations in the following Cases were burnt in the Clerk's Office of this Court on the night of the fourteenth of October last. It is ordered on motion of Phillip T. Schley, Attorney for Plaintiffs, that Copies thereof be & they are hereby established in lieu of said burnt Originals, to wit.

Randolphs & Underhill vs John G. Mulford. Assumpsit

Randolps & Scott vs The Same. Assumpsit

Edward Kellogg vs Dennis Sullivan. Assumpsit

John B. Jaques vs George W. Way. Assumpsit

[166]

Edward Kellogg & C° vs Bernard Matthewson. Assumpsit

Edward Kellogg vs Joseph T. Brown, William D. Hargraves, }
Timothy Collins, George H. Peabody, & Charles A. Peabody } Assumpsit

All of which said cases were brought to the October Term 1838 of this Court.

D. A. Cushman & Cº	}		Brown & Dimock	}	Ca sa in
vs	} Ca sa in Musgogee		vs	}	Muscogee
James Y. Smith	} Superior Court		James Y. Smith	}	Superior Court

It appearing to the Court that the Original Ca sas in the above cases were returned Non et inventus & since that time have been destroyed by fire. it is therefore ordered that the Clerk do issue alias ca sas in such cases.

Hannah S. Pitts }
    vs   } Certiorari in Justices Court of Muscogee County
Seth Tatum &   } of the 675 District G. M.
George Myers, Justices }

It appearing to the Court that the Justices Committed Error in the above case. It is on Motion ordered that the Certiorari be sustained & a New trial be had. Notice being given to the Opposite party.

John G. Dunlap }
    vs   } Assumpsit, Judgment, verdict, & Ca Sa
Stephen M. Ingersol }

It appearing to the Court that the following is a Copy in Substance of the original above stated Ca sa and that the Said original has been destroyed. it is ordered that the said Copy be established in place of said lost Original.

The Mayor & Council of }
the Town of Columbus }
    vs   } Ca Sa
Daniel Walling }

The defendant having been called & failed to appear, it is on motion of Counsel for Plaintiff Ordered that Plaintiff's Counsel have leave to enter up Judgment on defendant's bond against the defendant and William Walling, his Security, for the amount of Said bond. Said Judgment to be discharged upon the payment of the principal, interest, and cost due on said Ca sa.

Muscogee Superior Court October adjourned term 1838

The Court adjourned to meet again on Saturday next.

[167]   October adjourned Term Saturday 29th December 1838

The Court met according to adjournment, present the Honorable Marshall J. Wellborn, Judge of the Superior Courts of the Chattahoochee Circuit.

Benjaim P. Tarver   } Assumpsit & Verdict for the Plaintiff
        vs   } for One thousand Dollars with interest
Elijah Corley   } & Cost of suit

The Defendant, being dissatisfied with the verdict of the Jury rendered in the cause and paid all cost and demanded an appeal, brings James S. Calhoun and tenders him as his security, and they, Elijah Corley and James S. Calhoun, acknowledge themselves Jointly and severally bound to the Plaintiff for the eventual Condemnation money in said cause.

In Testimony whereof, they have hereunto set their hands and seals this 4th day of January 1838.

Test. Gerard Burch, Clk   Elijah Corley
                                                    J. Calhoun

Benjaim P. Tarver   } Assumpsit and Verdict for the Plaintiff
        vs   } for One thousand Dollars with interest
Elijah Corley   } & Cost of suit

The Defendant, being dissatisfied with the verdict of the Jury rendered in the above cause and having paid all cos, and demanded an appeal, brings James S. Calhoun and tenders him as his security, and they, the said Elijah Corley and James S. Calhoun, acknowledge themselves Jointly and severally bound to the Plaintiff for the Payment of eventual Condemnation money in said cause.

In Testimony whereof, they have hereunto set their hands and seals this 4th day of January 1838.

Test. Gerard Burch, Clk Elijah Corley
 J. Calhoun

James Jackson } Assumpsit and Verdict for the Plaintiff for
 vs } Two Hundred and fifty two dollars & eighteen
Arthur Fox Alfred } cents with interest, Protest fee, & Cost of suit

The Defendant, being dissatisfied with the verdict of the Jury rendered in the above cause and having Paid all cost and demanded an appeal, brings [blank] and tenders him as his security, and they, the said Arthur Fox Alfred and [blank] acknowledge themselves Jointly & severally bound unto the Plaintiff for the payment of the eventual condemnation money in said cause.

In Testimony whereof, they have hereunto set their hands and seals this 5th day of January 1838. (interlineations made before signature}

Test. Gerard Burch, Clk A. F. Alfred
 Elbert Wells

[168] Muscogee Superior Court ~~April term 1838~~

April Term 1836 Fi fas			April term 1838		
Alexander E. Patton }			Hiram Middlebrooks }		
vs	} Fi fa		vs	} Fi fa	
Sewell F. Wall }			John Nutt }		
Clifton & Kennedy }			Edwin L. De Graffinried }		
vs	} Fi fa		vs	} Fi fa	
James Portervint }			Seaborn J. Herron }		
Foster & Fogle }			G. H. & C. A. Peabody }		
vs	} Fi fa		vs	} Fi fa	
Moses Jones }			Daniel Peters }		

April term 1837

John W. Rinaldi vs Amasa A. Jones. Fi fa - Joseph S. Smith vs James K. Houghton. Fi fa

Cullen McMurphy, for the use of E. B. W. Spivey vs John McColl. Fi fa – Foster & Fogle vs James H. Jones, J^r. Fi fa

Thomas Hoxey vs Thomas Ashley. Fi fa – Lott & Peck vs Augustus A. Dill. Fi fa

October term 1837

William Owens vs John S. Bell. Fi fa – Sampson Lanier vs James Van Ness. Fi fa

G. H. & C. A. Peabody vs Joel W. Hand. Fi fa – Thomas Hoxey vs Allen Lawhon. Fi fa

E. & F. Bradley vs Thomas Ashley. Fi fa – Joseph S. Smith, Bird B. Mitchell. Fi fa

G. H. & C. A. Peabody vs Bird B. Mitchell. Fi fa – Elisha S. Norton vs Seaborn J. Herron. Fi fa

Elza Bland, Surviving Copartner of H. B. Millikin & Co vs George W. Jones. Fi fa - - Elisha S. Norton vs Seaborn J. Herron. Fi fa

G. H. & C. A. Peabody vs James H. Jones, J^r Fi fa - Jonathan P. Jackson vs James H. Jones. Fi fa

Elisha S. Norton vs Seaborn J. Herron. Fi fa – Darius Cox, for the use of Garland B. Terry vs Victor S. Townsley. Fi fa

April term 1836

Elisha S. Norton vs Seaborn J. Herron. Fi fa – John Dillingham, Administrator of George W. Dillingham vs Bridges Brannon. fifa

Elisha S. Norton vs S. J. Herron. Fi fa –

Continued on the next page.

Elisha S. Norton vs S. J. Herron. Fi fa – Joseph T. Killgore vs John Dillingham, Administrator of G. W. Dillingham, d^d

[169]

Georgia	} Rule to establish Copy Fi fas in the foregoing stated
Muscogee County	} cases. October adjourned term 1838

It appearing to the Court that the original fifas in the foregoing stated cases were destroyed by the burning of the Court House & Clerk's Office, and that the copies herewith submitted to the Court are in Substance Copys of the Originals.

It is on motion ordered that said Copies be established in lieu of the original Fi fas.

It appearing to the Court that the County of Muscogee is indebted to Edwin L. De Graffinried in the Sum of seven dollars for room rent for the Grand Jury during the adjourned October term 1838 of the Superior Court.

Whereupon it is ordered that the County treasurer do pay to the said Edwin L. De Graffinried the sum of money aforesaid.

Edward Cary }
      vs }
Abraham H. Falconer }

It appearing to the Court that the garnishee in this case was regularly served as such at the time of the commencement of this suit and that at the last term of the Court a Rule or order was granted and was duly served upon said Garnishee requiring him to answer on or before the first day of this term of this court, and he having failed so to answer. It is Ordered by the Court that the Plaintiff or his Council have leave to enter up Judgment against him.

Edward W. Wright }
  vs } Assumpsit & Bail to October term 1837
Van L. McKeen, maker & }
Thomas C. McKeen, endorser }

It appearing to the Court that insufficient Bail has been taken for one of the defendants by the Sheriff taking Van L. McKeen Bail for Thomas C. McKeen. On motion ordered that Asa Bates, Sheriff, and his Securities on his said bond be and are hereby taken and held as Special Bail for one of the defendants, Thomas C. McKeen, in the within named case.

Thomas A. Brannon }
  vs } Debt
Thomas C. McKeen }

I Confess Judgment to the Plaintiff for Seven hundred and twenty five dollars, with interest & Cost.

        Thom^s C. McKeen

[170]

Elliott W. Gregory }
  vs } Assumpsit
Charles E. & Henry Mims }

We, the Jury, find a verdict for the Plaintiff for Nine hundred and twenty one dollars & sixty one cents, with interest and cost of suit.

        Jn° McGough, F. M.

William Dougherty }
  vs } Assumpsit
William P. Malone }

I Confess Judgment to the Plaintiff for twenty two hundred & ten dollars, with interest and cost and three dollars Protest fees.

        Colquitt, Holt, & Echols, Def^t Att^{ys}

William Dougherty }
  vs } Debt
James R. Jones }

I confess Judgment to the Plaintiff for twenty two hundred & ten dollars, with interest & cost & three dollars protest fees.

        Colquitt, Holt, & Echols, Def^t Att^{ys}

[171] [blank page]

[172]

The Court adjourned to meet again on thursday next at ten O'clock.

        Marshall J. Wellborn, J. S. C. C. C.

[173] October adjourned Term Thursday 3rd day of January 1839

The Court met again according to adjournment. Present the Honorable Marshall J. Wellborn, Judge of the Superior Courts Chattahoochee Circuit.

N^{os}	Fifas Returned No Property to October Term 1838	Att^y	Shffs	Clk
4	Ulysses Lewis vs Whitly Foster	3	1.87½	6.25
8	Mayor & Council of the City of Columbus vs Daniel Walling pd	5	1.87½	6.25
19	James H. Shorter & Sophia H. Shorter, Admtr. & Admtrx. vs Moore & Tarver	2	1.25	3.75
23	George Knight & Co vs Edward J. Hardin	5	3.75	7.35
26	John E. Davis vs Daniel Walling P^r & Wm Walling, secty Ex^r	7	6.25	8.50
28	Robert McQueen vs Seaborn J. Herron	5	1.87½	6.25
29	B. B. Kirtland & Co vs M. G. Caldwell	3	3.12½	6.87½
35	Paulin Miedzielski vs Julius Holmes	5	3.12½	6.87½
36	James & Alfred McKeen vs Asa Wheler	5	3.12½	6.87½
37	William S. Hartsfield & Co vs Ben^j F. McDaniel	5	3.12½	6.87½
38	McGinnis G. Caldwell vs Julius Holmes	5	3.12½	6.87½
39	Pinhorn & Smith vs Ben^j F. McDaniel	5	3.12½	6.87½
40	Collins & Hannay vs Elisha S. Norton	5	1.87½	6.25
41	Hall & Moses vs Adolphus L. Heine	3	3.12½	6.87½

42	Jacob M. Johnson vs John H. Broadnax	5	3.12½	6.87½
44	Insurance Bank of Colmbus vs John H. Love p^d	5	1.87½	6.25
46	" " " vs James R. Butts p^d	5	1.87½	6.25
48	" " " vs Columbus Mills p^d	5	187½	6.25
49	Thomas J. Terry vs Patrick H. Smead	5	3.12½	6.87½
51	Steam Boat Hyperion & Owners vs Orrin W. Sage	3	1.87½	6.25
53	E. Wood vs Jacobi & Miedzielski	5	2.59	6.87½
59	James C. Holland vs Samuel M. Jackson	5	1.87½	6.25
61	Augustus Howard, Guard^n vs Bird B. Mitchell	3	1.87½	6.25
64	Augustus J. Brown vs Adonarian Treadwell & A. K. Ayer, secty	3	2.50	6.87½
67	C. W. Buckley vs M. D. Robinson	3	1.87½	6.25
69	Arthur B. Davis, for the use of the Bank of Columbus vs Boudery & Richards	5	2.50	6.87½
70	E. S. Greenwood & Co vs Carter J. Randolph	5	1.87½	6.25
71	The Bank of Columbus vs Bowdery & Richards	5	2.50	6.87½
72	Arthur B. Davis, for the use of the Bank of Columbus vs Bowdery & Richards	5	2.50	6.87½
78	Wm M. Tilleston & Co vs James Rhind	5	1.87½	6.25
80	Henry N. Langford vs Ben^j F. McDaniel	5	1.87½	6.25
86	Green J. Woodson, indorsee vs Henry C. Anderson	5	1.87½	6.25
87	Augustus L. Grant vs Joseph Davidson	5	1.87½	6.25
88	Henry M. Hunter vs Seaborn Ely	5	1.87½	6.25
89	Hamilton, Heard & Co vs Benjamin F. McDaniel	5	2.50	7.50
93	Hill & Dawson vs Seaborn Ely	3	1.87½	6.25
94	Wittich, Greenwood & Co vs John F. Vessels	5	1.87½	6.25

[174] Fifas Returned No Property to October Term 1838

96	Green J. Woodson, bearer vs Timothy Collins	5	1.87½	6.25
97	Green J. Woodson, bearer vs Caswell Johnson	5	1.87½	6.25
102	Daniel & Moody vs Patrick H. Smead	5	3.12½	6.87½
104	Thomas E. Taggart vs William McGee	5	1.87½	6.25
105	Nathan P. Willard vs Seaborn J. Herron	5	1.87½	6.25
106	Ben^j Hawley vs Alfred Landsberg	5	1.87½	6.25
107	Green J. Woodson, bearer vs Julius Holmes & David E. Walker	5	3.75	12.50
108	Willson & Cobb vs Charles A. Redd & Co	3	2.50	6.37½
112	Samuel E. Buckler vs Paulin Miedzielski	5	1.87½	5.25
113	Stebbins & Lockwood & Co vs James Rhind	5	0.00	6.25

116	The Bank of Columbus vs Bowdery & Richards	5	2.50	6.87½
117	The Bank of Columbus vs Bowdre & Richards	5	2.50	6.87½
121	The Bank of Columbus vs Bowdre & Richards	5	2.50	6.87½
124	John Locke vs A. Turner & Cº	3	1.87½	6.87½
127	Thomas Stocks vs E. L. De Graffenried	5	1.87½	6.25
128	Calhoun & Bass vs E. L. De Graffenried	5	1.87½	6.25
131	J. S. Calhoun vs James H. Berry	3	1.87½	6.25
140	N. H. Wildman & Cº vs Robinson & Williams	5	1.87½	6.87½
143	J. S. Calhoun & Cº vs E. L. De Graffenried	5	1.87½	6.25
144	William G. Porter vs Chisholm & Collins	5	2.50	6.87½
145	James Adams vs Caswell Johnson	3	1.87½	6.25
146	Thomas Orman vs Sullivan & Ryder	5	2.50	6.87½
147	Allen G. Bass vs Thomas Ashley	3	1.87½	6.25
148	Nicholas Howard vs Slaton Henley	5	1.87½	6.25
150	John C. Mangham vs Quincey A. Lawhon	5	3.12½	6.87½
151	William Foster vs Alpha K. Ayer & James V. Hogg	3	2.50	7.50
153	George Knight & Cº vs Edward J. Hardin	5	3.75	7.50
154	George Knight & Cº vs Edward J. Hardin	5	3.75	7.50
158	Richard Hooper vs Abel Turner	3	1.87½	6.25
160	The Bank of Columbus vs John Dillingham	3	3.12½	7.50
161	" " " " "	3	3.12½	7.50
162	" " " " "	3	3.12½	6.25
170	John Fontaine vs Jacobi & Miedzielski	3	2.50	6.87½
172	Johnson, Nuckolls, & Brother vs Seaborn Ely	3	1.87½	6.25
174	Seaborn Jones vs James D. Bryant & John M. Patrick	5	2.50	6.87½
180	Hriam Fuller vs C. S. Pryor, N. W. Howell, & Jnº H. Watson	5	1.87½	7.55
190	Beecher & Brown vs Henry C. Walsh	5	3.12½	6.87½
198	Owners of Steamer Reindeer vs Owners Steamer Free Trader	3	3.12½	7.50
199	William McGee vs Richard Head	5	3.12½	6.87½
200	Joseph T. Brown vs Wᵐ D. Raney	5	3.12½	6.87½

[175] Fi fas Returned to October Term 1838 No Property

201	Brown & Dimock vs James Y. Smith	3	3.12½	7.50
202	H. C. Phelps & Cº vs Benjamin F. McDaniel	5	3.12½	6.87½
203	Lovick L. Wittich vs Benjamin F. McDaniel	5	3.12½	6.87½
217	John C. F. Clark vs James E. L. Williamson	5	3.12½	6.87½

218	D. A. Cushman & C° vs James Y. Smith	3	3.12½	7.50
227	Paulin Miedzielski vs James D. Greenwood	5	1.87½	6.25
228	Edward Cary, Guard^n vs Wm Saulsbury & Wm D. Hargrove	3	1.87½	6.87½
229	Stout, Ingoldsby & C° vs Joel C. Wiggins	5	1.87½	6.25
230	Burton Hepburn vs John C. Jacobi	5	1.87½	6.25
231	James C. Watson vs Murdock Chisholm	3	1.87½	6.25
235	William Berry vs M. D. Robertson	3	1.87½	6.25
239	James C. Watson vs Malcom A. Chisholm	3	1.87½	6.25
244	Burton Hepburn vs Moore & Tarver	3	2.50	6.87½
246	James C. Watson vs Chisholm & Collins	3	2.50	6.87½
252	Thomas A. Brannon vs Thomas C. McKeen	3	1.87½	6.25
253	Jabob M. Johnson vs John H. Love	3	1.87½	6.25
254	Samuel M. Jackson vs Anthony Levie	3	1.87½	6.87½
255	Seaborn Jones vs Ann McGee & John Williams	5	2.50	6.87½
256	Wm H. Wilder & C° vs Wm W. Nichols	5	0.00	6.25
259	Wm H. Lewis vs James H. Iverson	5	1.87½	6.25
261	Wm H. Underwood, for the use &c vs Joseph Davidson	3	1.87½	6.25
262	Seaborn Jones vs E. S. Norton	5	1.87½	6.25
265	Mayor & Council of City of Columbus vs William Walling p^d	5	1.87½	6.25
269	Thomas Moore vs John H. Watson	5	0.00	6.25
276	Burton Hepburn vs Chisholm & Collins	3	2.50	6.87½
277	William H. Wilder vs William W. Nichols	5	0.00	6.25
280	Henry Hall vs Paulin Miedzielski	5	1.87½	6.25
282	Nichols & Ludlum vs Paulin Miedzielski	3	1.87½	6.25
283	Stovall & Hamlin vs C. W. Buckley & James Wood	3	0.00	6.87½
293	Preston & Nelms vs Adolphus L. Heine	3	1.87½	6.25
294	John Locke vs Abel Turner	3	1.87½	6.25
298	Wm W. Richards, L. A. Bowdery, & Thos Eckert vs Wm W. Nichols	5	1.87½	6.25
299	Carnes & Tatum vs John Cooper	5	1.87½	6.25
300	Carnes & Tatum vs Jonathan Davie	5	1.87½	6.25
301	Carnes & Tatum vs James J. Rorie	5	1.87½	6.25
302	Burton Hepburn vs Alexander Sullivan & Wm Sullivan	5	1.87½	6.87½
308	William Berry vs Augustus G. Lawrence	5	1.87½	6.25

311	John H. Williams vs Paulin Miedzielski	3	1.87½	6.25
314	J. T. Niles & Cº vs Alpha K. Ayer	3	1.87½	6.25

[176]

313	J. T. Niles & Cº vs Joseph Davidson	3	1.87½	6.25
315	Joseph D. Burs vs Ayer & Hogg	3	2.50	6.25
319	J. T. Niles & Cº vs James H. Jones, Junʳ	3	1.87½	6.25
322	Thomas James vs Alexander Gorman	5	3.12½	6.87½
323	Grigsby E. Thomas vs John Wister	3	3.12½	6.87½
331	Joseph T. Brown vs Thomas J. Bowdery	5	3.12½	6.87½
332	Joseph D. Hughes vs James H. Jones, Jr A. K. Ayer	3	2.50	6.87½
333	Thomas Moore vs N. W. Howell	3	1.87½	6.25
336	Stewart & Fontaine vs E. S. Norton	3	1.87½	6.25
339	G. L. Middlebrook & Cº vs Bowdre & Richards	5	2.50	9.12½
340	N. G. Woods vs Chisholm & Collins	5	2.50	6.87½
341	Ayer & James vs E. L. De Graffenried	5	1.87½	6.25
343	George Hargraves vs Alpha K. Ayer	3	1.87½	6.25
344	Stewart & Fontaine vs John Townsend	5	1.87½	6.25
345	Benjamin W. Clapp vs DeGiles & Gorman	3	1.87½	6.87½
346	Jacob Fogle vs Henry C. Walsh	5	1.87½	6.25
347	Stewart & Fontaine vs John M. Patrick	3	1.87½	6.25
350	Benjamin W. Clapp vs Paulin Miedzielski	3	1.87½	6.25
353	Foster & Fogle vs Henry C. Anderson	3	1.87½	6.25
354	John G. Mulford vs Jacob M. Guerry pᵈ	3	1.87½	6.25
355	Edward E. Powers vs James H. Iverson	3	1.87½	6.25
357	McClary, Asher & Cº vs Jacobi & Heine, Jnº H. Watson	3	5.00	8.12½
358	Edward Kellogg & Cº vs Clark, Tarver & Cº	5	3.12½	7.50
359	Edward Kellogg & Cº vs William V. Rainey	5	1.87½	6.25
361	John Shottles vs Caswell Johnson	3	3.12	6.87½
362	J. W. M. Berrien vs George W. Lively	5	3.12½	6.87½
363	E. S. Norton vs Seaborn J. Herron	3	1.87½	6.25
365	E. S. Norton vs Seaborn J. Herron	3	1.87½	6.25
366	Darias Cox, for the use of G. B. Terry vs Victor S. Townsley	3	1.87½	6.25
367	Jonathan P. Jackson vs James Jones, Jʳ	5	1.87½	6.25
370	Moore & Tarver vs Timothy Collins	5	1.87½	6.25

372	Daniel McDougald vs Jacobi & Miedzielski	5	2.50	6.87½
374	Moore & Tarver vs Henry L. Lestarjett	3	1.87½	6.25
375	N. G. Woods, indorsee vs Jacob M. Guerry	3	1.87½	6.25
377	Green J. Woodson, indorsee vs Alpha K. Ayer	5	1.87½	6.25
378	A. L. Heine vs Edward J. Hardin	5	1.87½	6.25
379	Theodore S. Gold, bearer vs Henry L. Lestarjett	3	1.87½	6.25
380	Richard Jones vs George Purklin	5	1.87½	6.25
382	N. G. Woods, indorsee vs E. C. Roberts & L. S. Vanzant	5	1.87½	6.87½

[177] Fi Fas to October Term 1838 No Property		Atty	Shffs	Clks
383	L. C. Morton vs Wm W. Nichols	5	0.00	6.25
384	Green J. Woodson vs James E. Glenn, J^r	5	1.87½	6.25
388	Moore & Tarver vs Timothy Collins	5	1.87½	6.25
390	Thomas McCarthy vs George C. Marler, W^m McGee, & Moses Garrett	5	2.50	7.50
391	Hubbard Odum, indorsee vs James R. Butts, indorser	5	1.87½	6.25
392	Raymond & Allison vs John C. Jacobi	3	1.87½	6.25
393	Richard Rowell vs Thomas Ashley Exu	3	1.87½	6.25
394	John Dillingham & Co vs Micajah A. Thorne	5	3.12½	6.87½
397	Moore & Tarver vs Timothy Collins	5	1.87½	6.25
406	Daniel McDougald vs Jacobi & Miedzielski	3	2.50	6.87½
407	Young, Smith & Co vs DeGilse & Gorman	5	0.00	6.87½
408	James E. Sloan vs Alfred Landsberg	5	1.87½	6.25
409	N. G. Woods vs Chisholm & Collins Exu	5	2.50	6.87½
410	Moore & Tarver vs Timothy Collins	5	1.87½	6.25
418	J. T. Niles & Co vs Elisha Tarver	5	1.87½	6.25
420	Felix Gregory Berteau vs Paulin Miedzielski	3	1.87½	6.25
421	The Farmers Bank of Chattahoochee vs Ben^j Fort	3	1.87½	6.25
422	H. C. Phelps & Co vs Alfred Landsberg	3	3.75	6.25
423	George Sears vs Jacobi & Heine	3	5.00	8.12½
425	Wm B. Robinson & Co vs Adolphus L. Heine	5	3.12½	6.25
426	Henry King vs Benjamin F. McDaniel	5	3.12½	6.87½
427	Hyde, Hickok, Grumman vs DeGilse & Gorman	3	3.75	8.12½
429	E. S. Greenwood & Co vs Thomas C. McKeen	5	1.87½	6.25
430	William Nelms vs James Rhind	5	1.87½	6.25
434	E. McKinstry vs William J. McMillan	5	1.87½	6.25
435	Ezra C. Reid vs Paulin Miedzielski	5	1.87½	6.25

436	James H. Shorter, Admtr. & Sophia H. Shorter, Admtrx. ~~vs John C. Jacobi~~ of Eli S. Shorter, Dec^d vs James S. Moore	5	1.87½	6.87½
437	John Sims vs James Van Ness	5	1.87½	6.25
442	Ja^s H. Shorter, Admtr. & Sophia H. Shorter, Admtrx. vs John C. Jacobi	5	1.87½	6.25
443	" " " " " " vs Joseph B. Webb	5	1.87½	6.25
444	J. B. Green & Co vs William McGee	5	1.25	5.00
449	H. C. Phelps & Co vs Alfred Landsberg	3	3.12½	8.75
452	Benjamin P. Tarver vs G. W. Tyson & Co	5	2.50	6.87½
453	J. W. M. Berrien, by his Att^y at Law G. E. Thomas vs Ge^o W. Lively	5	1.87½	6.87½

Whereas it appears to the Court that each of the foregoing & above stated Fi fas have heretofore been returned into the Clerk's Office of this Court by the Sheriff of said County with a return of Nulla Bona

[178] on them & that the costs of the Officers of Court have not been paid on each of said fi fas. It is therefore on motion ordered by the Court that the Clerk of this Court have leave to issue instanter fi fas for the Cost now due on each of said cases against the Plaintiffs thereon & their Attorneys where they are liable by Law.

October Adjourned Term 1838
Executions Returned No Property to April Term 1839

N^{os}		Att^y	Shiffs	Clk
12	James K. Daniel vs Thomas C. Evans	5	1.87½	6.25
14	Battle A. Sorsby vs Charles F. Spiller	5	1.87½	6.25
15	William Nelms vs James Rhind	5	1.87½	6.25
18	Dikerman & Mills vs John G. Mulford	5	1.87½	6.25
27	Revarius H. L. Buchannon vs Templeton Reid	5	1.87½	6.25
64	Wiley E. Jones vs Joseph Davidson	3	1.87½	6.25
72	Stewart & Fontaine vs Jacob D. Paul	5	1.87½	6.25
75	Daniel Hightower vs Thomas James	3	1.87½	6.25
78	Simeon Peteet vs Joseph Davidson	3	1.87½	6.25
82	George Hargraves vs John J. Willson	3	1.87½	6.25
95	Austin M. Walker vs Carnes & Tatum	5	2.50	6.87½

112	Jacob Fogle vs Lucian A. Boudre	5	1.87½	6.25
117	Thomas C. Winthrop vs G. H. & C. A. Peabody	5	2.50	6.87½
119	E. & F. Bradley vs John M. Patrick, Junr	5	1.87½	6.25
120	E. & F. Bradley vs Wm W. Nichols	5	1.87½	6.25
124	A. Mims & Co, for the use of Union Bank of Florida vs James H. Jones, J^r & Robert W. Carnes	5	2.50	6.87½
129	Barker & Morgan vs J. T. Niles & Co	5	2.50	6.87½
149	John T. Myrick vs William W. Nichols	5	1.87½	6.25
155	William M. Roberts vs John B. Hoffman	5	3.12½	6.87½
160	E. & F. Bradley vs John M. Patrick, Senr	5	1.87½	6.25
161	James Harrial vs Robinson & Halcomb	5	1.87½	6.87½
164	E. & F. Bradley vs Anthony Levi	5	1.87½	6.25
170	Maltby & Starr vs G. H. & C. A. Peabody	5	2.50	6.87½
172	Olcott, Heyer & Co vs John B. Peabody	5	1.87½	6.25
176	Henry Matthews vs John R. Lloyd	5	1.87½	6.25
179	Baker, Johnson & Co vs Carnes & Tatum	5	2.50	6.87½
185	William G. Porter vs Moore & Tarver	5	2.50	6.87½
187	Barker & Morgan vs J. T. Niles & Co	5	2.50	6.87½
195	The Bank of Columbus vs C. W. Buckley & Co	3	3.12½	7.00
199	John Hitchcock & Son vs John Dillingham & Co	5	1.87½	7.50
200	Joseph Whitney & Co vs William S. Hartsfield & Co	5	0.00	12.50
207	Jesse B. Johns vs Jefferson Painter	5	1.87½	6.25
208	Smith, Grimes & Co vs M. D. Robinson	5	1.87½	6.25
210	Allen & Young vs John R. Lloyd & Co	5	2.50	6.87½

[179] Fi Fas Returned No Property to April Term 1839

211	Joseph Cheesman vs Chisholm & Collins	3	1.87½	6.87½
212	R. & G. Barker & Co vs John G. Mulford	5	0.00	6.25
213	John D. Howell vs Timothy Collins	5	1.87½	6.25
215	Jacobus & Gaithwaite vs John Dillingham & Co	5	2.50	7.50
217	McClary & Asher vs Ayer & Hogg	3	2.50	6.87½
218	George W. Heard vs Joseph Burton	5	3.12½	6.87½
221	Allen J. Mims vs M. D. Robinson	3	1.87½	6.25
224	Thomas J. Terry, Admtr. vs James H. Jones, J^r	5	1.87½	6.25
226	Hampton W. Hill vs Robert W. Carnes	5	1.87½	6.25
229	William H. Lovejoy vs James C. McGilory	5	1.87½	6.25
230	Calhoun & Bass vs Nicholas M. Lewis	5	1.87½	6.25
231	Henry Matthews vs William Pride	3	1.87½	6.25

241	Ayer & Hogg vs Wᵐ J. McMillan	3	1.87½	6.25
247	James A. Bradford vs John R. Lloyd	5	1.87½	6.25
248	Calhoun & Bass vs John J. Willson	3	1.87½	6.25
249	James S. Calhoun vs William McGee	5	1.87½	6.25
250	Farmers Bank Chattahoochee vs Joseph Davidson	5	1.87½	6.25
252	Farmers Bank Chattahoochee vs John J. Willson	3	1.87½	6.25
253	Sterling Edwards vs Mansel H. Torrence	5	1.87½	6.25
256	Battle A. Sorsby vs George W. Way	5	0.00	6.25
258	Arthur B. Davis vs John R. Lloyd & Cº	3	2.50	6.87½
259	Richard S. Williams vs John B. Peabody	3	1.87½	6.25
260	William Atkinson vs Thomas C. McKeen	3	1.87½	6.25
261	Edward Kellogg & Cº vs Hiram Fuller	3	1.87½	6.25
262	A. L. Heine vs E. Wheelock	3	1.87½	6.25
266	A. L. Heine vs Jacobi & Miedzielski	3	3.75	8.75
268	Eli Wainwright vs Moore & Tarver	5	2.30	6.87½
269	Levi Cook & Cº vs John G. Mulford	3	0.00	6.25
270	William T. Gould vs Wᵐ S. Hartsfield & Cº	5	0.00	7.50
271	Doremus, Suydam, & Nixon vs Wᵐ S. Hartsfield & Cº	5	0.00	7.50
272	Battle A. Sorsby vs C. W. Buckley & Cº	3	0.00	6.87½
273	Joseph T. Atwell vs A. L. Heine	3	0.00	6.25
275	Wetherel, Fowle & Cº vs Chisholm & Collins	3	2.50	6.87½
277	N. & J. White vs John Dillingham & Cº	5	2.50	7.50
279	R. & G. Barker vs John G. Mulford	5	3.12½	7.50
281	Edward Kellogg & Cº vs Carnes & Tatum	5	2.50	6.87½
282	Thomas H. Hall vs Joseph Davidson	5	1.87½	6.25
285	Battle A. Sorsby vs Samuel E. Peacock	5	1.87½	6.25
289	Insler & Jaques vs James D. Greenwood	5	1.87½	6.25

[180]

290	A. & S. Thorp vs Jacobi & Heine	5	2.50	6.87½
294	S. P. Church vs Carnes & Tatum	5	2.50	6.87½
297	Stewart & Fontaine vs John Duncan	5	1.87½	6.25
298	Pryor Reaves vs Treadwell & Ayer	3	1.87½	6.87½
302	Stewart & Fontaine vs Ayer & Hogg	5	2.50	6.87½
305	William L. Wynn vs Robert W. Carnes	5	1.87½	6.25
307	J. S. Smith & Cº vs S. R. Bonner	5	1.87½	6.25
311	Wᵐ S. Hartsfield & Cº vs Jacob M. Guerry	3	1.87½	6.25

312	T. & M. Evans vs Sheldon Swift	3	1.87½	6.25
317	Francis Jepson vs John R. Lloyd & Cº	3	2.50	6.87½
320	Bogert & Forbes vs Matthew M. Hitchcock	5	3.12½	6.87½
321	Theobald Howard vs Raney C. Ragland	5	3.12½	6.87½
325	Burton Hepburn vs John B. Peabody	5	1.87½	6.25
327	Stewart & Fontaine vs William McGee	5	1.87½	6.25
328	Bank of Darien vs James Wood	3	1.87½	6.25
331	G. W. B. Towns vs Luther Blake	3	1.87½	6.25
332	William P. Yonge vs James M. Landrum	5	0.00	6.25
333	Elizabeth Billups vs Michael Hoffman & A. L. Heine	3	2.50	6.87½
335	Burton Hepburn vs A. L. Heine exu	5	1.87½	6.25
336	John T. Blount vs M. D. Robinson	5	1.87½	6.25
341	Amasa Walker & Cº vs Chisholm & Collins	3	2.50	6.87½
342	Edward Kellogg & Cº vs Moore & Tarver	5	2.50	6.87½
345	R. & G. Barker & Cº vs John B. Peabody	3	1.87½	6.25
346	Clark, Tarver & Cº vs Paul H. Tiller	5	1.87½	6.87½
347	R. & G. Barker vs Timothy Collins & Luther Blake	5	2.50	6.87½
351	Packer, Prentice & Cº vs John G. Mulford	5	0.00	6.25
369	Rose, McKnight & Cº vs John G. Mulford	3	3.12½	7.50
370	R. & G. Barker vs John B. Peabody	3	1.87½	6.25
373	Seaman & Ward vs G. H. & C. A. Peabody	3	2.50	6.87½
374	Randolph & Underhill vs Moore & Tarver	5	2.50	6.87½
376	John B. Guedron vs Joseph B. Webb	5	1.87½	6.25
377	Daniel Johnson vs Creswell Johnson	5	3.12½	6.87½
378	James K. Daniel vs Thomas C. Evans, endorser	5	1.87½	6.25
379	George Smith vs John R. Lloyd	5	1.87½	6.25
380	James K. Daniel vs Thomas C. Evans, endorser	5	0.00	6.25
381	Benjamin P. Tarver vs Henry L. Lestarjett	3	1.87½	6.25
382	Hiram Manly vs Chisholm & Collins	5	2.50	6.87½
384	Randolph & Hoffman vs Archibald Baggerly	5	1.87½	6 25
385	William E. Boren vs J. H. Jones & J. H. Iverson	5	2.50	6.87½

[181]   Fi Fas Returned Np Property to April Term 1839

389	John English vs James Van Ness	3	1.87½	6.25
392	J. C. Plant & Cº vs John B. Peabody p^d	5	1.87½	6.25
395	Stewart & Fontaine vs Ivey Thomas	5	1.87½	6.25
396	George W. B. Towns vs John Nutt	5	1.87½	6.25

400	Stewart & Fontaine vs Anthony Levi	5	3.12½	6.87½
402	William D. Hargraves vs Nelson Baird	5	1.87½	7.50
403	James Whitfield vs John B. Peabody	5	1.87½	6.25
406	Hall & Moses vs George W. Ross	5	0.00	6.25
409	James R. Sloan vs John R. Lloyd	5	1.87½	6.25
411	Harper, Thornton, & Livingston vs A. K. Ayer	3	1.87½	6.25
415	Shipman, Crane & C° vs G. H. & C. A. Peabody	5	2.50	6.87½
419	Augustus Hayward vs Carnes & Tatum	5	2.50	6.87½
421	Benjamin P. Tarver vs John M. Patrick	5	1.87½	6.25
424	William H. Wilder vs Wm W. Nichols	5	1.87½	6.25
425	Thomas Fleming vs James H. Jones	5	1.87½	6.25
427	Benjamin Cropp vs Dennis Sullivan	5	1.87½	6.25
428	Hezekiah Hawley vs Henry Allen	5	3.12½	6.87½
430	John B. Guedron vs Carter J. Randolph	5	1.87½	6.25
431	" " vs James H. Iverson	5	1.87½	6.25
432	" " vs John J. Willson	5	1.87½	6.25
433	" " vs N. W. Howell	5	1.87½	6.25
434	Henry Matthews vs James H. Jones	5	1.87½	6.25
435	Henry Matthews vs Luther Blake & Ja^s H. Iverson	5	2.50	6.87½
437	Henry Bird vs George W. Way	5	1.87½	6.25
439	James N. Bethune vs Slaton Henly	5	1.87½	6.25
441	Robert McQueen vs Joseph Davidson	5	1.87½	6.25
442	James Y. Smith vs John R. Lloyd	5	1.87½	6.25
443	James Rankin vs John J. Willson	3	1.87½	6.25
444	James Kirlin vs Jacob M. Guerry	5	1.87½	6.25
448	Garret Hallenbeck vs Jacob M. Guerry & L. Blake	5	2.50	6.87½
449	Ja^s S. Norman, Admtr. of J. S. W. White vs John J. Willson	3	1.87½	6.25
453	J. C. Plant & C° vs G. H. & C. A. Peabody	5	0.00	6.87½
460	Daniel C. Campbell vs Wm S. Hartsfield & C°	5	0.00	7.50
461	John B. Guedron vs Thomas J. Bowdery, James Gorman, makers & William J. McMillan	5	2.50	7.50
462	Jacobus & Gaithwaite vs G. H. & C. A. Peabody	5	2.50	6.87½
464	Thomas Fleming & C° vs James H. Iverson	5	3.12½	6.87½
472	L. J. Davis vs E. A. D. Brown	5	1.87½	6.25
474	Bennedict & Wetmore vs Carnes & Tatum	5	2.50	6.87½

[182]

478	John D. Howell vs George W. Ross	5	1.87½	6.25
479	E. & F. Bradley vs John Nutt & J. B. Peabody	5	2.50	6.87½
480	E. & F. Bradley vs John R. Lloyd	5	1.87½	6.25
486	James E. Sloan vs John R. Lloyd	5	1.87½	6.25
487	John B. Guedron vs Paul H. Tiller	5	1.87½	6.25
488	John B. Guedron vs John R. Lloyd	5	1.87½	6.25
489	John B. Guedron vs Erasmus Benten	5	1.87½	6.25
492	Insurance Bank of Columbus vs Joseph B. Webb X	3	1.87½	6.25
504	Elisha Betts vs Jona. Niles & Son & S. R. Bonner	5	3.12½	7.50
511	Robbins, Painter & C° vs John E. Davis	5	3.12½	6.87½
512	William H. Smith vs Anthony Levie	5	1.87½	6.25
518	Wade & C° vs Ephraim Mandell	5	3.12½	6.87½
520	Jacob Fogle vs Ephraim Mandell P^d	5	3.12½	6.87½
525	Robert McQueen vs James Willis	5	3.12½	6.87½
526	Alfred P. Reid vs Raney C. Ragland	5	3.12½	6.87½
532	Wm J. McMillan vs Lodwick R. Cashan	5	1.87½	6.25
533	Foster & Fogle vs John C. Jacobi P^d	5	3.12½	6.87½
536	Sampson L. Lampkin vs John J. Willson	5	1.87½	6.25
538	George Field vs Sullivan & Ryder	5	2.50	6.87½
540	David Z. Ward vs Wm H. Alston & S. R. Bonner	5	2.50	6.87½
550	Stewart & Fontaine vs James W. Glenn	5	1.87½	6.25
551	Garland B. Terry vs James H. Jones, Ju^r	5	1.87½	6.25
556	John Jones vs Patrick J. Murray	3	3.12½	6.87½
557	Young, Smith & C° vs John B. Peabody	5	1.87½	6.25
558	Duncan & Hart vs Mansel H. Torrence	5	1.87½	6.25
560	Elizabeth Billups vs Joseph Davidson	3	3.12½	6.87½
563	Charles Swan vs John R. Lloyd	5	1.87½	6 25
564	Thomas Fleming & C° vs James Van Ness	3	1.87½	6 25
567	Shotwell B. Clarkson vs Patrick J. Murray	5	3.12½	6.87½
568	Francis A. Loisie vs William O. Mills	3	3.12½	8.12½
569	Thomas Fleming & C° vs Jacob M. Guerry	3	1.87½	6.25
573	George Field vs Chisholm & Collins	5	1.87½	6.87½
574	D. Hungerford & C° vs William Rogers	5	1.87½	6.25
577	Stewart & Fontaine vs Anderson Spear	5	1.87½	6.25
580	S. R. Bonner vs William Green	5	1.87½	6.25
581	Stewart & Fontaine vs Cornelius Watkins	5	1.87½	6.25
583	John B. Peabody vs Timothy Collins &			

	R. G. Mitchell	5	2.50	6.87½
584	James Y. Smith vs Dennis Sullivan	5	1.87½	6.25
587	William T. Richardson vs Thomas C. McKeen	5	1.87½	6.25

[183]   Thursday 3rd day of January 1838

588	Emanuel Ezekiel vs John Dickerson, endorser	5	3.12½	6.87½
589	Stewart & Fontaine vs Noah Pitman	5	1.87½	6.25
590	Martin Brooks vs Henry Allen	5	3.12½	6.87½
593	Garland B. Terry vs Anthony Levie	5	1.87½	6.25
598	Foster & Fogle vs Henry Kendall P^d	5	1.87½	6.25
600	George Hargraves vs Henry Allen Lawhon	5	1.87½	6.25
602	Fellows, Wadsworth & C° vs Wm S. Hartsfield & C°	5	0.00	7.50
606	H. Mims & C° vs Umphry Rowell	5	1.87½	6.25
610	Fellows, Wadsworth & C° vs G. H. & C. A. Peabody	5	2.50	6.87½
613	Beck & Clark vs Wm W. Colson	5	1.87½	6.25
614	Eaton Flewellen vs John R. Lloyd	5	1.87½	6.25
615	Turentine, Andrews, & Watson vs Wm Brazil	5	1.87½	6.25
616	Henry Matthews vs Joseph B. Webb	5	1.87½	6.25
617	Union Bank of Florida vs John T. Walker	5	1.87½	6.25
620	William Patrick vs Henry L. Lestarjett	5	1.87½	6.25
621	R. C. Wetmore vs John Dillingham & C°	5	2.50	6.87½
623	Baldwin, Phelps & C° vs Robinson & Halcomb	5	2.50	6.87½
627	D. Hungerford & C° vs John G. Dillingham	5	1.87½	6.25
628	Fewtrall Hall vs Daniel Loften	5	1.87½	6.25
634	Lewis Dowdle vs Henry C. Phelps	5	1.87½	6.25
635	Preston & Nelms vs Joseph Davidson	5	1.87½	6.25
637	Stewart & Fontaine vs Jesse Mann	5	1.87½	6.25
638	James Harriel vs Thomas J. Hand	5	1.87½	6.25
639	Henry King vs Lemuel Jepson	5	1.87½	6.25
640	William Patrick vs David Golstein	5	1.87½	6.25
642	D. Hungerford & C° vs A. K. Ayer	3	1.87½	6.25
644	W^m & W. Toney vs Joseph Davidson	5	1.87½	6.25
646	Starr & Reese vs Chisholm & Collins	5	2.50	6.87½
647	John M. Flournoy, Admtr. vs Jacobi & Miedzielski	5	2.50	6.87½
651	The Bank of Darien vs C. W. Buckley	3	0.00	6.25
652	Ayer & Hogg vs Bird B. Mitchell	3	1.87½	6.25
653	Wm S. Hartsfield & C° vs Caswell Johnson	3	1.87½	6.25
656	Burton Hepburn vs Joseph B. Webb Exn	5	1.87½	6.25

663	Lewis J. Davies vs John McGee	5	1.87½	6.25
664	Jeremiah McCoy vs Augustus G. Lawrence	5	1.87½	6.25
665	Henry Samford, Jʳ vs Rufus K. Mills	5	1.87½	6.25
666	John B. Guedron vs Thomas C. McKeen	5	1.87½	6.25
667	G. H. & C. A. Peabody vs Lucian A. Bowdery	5	1.87½	6.25
668	Hamilton, Hurd & Cº vs John R. Lloyd	5	1.87½	6.25

[184]

669	David Church vs A. K. Ayer & Milton J. Tarver	5	2.50	6.87½
671	Hamilton, Hurd & Cº vs Luther Blake	5	2.50	6.87½
	T. G. Gordon vs G. B. Terry, N. Terry, G. W. Short	5	5.62½	8.75
676	Hill, Dawson & Cº vs Benajah Skinner	5	1.87½	6.25
677	George Hargraves vs Wᵐ W. Nichols	5	1.87½	6.25
679	Young, Smith & Cº vs A. L. Heine	5	1.87½	6.25
75	Daniel Hightower vs Thomas James	3	1.87½	6.25
680	Wᵐ Myrick vs Robinson & Hand	5	2.50	6.87½
686	Burton Hepburn vs John J. Willson	5	1.87½	6.25
690	George Hargraves vs Alpha K. Ayer	3	1.87½	6.25
693	John B. Guedron vs Wᵐ McGee	5	1.87½	6.25
695	Jeremiah McCoy vs Aug. G. Lawrence & Thº J. Hand	5	2.50	6.87½
698	Kennith McKenzie vs Dennis Sullivan	5	1.87½	6.25
699	Hardin & Taylor vs A. L. Heine	5	1.87½	6.25
701	Farmers Bank of Chattahoochee vs John A. Campbell	5	1.87½	5.25
702	James S. Calhoun vs John Rounds	5	1.87½	5.25
703	James S. Calhoun vs C. W. Buckley & Cº	5	0.00	6.87½
704	Benjamin P. Tarver vs Hand & Lawrence	5	2.50	6.87½
706	James Kirlin vs John R. Lloyd	5	1.87½	6.25
707	Thomas R. Gould vs John T. Colquitt	5	1.87½	6.25
709	Charles H. Stewart vs Jesse Mann	5	1.87½	6.25
713	Egbert B. Beall vs Joel C. Wiggins	5	1.87½	6.25
716	John B. Guedron vs Jacob M. Guerry	5	1.87½	6.25
718	Stephen, Corlius, & Dennison vs Alexander & Wiggins	5	3.75	11.87½
719	Balock Bullock vs Samuel C. Scott & Talifear Scott	5	6.25	11.87½
725	Baldwin, Phelps & Cº vs Alexander & Wiggins	5	3.75	11.87½
731	Robert B. Alexander vs John J. Willson & James Rhind	5	3.75	11.87½

732	Ezekiel B. Stoddard vs Robinson & Williams	5	3.75	11.87½
735	Robert McAlpin vs Thomas C. McKeen	3	1.87½	6.25
736	William Nelms vs Thomas R. Gould	5	1.87½	6.25

It appearing to the Court that executions have been issued in all of the foregoing Cases against the several defendants & have been Returned with the entries of "No Property." It is ordered that Fi fas or ca sas be issued against the several Plaintiffs aforesaid for the amount of the Costs in their several Cases and that the Cost due in each case be collected out of the Plaintiff or Plaintiffs in that Case.

[185]

[blank page]

[186]

[blank page]

[187]

[blank page]

[188]

[blank page]

[189]

[blank page]

[190]

[blank page]

[191-196]

[blank pages not microfilmed]

[197] Thursday the 3rd day of January 1839

[blank page]

[198]

The Court adjourned untill Court in Course.

Marshall J. Wellborn, J. S. C. C. C.

[199]

James Jackson } Assumpsit and Verdict for the Plaintiff for for
vs } Two Hundred and fifty five dollars and fifty cents
Arthur Fox Alfred } Principal, with interest & cost of suit

The Defendant, being dissatisfied with the verdict of the Jury rendered in the above cause and having paid all Costs and demanded an appeal, brings Elbert Wells and tenders him as his security, and they, the said Arthur Fox Alfred and Elbert Wells, acknowledge themselves Jointly and severally bound unto James Jackson, the Plaintiff, for the payment of the eventual Condemnation money in said cause.

In Testimony whereof, they have hereunto set their hands and seals this 5th day of January 1839. (interlineations made before signature)

Test. Gerard Burch, Clk   A. F. Alfred
                                 Elbert Wells

James Jackson } Assumpsit and verdict for the Plaintiff for
vs } Two Hundred & fifty two dollars and eighteen
John B. Peabody, endorser} cents Principal, with interest and Cost of suit

The Defendant, being dissatisfied with the verdict of the Jury rendered in the above cause and having paid all costs and demanded an appeal, brings [blank] and tenders him as his security, and they, the said John B. Peabody and [blank], acknowledge themselves Jointly and severally bound unto James Jackson, the Plaintiff, for the payment of the eventual Condemnation money in said cause.

In Testimony whereof, they have hereunto set their hands and seals this 5th day of January 1839.

Test. Gerard Burch, Clk
John B. Peabody
Elbert Wells

James Jackson } Assumpsit and verdict for the Plaintiff for
vs } Two Hundred and fifty five dollars and fifty
John B. Peabody, endorser } cents Principal, with interest & cost of suit

The Defendant, being dissatisfied with the verdict of the Jury rendered in the above cause and having paid all costs and demanded an appeal, brings [blank] and tenders him as security, and they, the said John B. Peabody and [blank], acknowledge themselves Jointly and severally bound unto James Jackson, the Plaintiff, for the Payment of the eventual Condemnation money in said cause. In Testimony whereof, they have hereunto set their hands and seals this 5th day of January 1839.

Test. Gerard Burch, Clk
John B. Peabody
Elbert Wells

[200]

D. Hungerford & Co }
vs } Debt and Judgment in favour of the Plaintiffs
Pool, Lively, & McCrary } for the Sum of three thousand eight hundred and twenty Seven dollars & eighty cents principlal debt, also ninety nine dollars & fifty two cents interest thereon up to Judgment, to wit, to the 10th December 1838, with the cost of suit & three dollars Cost of protest.

The defendants in this case comes and craves a Stay of Execution and tenders Robert McCrary for their Security. And they, the said Pool, Lively, & McCrary, binds themselves Jointly & Severally for the payment of the Same to the said Plaintiffs, and if not paid at or before the expiration of Sixty days from this date then the said Robert McCrary, Security on the stay, will do it for them.

In Witness whereof, they the said Pool, Lively, & McCrary and Robert McCrary, Security aforesaid, have hereunto set their hands and Seals this 5th January 1839

Test.   W. W. Pool
                                     P. R. McCrary
                                     Robert McCrary

D. Hungerford & Co }
          vs   } Assumpsit and Judgment in favour of the
Pool, Lively, & McCrary } Plaintiffs for the sum of eight hundred and eighty four dollars and ten cents Principal Debt, also one hundred and fourteen dollars and ninety three cents interest thereon up to Judgment, to wit, the 1st January 1839, with cost of suit.

The defendants in this case comes and craves a Stay of Execution and tenders Robert McCrary for their security and they, the said Pool, Lively, & McCrary, binds themselves Jointly & Severally for the Payment of the same to the said Plaintiffs and if not paid at or before the expiration of Sixty days from this date then the said Robert McCrary, security on the Stay, will do it for them.

In Witness whereof, they the said Pool, Livly, & McCrary and Robert McCrary, security aforesaid, have hereunto set their hands and seals this 5th January 1839.

Test.   W. W. Pool
                                     P. R. McCrary
                                     Robert McCrary

Jacob M. Johnson }
          vs   } Judgmt Octr Term 1837
John H. Love   }

                         Principal Debt $239.92
                         Interest to the 24th April 1838   63.97

It appearing to the Court that the Original Fi fa by destroyed by fire at the late burning of the Clerk's Office and Court House for Muscogee County. It is therefore Ordered by the Court that the Clerk do issue an alias fi fa in lieu of the said Original.

[201]

John B. Baird }
    vs   } Assumpsit and confession of Judgment for the
Thomas C. Evans } Plaintiff for Thirteen Hundred & eleven dollars & twelve cents Principal, with interest & Cost of suit and protest fee.

The Defendant, being dissatisfied with the Confession of Judgment rendered in the above cause and having paid all cost and demanded an appeal, brings Matt R. Evans and tenders him as his security and they, the said Thomas C. Evans and Matt R. Evans, acknowledge themselves Jointly and severally bound unto the Plaintiff for the Payment of the eventual condemnation money in said cause. In Testimony whereof, they have hereunto set their hands and seals this 7th day of January A. D. 1839.

Test. Gerard Burch, Clk   Th^o C. Evans
                                          Matt R. Evans

John B. Baird   }
    vs   } Assumpsit and Verdict for the Plaintiff for
Edwin L. De Graffenried } Thirteen Hundred and eleven dollars and twelve cents Principal, with interest & cost of suit and protest fee.

The Defendant, being dissatisfied with the verdict of the Jury rendered in the above cause and having paid all costs and demanded an appeal, brings Matt R. Evans and tenders him as his security and they, the said Edwin L. DeGraffenried and Matt R. Evans, acknowledge themselves Jointly and severally bound unto the Plaintiff for the Payment of the eventual condemnation money in said cause. In Testimony whereof, they have hereunto set their hands and seals this 7th day of January A. D. 1839.

Test. Gerard Burch, Clk   E. L. De Graffenried
                                          Matt R. Evans

John B. Baird }
    vs   } Assumpsit and Confession of Judgment to the Plaintiff
Matt R. Evans } for Thirteen Hundred & eleven dollars & twelve cents Principal, with interest & cost of suit and Protest fee.

The Defendant, being dissatisfied with the confession of Judgment rendered in the above cause and having paid all costs and demanded an appeal, brings Thomas C. Evans and tenders him as his security and they, the said Matt R. Evans and Thomas C. Evans, acknowledge themselves Jointly and severally bound unto the Plaintiff for the Payment of the eventual Condemnation money in said cause. In Testimony whereof, they have hereunto set their hands and seals this 7th day of January 1839.

Test. Gerard Burch, Clk   Matt R. Evans
                                           Thº C. Evans

[202]

Marshall J. Wellborn   }
           vs   } Assumpsit and Judgment in favour of the
Benjamin V. Iverson, Principal } Plaintiff for the sum of Three thousand
Alfred Iverson   } four Hundred and Eighty Dollars Principal
Jacob M. Guerry   } debt, also Two hundred and seventy Eight
John J. Boswell, and   } dollars and forty cents interest thereon up to
Thomas C. Evans, Securities   } Judgment, to wit, to the 20th day of
December 1838, with the cost of suit.

The Defendants in this case comes and craves a stay of Execution and tenders John L. Lewis for their security and they, the said Benjamin V. Iverson, Principal, Alfred Iverson, Jacob M. Guerry, John J. Boswell, and Thomas C. Evans, securities, binds themselves Jointly & severally for the Payment of the same to the said Plaintiff, and if not paid at or before the expiration of sixty days from this date then the said John L. Lewis, security on the Stay, will do it for them. In Witness whereof, they the said Benjamin V. Iverson, Principal, Alfred Iverson, Jacob M. Guerry, John J. Boswell, and Thomas C. Evans, securities, and John L. Lewis, security as aforesaid, have hereunto set their hands and seals this 7th day of January 1839.

Test.   Benjamin V. Iverson
                                           A. Iverson
                                           J. M. Guerry
                                           J. J. Boswell
                                           Thº C. Evans
                                           John L. Lewis

Parish, Marshall & Co }
     vs } Assumpsit & Judg^t in favour of the Plff for the
Alfred Iverson, maker } sum of thirteen hundred & ninety two dollars
Ben^j V. Iverson, Indorser } & seventy two cents principal & two hundred &
sixteen dollars & sixty nine cents interest thereon up to Judg^t, to wit, to the
10th Decr 1838, with cost of suit.

The Def^{ts} in this case come into Court and crave a stay of Execution & tender John J. Boswell for their security and they, the said Alfred Iverson, maker, & B. V. Iverson, Indorser, ~~bind themselves~~ & John J. Boswell, Security on the Stay, bind themselves jointly & severally for the payment of the same to the said Plff^s, & if not paid at or before the expiration of Sixty days from this date, then the said John J. Boswell will do it for them. In Witness whereof they, the said Alfred Iverson, Maker, B. V. Iverson, In^d, & J. J. Boswell, st^y, have hereto set their hands & Seals this 7th day of Jany 1839.

Test.   A. Iverson
                                  B. V. Iverson
                                  J. J. Boswell

[203]

A. L. Heine }
     vs } Attachment in Muscogee Superior Court
James H. Mitchell, Surviving }
Copartner of Norton & Mitchell }

It appearing to the Court that the original attachment in this Case has been destroyed by fire and that a copy of the same and of the entries thereon has been filed in the Clerk's Office with the Clerk. It is is therefore ordered by the Court that said Copy be and is established in lieu of said Original.

[204]

[blank page]

[205]

Seaborn Thorn }
    vs } Assumpsit and Judgment in favour of the Plff^s
Jacob M. Guerry (Maker) } for the sum of Three thousand five hundred
Alfred Iverson } dollars Principal, and also Five Hundred &
Robert Iverson & } sixteen dollars & sixty six cents interest
John W. Turner, securities } thereon up to Judgment, to wit, to the 10th day of December 1838, and Cost of suit and Three dollars Protest fee.

The Defendants in this case comes and craves a Stay of Eceution and tenders John J. Boswell for their security and they, the said Jacob M. Guerry (maker), Alfred Iverson, Robert Iverson, & John W. Turner, securities, binds themselves Jointly & severally for the Payment of the same to the Plaintiff and if not Paid at or before the expiration of sixty days from this date then the said John J. Boswell, security on the stay, will do it for them. In Witness whereof they, the said Jacob M. Guerry (maker), Alfred Iverson, Robert Iverson, & John W. Turner, securities, and John J. Boswell, security on the stay, have hereunto set their handsand seals this 7th day of January A. D. 1839.

                                        Alfred Iverson
                                        J. M. Guerry
                                        John W. Turner
                                        B. V. Iverson
                                        J. J. Boswell

James Neal }
    vs } Assumpsit and Judgment in favour of the Plaintiff for the
John J. Boswell } sum of Six Hundred dollars Principal debt, also forty Eight dollars for his interest up to this date, to wit, 28th December 1838, & cost of suit.

the defendant comes & craves a Stay of execution & tenders Alfred Iverson for his Security & they, the said John J. Boswell and Alfred Iverson, security on the stay, binds themselves Jointly & severally for the payment of the same to the Plaintiff, and if not paid at or before the Expiration of sixty days from this date then the said Alfred Iverson, security as aforesaid, will do it him. In

Witness whereof the, the said John J. Boswell and Alfred Iverson, Security on the stay, have hereunto set their hands and seals this 7th day of December 1839.

Test.   J. J. Boswell
                                        A. Iverson

[206]

William Holland   }
         vs   } Assumpsit and Judgment for the Plaintiff for
Benjamin V. Iverson   } Eight Hundred and sixty dollars & forty Eight cents Principal debt, also sixty dollars and sixty cents thereon up to Judgment, to wit, to the 1st day of January 1839, & cost of suit.

The Defendant in this case comes & craves a stay of Execution and tenders [blank] for his security and they, the said Benjamin V. Iverson and [blank] binds themselves Jointly & severally for the Payment of the same to the Plaintiff, and if not Paid at or before the expiration of sixty days from this date then the said [blank], security on the stay, will do it for him. In Witness whereof they, the said Benjamin V. Iverson and [blank], security on the stay, have hereunto set their hands and seals this 7th day of January A. D. 1839.

Test.   B. V. Iverson
                                        J. J. Boswell

William Holland   }
      vs   } Assumpsit and Judgment for the Plaintiff for
Alfred Iverson   } Eight hundred and ~~fifty~~ sixty six dollars and forty Eight cents principal.

[blank]

                                        Alfred Iverson
                                        J. J. Boswell

William Holland   }
      vs   } Assumpsit and Judment for the Plaintiff for
Thomas C. Evans   } Eight hundred and sixty six dollars and forty Eight cents Principal.

[blank]

Th⁰ C. Evans
J. J. Boswell

[207]

Burton Hepburn }
    vs   } Assumpsit & Judgment for eleven thousand
Clarles L. Bass } one hundred & seventy three dollars & twenty seven
cents.

[blank]

Charles L. Bass
T. & M. Evans

Burton Hepburn }
    vs   } Assumpsit & Judgment eleven thousand one
Seaborn Jones } hundred & seventy three dollars & twenty seven Cents.

[blank]

By J^s Calhoun for Seaborn Jones
T. & M. Evans

Burton Hepburn }
    vs   } assumpsit And Judgment for the Plaintiff for
James S. Calhoun} eleven thousand one hundred & Seventy three dollars &
twenty seven cents.

[blank]

[208]

J^s Calhoun
T. & M. Evans

Bogert & Kneeland }
  vs   } assumpsit
Augustus Howard }

Judgment to the Plaintiff for two thousand Seven hundred & twenty six & ninety cents, with interest & cost of suit.

Bogert & Kneeland }
  vs   } assumpsit
T. & M. Evans }

Judgment for the Plaintiff for the sum of two thousand Six hundred & Eighty two dollars & forty two cents, with interest & cost of Suit.

        T. & M. Evans
        J^s Calhoun

James H. Shorter }
  vs   } assumpsit
T. & M. Evans }

Judgment for the Plaintiff for the sum of Seven thousand five hundred dollars, with interest & Cost of Suit.

[209]

[blank]

        T. & M. Evans
        J^s Calhoun

Bogert & Kneeland }
  vs   } Assumpsit. Judgment for the Plaintiff for the sum of
T. & M. Evans } two thousand Seven hundred & twenty six dollars & ninety Cents, with interest & Cost of suit.

[blank]

        T. & M. Evans
        J^s Calhoun

Insurance Bank of Columbus }
  vs { Assumpsit and Judgment for the Plaintiff
James S. Calhoun & } for the sum of Nine thousand dollars
Charles L. Bass } Principal

[blank]

        J^s Calhoun & Charles L. Bass
        T. & M. Evans

Insurance Bank of Columbus }
  vs { Assumpsit and Judgment for the Plaintiff
Edward Cary } for the sum of nine thousand dollars.

[210]

[blank]

        Edwd Cary
        T. & M. Evans

William Berry }
  vs } Assumpsit and Judgment for the Plaintiff
Charles L. Bass } for Four thousand seven hundred and forty
& Edward Cary } four dollars and fifty cents Principal.

[blank]

        Edwd Cary
        T. & M. Evans

William Berry }
  vs } Assumpsit and Judgment for the Plaintiff for Four
Seaborn Jones } thousand seven hundred and forty four dollars and fifty
cents Principal.

[blank]

        By J^s Calhoun for Seaborn Jones
        T. & M. Evans

Insurance Bank of Columbus }
    vs } Assumpsit and Judgment for the Plaintiff
Thomas C. Evans & } for Nine thousand dollars Principal.
Matt R. Evans }

[211]

[blank]

                         T. & M. Evans
                         J^s Calhoun

Insurance Bank of Columbus }
    vs } Assumpsit and Judgment for the Plaintiff
Burton Hepburn } for nine thousand dollars Principal.

[blank]

                         B. Hepburn
                         Calhoun & Bass

Hall & Moses }
    vs } Assumpsit and Judgment for the Plaintiff for the sum
Seaborn Jones } of Two thousand three hundred & forty three dollars and forty five Cents Principal.

[blank]

                         By J^s Calhoun for Seaborn Jones
                         T. & M. Evans

Hall & Moses }
    vs } Assumpsit and Judgment for the Plaintiff for Two
Calhoun & Bass } thousand three hundred & forty three dollars and forty five cents Principal.

[212]

[blank]

        Calhoun & Bass
        T. & M. Evans

James Kirlin }
  vs   } Debt and Judgment For the Plaintiff for Three
Calhoun & Bass } Hundred and seventy dollars and Eighty three cents
Principal.

[blank]

        Calhoun & Bass
        T. & M. Evans

Insurance Bank of Columbus}
   vs   } Assumpsit and Judgment for the Plaintiff
James S. Calhoun   } Two thousand dollars Principal.

[blank]

        J^s Calhoun
        T. & M. Evans

Lorenzo D. Buckner }
  vs   } Assumpsit and Judgment for the Plaintiff for
Charles L. Bass } Five thousand dollars Principal.

[213]

[blank]

        Charles L. Bass, T. & M. Evans
        T. & M. Evans

Lorenzo D. Buckner }
  vs   } Assumpsit and Judgment for the Plintiff for
T. & M. Evans } Five thousand dollars Principal.

[blank]

       T. & M. Evans
       J^s Calhoun

Lorenzo D. Buckner }
  vs   } Assumpsit and Judgment for the Plaintiff for
Edward Cary   } Five thousand dollars Principal.

[blank]

       Edwd Cary
       T. & M. Evans

Lorenzo D. Buckner }
  vs   } Assumpsit and Judgment for the Plaintiff for
Seaborn Jones } Five thousand dollars Principal.

[blank]

       Edwd Cary
       T. & M. Evans

[214]

       By J^s Calhoun for Seaborn Jones
       T. & M. Evans

Hall & Moses   }
  vs   } Debt and Judgment for the Plaintiff for the sum of
Calhoun & Bass } Two hundred and forty one dollars and seventy three
cents Principal.

[blank]

       Calhoun & Bass
       T. & M. Evans

James H. Shorter }
    vs } Assumpsit and Judgment for the
Calhoun & Bass, Principals & } Plaintiff for the sum of One thousand
John L. Lewis, endorser & security } dollars Principal.

[blank]

                          Calhoun & Bass
                          John L. Lewis
                          John H. Ware

James H. Shorter }
    vs } Assumpsit and Judgment for the Plaintiff for the sum
James S. Calhoun } of Fourteen Hundred and forty dollars Principal.

[blank]

[215]

                          J^s Calhoun
                          T. & M. Evans

Samuel Thompson }
    vs } Assumpsit and Judgment for the Plaintiff for the sum of
Calhoun & Bass } thirteen Hundred and seventy eight dollars and Eighty
two cents.

[blank]

                          Calhoun & Bass
                          T. & M. Evans

George Hargraves }
    vs } Assumpsit and Judgment for the Plaintiff for Five
James S. Calhoun } Hundred dollars Principal.

[blank]

                          J^s Calhoun
                          T. & M. Evans

[216]

James H. Shorter }
    vs } Assumpsit and Judgment for the Plaintiff for
Thomas G. Gordon }

[blank]

                              Thos G. Gordon
                              J^s Calhoun

James H. Shorter }
    vs } Assumpsit and Judgment for the Plaintiff for
James S. Calhoun, endorser } fourteen hundred & forty dollars principal debt.

[blank]

                              J^s Calhoun
                              Thos G. Gordon

[217]

T. & M. & J. Allyn }
    vs }
D. Hungerford & C° }

Debt and Judgment for the Plaintiff for Eleven hundred & thirty seven dollars & thirty one cents Principal debt, also one hundred and forty seven dollars and Eighty one cents interest thereon to Judgment, to wit, to the 25th day of December 1838, and cost of suit. The Defendants in this case comes and craves a stay of Execution and tenders Lester L. Cowdery as his security and they, the said D. Hungerford & C°, binds themselves Jointly and severally for the Payment of the same to the Plaintiffs and if not Paid at or before the Expiration of sixty days from this date then the said Lester L. Cowdery will do it for him. In Witness whereof they, the said D. Hungerford & C° and Lester L. Cowdery, have hereunto set their hands and seals this 7th day of January A. D. 1839.

                              D. Hungerford & C°
                              Lester L. Cowdery

Crawford & McKim }
   vs   }
W^m & W. Toney }

Debt and Confession of Judgment to the Plaintiffs for Five thousand and sixty one dollars and fifteen cents Principal, with interest & cost of suit. The Defendants, being dissatisfied with the Confession of Judgment rendered in the above cause, and having Paid all Costs and demanded an appeal, brings [blank] and tenders him as their security, & the said W^m & W. Toney and [blank] acknowledge themselves Jointly & severally bound unto the Plaintiffs for the Payment of the eventual Condemnation money in said cause. In Testimony they have hereunto set their hands and seals this 8th day of January A. D. 1839.

[blank]

James Corry }
  vs   } Assumpsit & verdict of the Jury for the Plff for the
T. & M. Evans } Sum of Eighteen hundred & Seventy five dollars,
Calhoun & Bass } with interest, cost of suit, & protest fee.
& Ge° W. Ross }

[blank]

7th January 1839   Th° C. Evans

[218]   Charles L. Bass
              J^s Calhoun
              Matt R. Evans
              John H. Ware

[219]

[blank page]

[220]

[blank page]

[221] April Term 1839
Muscogee Superior Court Monday 15th April 1839

The Court met according to adjournment, present the Honorable Marshall J. Wellborn, Judge of the Superior Courts of the Chattahoochee Circuit.

The names of the following persons being called and having answered, when the Oaths of Grand and Special Jurors were administered to them by the Solicitor General.

1. James M. Chambers, foreman
2. John H. Ware
3. George Hargraves, Junr
4. Edward Delony
5. Garland B. Terry
6. Darias Cox
7. Thomas McGinty
8. G. W. E. Bedell
9. Samuel Boykin
10. William S. Chipley
11. James S. Calhoun
12. Thomas J. Shivers
13. Martin Brooks
14. William F. Luckie
15. William B. Bacon
16. Rhodam A. Green
17. Thomas Preston, Tallisman
18. Abraham Levison, T^n

George W. Short Sworn Bailiff to the Grand & Special Jurys.

The names of the following persons were called and answered to, when the Oath of Petit Jurors for the trial of civil cases were administrated by the Solicitor General.

N° 1
1. John L. Walton
2. Thomas Kendall
3. William J. Rylander
4. Thomas Nix
5. George W. Brown
6. Zachariah Watkins
7. Richard Greer
8. Samuel Hemphill
9. James Kemp
10. David Wall
11. Joseph Biggers
12. Robert C. Patterson

N° 2
1. Vincent P. Rockquemore
2. James C. McGibbony
3. William H. Alston
4. Bartlett Wicks
5. William Pride
6. James Ward
7. Daniel D. Ridenhour
8. Umphry Rowell
9. Menoah D. Robison
10. Jessee Osteen
11. William Liggon
12. Zachariah Butler

Adons H. Belyeu sworn Bailiff.

[222]

The Bank of Columbus }
   vs   } Assumpsit
Pool, Lively & C° }

I confess Judgment to the defendant, reserving the right of Appeal.

         G. E. Thomas, Plff^s Att^y

Frederick Richster }
   vs   } Assumpsit & Bail
Jacobi & Heine }

I Confess Judgment to the defendant, reserving the right of Appeal.

         G. E. Thomas, Plff^s Att^y

Brown & Dimock }
   vs   } Ca sa from Muscogee Superior Court And motion
James Y. Smith } to take the benefit of the Insolvent debtors act.

D. A. Cushman & C° }
   vs   } Ca sa And motion to take the benefit of the
James Y. Smith, } Insolvent debtors act from Muscogee Superior Court.
Lewis C. Allen & }
James H. Campbell, }
Securities   }

The petition of James Y. Smith respectfully Sheweth that he has filed in the Clerk's Office a schedule of all his property and has given notice to his creditors in terms of the law. he therefore prays your Honor that he may be admitted to take the benefit of an act entitled an act for the relief of honost debtors passed in 1823, and as in duty bound your petitioner will ever pray &c.

         Campbell, McDougald, & Watson, Def^{ts} Att^{ys}

Seaborn Thorn }
    vs } Assumpsit
John L. Lewis, endorser }

Jury N° 1. We, the Jury, find for the Plaintiff the sum of Three thousand and five hundred dollars, with interest & Cost of suit.

                        Wm J. Rylander, foreman

Penina Thomas, Executrix of }
Stephens Thomas, deceased }
    vs } Assumpsit
John J. Willson }

Jury N° 1. We, the Jury, find for the Plaintiff Five thousand dollars, with interest & Cost of suit and three dollars for Cost of Protest.

                        Wm J. Rylander, foreman

N. S. Williams }
    vs } Trover &c
Lewis Townsen }

We Confess Judgment to the defendant for Cost of suit, reserving the right of appeal.

                        Colquitt, Holt, & Echols, Plaintiffs Attorneys

[223]   Monday 15th April 1839

Calhoun & Bass }
    vs } Assumpsit
Micajah W. Thweatt }

I Confess Judgment to the Plaintiffs for Two Hundred $^{43}/_{100}$ Dollars, with interest & Cost of suit. 15 April 1839

                        Colquitt, Holt, & Echols, Def^{ts} Att^{ys}

Silas B. Stilwell, bearer }   Silas B. Stilwell, bearer }
    vs   } Assumpsit   vs   } assumpsit
Samuel Lytle   }   John T. Walker   }

Silas B. Stilwell }
    vs   } assumpsit
Allen G. Bass }

Francis S. Sewell, bearer }
    vs   } assumpsit
William B. Robison & C°}

Silas B. Stilwell, bearer }
    vs   } assumpsit
William B. Robison & C°}

Silas B. Stilwell, bearer }
    vs   } assumpsit
W^m & W. Toney }

Georgia   }
Muscogee County } Rule to establish the writs in the above cases for October term 1838. It appearing to the Court that the Original writs &c were destroyed in the burning of the Court House and Clerk's Office and that the Copies herewith Submitted to the Court are according to the admissions of parties defendants Copies in Substance of the original writs &c destroyed. it is on motion ordered that said Copies be established in lieu of the Originals.

The Court adjourned to meet again to morrow morning at nine O'clock.

[224]   Tuesday 16th day of April 1839

The Court met this morning according to adjournment. Present the Honorable Marshall J. Wellborn, Judge of Said Court.

N. G. Woods }
    vs   } Assumpsit to April term 1838
Noel Mathews }

We consent that the within Copy declarartion be established in lieu of the lost original, waving entry of Sheriff's Service April term 1839.

J. N. & J. M. Bethune, Def[ts] Att[ys]

On Motion, it is ordered that the within declaration be established in lieu of the lost Original.

N. G. Woods }
    vs } Assumpsit to April term 1838
Thomas C. Evans }   April term 1839
Endorser }

It appearing to the Court that the Original Declaration of which the within is a Copy in Substance has been destroyed in the late Conflagration of the Clerk's Office. It is therefore on motion Ordered that the within Copy Declaration be established in lieu of the said lost original.

Kenith McKinzie, Nicholas Howard, & Launcelot Gambril were Summoned by the Sheriff as Tallismen to serve on the Grand Jury at this term, they being Sworn in Open Court as Grand & Special Jurors, Joined the body of the Grand Jury.

Stewart & Fontaine }
    vs } Attachment
Henry Robinson }

We, the Jury, find for the Plaintiffs thirty five dollars and nineteen Cents, with interest & Cost of Suit.

William J. Rylander, foreman

The Mayor & Council of }
the Town of Columbus }
    vs } assumpsit
Thomas C. Evans }

We, the Jury, find for the Plaintiff thirteen hundred & Seventy dollars & Seventy five cents, with interest & costs.

William J. Rylander, foreman

[225]   Tuesday 16th day of April 1839

James S. Calhoun }
      vs   } Assumpsit
M. D. Robison & }
Thomas J. Hand }

I Confess Judgment to the Plaintiff for the sum of three thousand & eighty dollars and ninety one cents, with interest & Cost. 15th April 1839

J. N. & J. M. Bethune, Def^{ts} Att^{ys}

Muscogee Superior Court O

North, Manning, & Hoyt vs John B. Peabody. Debt
The same vs A. F. Alfred, G. W. Short, & S. E. Buckler. Assumpsit
The same vs Ephraim C. Bandy. Assumpsit
Bank of Milledgeville vs Thos G. Gordon, Thos C. Evans, & S. Jones. Assumpsit
James R. Butts vs Starr & Reese. Assumpsit
Richard K. Hines vs Starr & Reese. Assumpsit

Georgia   }
Muscogee County } Personally appeared in Open Court Franklin A. Nisbet, who being duly sworn deposeth & saith, that the declarations in the above Cases were Consumed in the Clerk's Office and that the declarations now herewith shown the Court are in substance true Copies of the said lost Originals. Sworn to in Open Court 16th April 1839.

Gerard Burch, Clk   Franklin A. Nisbet

It appearing to the Court that the Original declarations in the above Stated cases have been lost. it is on motion of F. A. Nisbet Ordered that the above mentioned Copies be established in lieu of the lost Originals.

The State }
   vs } Larceny after a Trust
William N. Jackson }

True Bill.   James M. Chambers, Foreman

The State }
   vs } Assault & Battery
James Monroe }

True Bill.   James M. Chambers, Foreman

L. J. Davies vs Henry Allen. Assumpsit now pending in Muscogee Superior Court
Martin Brooks vs Henry Allen. Ca Sa
Hezekiah Hawley vs Henry Allen. Ca Sa

             Muscogee Superior Court April Term 1839

It appearing to the Court that Henry Allen, the defendant in the above cases, having filed a Schedule of his property & effects with the Clerk of this Court ten days prior to the Sitting of said Court & having served the aforesaid Creditors with a Notice that he

[226] would move this Court at this Term to be admitted to take the Oath prescribed for the Relief of Insolvent debtors ten days previous thereto. It is therefore ordered by the Court that the said Henry Allen be now admitted to said Oath.

I, Henry Allen, do Solemnly Swear in the presence of Almighty God that I am not possessed of any Real or personal Estate, Debts, Credits, or Effects, securities or Contracts whatsoever, my wearing apparel, bedding for myself & family, & the working tools or implements of my trade or calling, together with the necessary equipments for a Malitia Soldier excepted, other than are Contained in this schedule now delivered, & that I have not, directly or indirectly, Since my imprisonment or before Sold, leased, assigned, or otherwise disposed of or made over in trust for myself, or otherwise any part of my lands, estates, Goods, Stocks, money, debts, Securities, or contracts whereby any money may hereafter become payable, or any real or personal estate whereby to have or expect any benefit or profit to myself, wife, or my heirs. So help me God.

Sworn to in open Court & Subscribed this 16th April 1839.

Marshall J. Wellborn, J. S, C. C. C.   Henry Allen

It appearing to the Court that James Y. Smith has been arrested by virtue of two Ca Sa's from Muscogee Superior Court, One in favour of Brown & Dimmock vs James Y. Smith and the other in favour of D. A. Cushman & C° vs James Y. Smith, and the said James Y. Smith having given bond and security for his appearance at this term of the Court to avail himself of the benefit of an act entitled an act for the relief of Honest Debtors passed in eighteen hundred and twenty three. And it further appearing to the Court that the said James Y. Smith hath filed his Schedule and given notice to his Creditors in terms of the law to avail himself of the benefit of said act. It is therefore on motion ordered that the said James Y. Smith be admitted to take the oath prescribed for the relief of Honest debtors and be thence discharged.

I, James Y. Smith, do Solemnly Swear in the presence of Almighty God that I am not possessed of any real or personal estate, debts, credits, or effects, securities or Contracts whatever, my wearing apparel, bedding for myself and family, and the working tools or implements of my trade or Calling, together with the necessary equipments for a Malitia Soldier excepted, other than are Contained in the schedule now delivered, and that I have not, directly or indirectly, Since my imprisonment or before Sold, leased, assigned, or otherwise disposed of or made over in trust for myself, or otherwise any part of my Lands, estates, Goods, Stock, money, debts, Securities, or contracts whereby any money may hereafter become payable, or any real or personal estate whereby to have or expect any benefit or profit to myself, wife, or my heirs. So help me God.

Sworn to in open Court & Subscribed this 16th day of April 1839.

Marshall J. Wellborn, J. S, C. C. C.   James Y. Smith

[227]   Tuesday 16th day of April 1839

On motion it it ordered that the Said James Y. Smith be discharged from further Custody, he having taken and Subscribed the oath prescribed for the relief of Honest debtors and that an exhonereteur be entered upon each of the bonds given in the above stated cases for his appearance at this Court.

Henry Moffett }
    vs } Assumpsit
Calhoun & Bass }

I confess Judgment to the defendants, with cost of suit, reserving the right of Appeal.

                        John Schley, Plff^s Att^y

Henry Moffett }
    vs } Assumpsit
James S. Calhoun }

I Confess Judgment to the Plaintiff for the sum of two Hundred & fifteen dollars & nineteen cents, with interest & cost of suit, reserving the right of Appeal.

                        Seaborn Jones, Def^{ts} Att^y

Thos G. Gordon }
    vs } Assp^t & Bail
Garland B. Terry }
Nathaniel Terry }
and George W. Short }
security }

Whereas John Langdon Lewis is security on the Bail Bond for Nathaniel Terry, one of the defendants in this case, and the plaintiff Consents that said Lewis be exonereted from his liability as bail aforesaid. It is ordered by the Court that said John L. Lewis be exonarated from all liability as bail aforesaid for said Nathaniel Terry, one of the Defendants.

John T. Robertson }
    vs } Debt
James N. Bethune }

We, the Jury, find a verdict for the defendant.

                        William J. Rylander, foreman

The Court Adjourned to meet again to Morrow Morning at Nine O'Clock.

Marshall J. Wellborn, J. S. C. C. C.

[228] Wednesday April 17th 1839

The Court met this morning according to Adjournment. Present the Honorable Marshall J. Wellborn, Judge of said Court.

James Bradford }
    vs   } Ca sa   Muscogee Superior Court
Nelson Baird }   April Term 1839

It appearing to the Court upon the petition of Nelson Baird that he has been arrested by virtue of a Ca Sa in favour of James A. Bradford vs Nelson Baird, and it further appearing that the Said Nelson Baird has given bond and Security for his appearance at this term of the court to avail himself of the benefit of an act entitled an act for the relief of honest debtors passed in 1823. And it further appearing that he has filed his Schedule in the Clerk's Office of the Superior Court of said County and notified his Creditors of Such his intention in terms of the law.

It therefore on motion ordered that the Oath prescribed for the relief of Honest debtors be administered to the said Nelson Beard.

I, Nelson Baird, do Solemnly Swear in the presence of Almighty God that I am not possessed of any real or personal estate, debts, credits, or effects, Securities or Contracts whatever, my wearing apparel, bedding for myself and family, and the working tools or implements of my trade or Calling, together with the necessary equipments for a Malitia Soldier excepted, other than are Contained in the Schedule now delivered, and that I have not, directly or indirectly, Since my imprisonment or before Sold, leased, assigned, or otherwise disposed of or made over in trust for myself, or otherwise any part of my lands, estates, Goods, Stock, money, debts, Securities, or contracts whereby any money may hereafter become payable, or any real or personal estate whereby to have or expect any benefit or profit to myself, wife, or my heirs. So help me God.

Sworn to and Subscribed in open Court this 17th day of April 1839.

Marshall J. Wellborn, J. S, C. C. C.   Nelson Baird

On motion it it ordered that the Said Nelson Baird be released from custody under the Ca sa in the above Stated Case and that an exhonereteur be entered upon the bond given for his appearance in the above Stated case.

Spivy Fuller }
    vs } Assumpsit
Jonathan A. Hudson }

We, the Jury, find for the Plaintiff nine hundred and twenty eight dollars, with interest and Cost of Suit.

                            William J. Rylander, foreman

[229]   Wednesday 17th April 1839

Petit Jury N° 1	Petit Jury N° 2
1. William J. Rylander, foreman	1. Menoah D. Robinson, foreman
2. Joseph Biggers	2. William H. Alston
3. George W. Brown	3. Zachariah Butler
4. Richard Greer	4. James C. McGibony
5. Samuel Hemphill	5. Little Berry Harris
6. James Kemp	6. William Pride
7. Thomas Kendall	7. Daniel D. Ridenhour
8. Thomas Nix	8. Umphry Rowell
9. Robert C. Patterson	9. Vincent P. Roquemore
10. John L. Walton	10. Jessee Osteen
11. David Wall	11. Bartlett Wicks
12. Zachariah Watkins	12. James Ward

Foster & Fogle }
    vs }
Henry Kendall & }
Wm H. Harper, security }
in Ca sa Bond }

It appearing to the Court that the defendant, Henry Kendall, was arrested by virtue of a ca sa in this case and gave Bond in terms of the Law of an act entitled "an act for the relief of honest debtors" for his appearance at this term of this Court and he having failed to appear or to give Notice or file his schedule in terms of said act. It is ordered by the Court that the Plaintiff order up Judgment upon said bond for the amount of the same, to be discharged upon payment of the Principal, interest, and all cost.

John Doe, ex dem }
Saml Nixon }
     vs } Ejectment
Richard Roe, casual ejector }
& Josiah Evans, tenant }
in possession }

Jury N° 1. We, the Jury, find for the Plaintiff the premises in dispute & Cost of suit. 17 April 1839

                       Wm J. Rylander, foreman

Ayer & Hogg }
     vs } In Muscogee Superior Court April term 1839
H. B. Millikin }

James H. Campbell, Administrator on the estate of H. B. Millikin, deceased, comes in at this term of the Court and consents to be made a party in the above Stated case. It is therefore on motion ordered by the Court that he be made a party defendant as administrator aforesaid.

[230]

Ayer & Hogg }
     vs } Debt
H. B. Millikin & }
J. H. Campbell, Admtr. &c }

I Confess Judgment to the Plaintiff in the Sum of fifty eight dollars and fifty nine cents principal, besides interest and costs of Suit, to be levied and collected out of Assets liable to the Judgment & Shall come to my hands.

                       J. H. Campbell

John C. Mangham }
     vs } Assumpsit
Joseph T. Brown }

We, the Jury, find for the Plaintiff the Sum of fifty seven dollars and ninety five cents, with interest & costs.

M. D. Robison, forman

Thomas McCarty }
    vs   } assumpsit
John S. Allen   }

I confess Judgment to the Plaintiff for the sum of fifty seven dollars principal, with interest and cost of Suit.

Nicholas L. Howard, Def[ts] Att[y]

Burton Hepburn }
    vs   } assumpsit
Luther Blake   }

We, the Jury, find for the Plaintiff the Sum of Eight hundred dollars, with interest and Cost of suit, also three dollars protest fee.

M. D. Robison, forman

Burton Hepburn }
    vs   } Assumpsit
Alfred Iverson }

We, the Jury, find for the Plaintiff the Sum of eight hundred dollars, with interest & Cost.

M. D. Robison, forman

Burton Hepburn   }
    vs   } assumpsit
Benjamin V. Iverson }

We, the Jury, find for the Plaintiff the Sum of eight hundred dollars, with interest & cost of suit.

M. D. Robison, forman

Thomas B. Greenwood }
  vs   } assumpsit
James Boykin   }

We, the Jury, find for the Plaintiff fifty dollars, with Cost of Suit.

          M. D. Robison, forman

[231]   Wednesday 17th day of April 1839

Stewart & Fontaine }
  vs   } Debt
J. P. Hitchcock }

I confess Judgment to the Plaintiff for fifty and forty Six cents principal, with interest and cost of suit.

          Jesse P. Hitchcock, Def[t]

Burton Hepburn }
  vs   } Assumpsit
John J. Boswell }

We, the Jury, find for the Plaintiff the sum of Eight hundred dollars, with interest & cost.

          M. D. Robison, forman

H. Matthews }
  vs   } Debt
S. M. Jackson }

I Confess Judgment to the Plaintiff for One hundred and forty eight dollars and seventy five cents principal, with interest & Cost of suit.

          Sam M. Jackson

Guyard & Jordan }
  vs   } Debt
W[m] J. Rylander }

I Confess Judgment to the Plaintiff the sum of sixty seven dollars and forty cents, with interest & Cost.

> Jn° Schley, Def^{ts} Att^y

Neill McNair }
    vs } Debt
Reuben H. McCoy }

It appearing to the Court that the Original declaration in this ~~suit~~ Case has been lost or destroyed. It is therefore on motion ordered by the Court that the within be established instanter in lieu of said lost Original. April Term 1839

Neill McNair }
    vs } Debt
Reuben H. McCoy }

We, the Jury, find for the Plaintiff the sum of Seventy four dollars. with interest & Costs.

> William J. Rylander, foreman

Elizabeth Billups }
    vs } Attachment
Henry D. Baldwin }

We, the Jury, find for the Plaintiff the sum of one hundred and twenty five dollars, with interest and cost of suit.

> William J. Rylander, form

Neill McNair }
    vs } Debt
Henry G. McCoy }

We, the Jury, find for the Plaintiff the sum of Two hundred and five dollars and Sixteen and a half cents, with interest & Costs.

> M. D. Robinson, foreman

[232}

George Field }
    vs   } Assumpsit
Seaborn Jones }

I confess Judgment to the Plaintiff for the sum of Seventeen hundred and ninety six dollars, with interest & Cost of suit and three dollars Cost of Protest.

Seaborn Jones

George Field }
    vs   } Assumpsit
T. & M. Evans }

We Confess Judgment to the Plaintiff for the sum of seventeen hundred and ninety six dollars, with interest & Costs of suit.

Seaborn Jones, Def^{ts} Att^y

Guyard & Jordan }
    vs   } Debt
Michael N. Clarke }

We, the Jury, find for the Plaintiff the sum of fifty five dollars and thirty five cents, with interest and cost of suit.

William J. Rylander, foreman

George Field }
    vs   } Assumpsit
T. & M. Evans }

We Confess Judgment to the plaintiff for the sum of Seventeen hundred and eighty eight dollars, with interest and cost of suit.

Seaborn Jones, Def^{ts} Att^y

Bennedict & Wetmore }
  vs   } Assumpsit
A. F. Brannon & C° }

We, the Jury, find for the Plaintiffs the Sum of four hundred and forty five dollars and sixty five cents, with interest and Cost of suit.

         M. D. Robinson, foreman

Robert Maitland & Son }
  vs   } Assumpsit
William W. Pool }

We, the Jury, find for the Plaintiff the sum of Six hundred and Six dollars & sixty six cents, with interest & Cost.

         William J. Rylander, foreman

Alexander Moss }
  vs } Assumpsit
James U. Glenn }

We, the Jury, find for the Plaintiff the sum of forty dollars and thirty four cents, with interest and Cost of suit.

         William J. Rylander, foreman

Bennedict & Wetmore }
  vs   } Assumpsit
Wm S. Hartsfield & C° }

We, the Jury, find for the Plaintiff the sum of thirteen hundred and fifty one dollars & twenty seven cents, with interest & Cost of suit.

         William J. Rylander, foreman

[233]   Wednesday 17th April 1839

William B. Davis }
    vs   } Debt
H. Mims & C°   }

We Confess Judgment to the Plaintiffs the sum of Sixty six dollars and twenty nine cents, with interest and Cost.

                                          J. N. & J. M. Bethune, Defts Attys

John Schley   }
    vs   } Assumpsit
George C. Hodges }

We, the Jury, find for the ~~defendant~~ Plaintiff the sum of five hundred and forty four dollars and twenty cents with interest and Cost of suit.

                                          William J. Rylander, foreman

John Schley   }
    vs   } Assumpsit
George C. Hodges }

We, the Jury, find for the Plaintiff the sum of four hundred dollars, with interest & cost of suit.

                                          William J. Rylander, foreman

Bennedict & Wetmore }
    vs   } Assumpsit
Wm & W. Toney   }

We Confess Judgment to the Plaintiff for the sum of Twenty two hundred & eighty eight dollars & twenty seven cents, with interest & cost of suit.

                                          Thomas & Shivers, Defts Attys

John Doe, ex dem }
of Samuel Nickson }
vs } Ejectment And verdict for the plaintiff
Richard Roe, Casual ejector } for the premises in dispute and Cost
& Josiah Evans, casual Ejector } of Suit

The defendant, being dissatisfied with the verdict of the Jury rendered in the above cause and having paid all Cost and demanded an Appeal, brings Eli B. W. Spivey and tenders him as his Security. And they, the said Josiah Evans and Eli B. W. Spivey, acknowledge them Selves Jointly & Severally bound to Samuel Nickson for the payment of the eventual condemnation money in said Cause. In Testimony whereof, they have hereunto Set their hands and Seals this 17th day of April 1839.

            Josiah Evans
            Eli B. W. Spivey

[234]

V. P. Rockquemore }
   vs   } Assumpsit   Term 1839
John Canty   }

We consent that the within Copy Declaration be established in lieu of the lost Original and that all entries thereon are waived and Service admitted, all exceptions to pleadings are also waived as well as also all exceptions to the entry of Appeal, want of Appeal bond &c, the case being admitted to be regularly on the Appeal, no exceptions to be taken.

         Colquitt, Holt, & Echols, Defts Attys
         Campbell, McDougald, & Watson, Plffs
         attys for D. Golightly

On motion ordered that the within Copy Declaration be established in lieu of the lost Original.

George Field }
   vs   } Assumpsit
Seaborn Jones }

~~We~~ I Confess Judgment to the Plaintiff for the sum of Seventeen hundred and eighty eight dollars, with interest and Cost of suit and three dollars protest fee.

Seaborn Jones

Bostwick & Taylor }
     vs   } Assumpsit
T. T. Gamage & C⁰ }

We, the Jury, find for the Plaintiff the sum of three hundred and Sixty dollars Sixty four cents, with interest & Cost of suit and three dollars protest fee.

William J. Rylander, forman

Junius Jordan   }
     vs   } Assumpsit
John H. Watson, maker }
& Thomas Moore   }
endorser & Security   }

We, the Jury, find for the Plaintiff the sum of Seventy dollars, with interest & Costs.

William J. Rylander, forman

E. D. Hurlbert & C⁰   }
     vs   } Assumpsit
John Dillingham, Admtr. }

I confess Judgment to Plaintiff in the sum of two thousand five hundred and twenty six dollars & forty six, to be recovered when assetts comes into the Hands of the Administrator, with cost of suit. 18ᵗʰ April 1839

Seaborn Jones, Defts Atty

Index

—
Victoria Alexandria, 6, 152, 155
Violet, 146
William IV, 151, 153
Abbercrombie
  Anderson, 170
  Charles, 170
  James, 15, 170
Adams
  James, 241
  Thompson T., 191
Adkinson
  D., 229
Alexander, 252
  Robert, 119
  Robert B., 89, 252
Alfred
  A. F., 235, 254, 276
  Arthur Fox, 235, 254
Allen, 99, 100, 203, 246
  Henry, 249, 251, 277, 278
  John S., 283
  Lewis C., 77, 99, 272
Alling
  C., 204
Allison, 244
Allsop
  Richard, 230
Allyn
  J., 50, 269
  M., 269
  T., 269
  T. M., 50
Alston
  William H., 228, 271, 281

  Wm. H., 250
Amos
  William, 134
  Wm., 135, 140, 141, 193
Anderson
  Henry C., 31, 230, 240, 243
Andrews, 16, 251
  Josephine, 208
  Montclaiborne, 208
  Samuel R., 55, 72, 112, 228
Anthony
  Lewis, 229
Arney
  A., 230
Asher, 12, 78, 243, 246
Ashley
  Thomas, 236, 241, 244
Atkins
  Thomas B., 230
Atkinson
  William, 163, 247
Atkison
  William, 112
Atwell
  Joseph T., 113, 247
Averitt
  Solomon, 24, 72, 226, 227
Ayer, 12, 54, 133, 205, 243, 246, 247, 251, 282
  A. K., 12, 95, 158, 240, 243, 249, 251, 252
  Alpha K., 11, 39, 94, 95, 129, 133, 158, 159, 160, 241, 243, 244, 252
Bacon

William B., 271
William E., 228
Baggerly
  Archibald, 248
Bailey
  Charles, 45
  Charles C., 63
  Saml. A., 18
  Samuel A., 17, 18, 68, 70, 71, 72, 112
Baird
  John B., 45, 46, 191, 257
  Nelson, 249, 280, 281
Baker, 246
  Arthur B., 44, 52, 80
  Willis P., 8, 175
Baldwin, 203, 251, 252
  H. D., 38
  Henry D., 285
  Richard C., 101
Ball
  Green B., 209
Bandy
  E. C., 114
  Ephraim C., 162, 228, 276
Bany
  Ephraim C., 80
Barberie
  John, 169
Barden
  William Y., 229
Barker, 78, 101, 246
  G., 45, 123, 203, 246, 247, 248
  R., 45, 123, 203, 246, 247, 248
Bartlett
  Myron, 78
Bass, 23, 24, 31, 37, 38, 60, 83, 85, 97, 100, 104, 127, 171, 193, 194, 199, 241, 246, 247, 265, 266, 267, 268, 270, 273, 279
  Allen G., 13, 28, 82, 241, 274
  Charles L., 21, 22, 29, 78, 91, 102, 123, 124, 185, 209, 262, 264, 266, 270
Bates
  Asa, 21, 65, 93, 124, 128, 163, 194, 195, 226, 238
Beall, 20
  Egbert B., 44, 252
Beard
  Nelson, 280
Beatie
  William J., 136
Beattie
  W. J., 136, 138
  William J., 136
Beauchamp
  Green, 138
Becase
  John L., 230
Beck, 251
  Samuel, 230
  Stephen, 6, 8
Beckham
  A. G., 92
  Albert G., 202, 228
Bedell
  G. W. E., 103, 271
  George W. E., 158, 159, 205, 228
Beecher, 241
Bell
  John S., 236
Belyeu
  Adons H., 272
Benedict, 37
Bennedict, 82, 97, 249, 287, 288
Bennett

Micajah, 116, 162
Benning
  Henry L., 32, 105, 106, 129, 139, 141, 157, 175
Benten
  Erasmus, 250
Benton
  John, 6
Bernard
  Samuel, 201
Berrien
  J. W. M., 243, 245
Berry
  James, 229
  James H., 241
  William, 91, 242, 264
Berteau
  Felix Gregory, 244
Bethune, 118
  J. D., 126
  J. M., 10, 12, 14, 15, 19, 20, 56, 58, 64, 66, 96, 105, 110, 187, 189, 199, 207, 275, 276, 288
  J. N., 10, 12, 14, 15, 19, 20, 56, 58, 64, 66, 79, 96, 105, 110, 187, 189, 199, 207, 275, 276, 288
  James N., 13, 21, 55, 79, 125, 200, 249, 279
  Jas. N., 15
  John, Sr., 108
  Joseph D., 57, 156, 200, 208, 212
Betts
  Elisha, 250
Biggers
  A. J., 229
  B. J., 230
  H. F., 229
  Joseph, 271, 281

T. J., 77
Billups
  Elizabeth, 38, 54, 55, 248, 250, 285
  Elizabeth A., 213, 219
Bird
  Henry, 171, 249
Bishop
  James B., 92
Blackwell, 138
Blair
  James, 101, 151, 153
  William, 101, 153, 154, 155
Blake
  L., 249
  Luther, 14, 34, 44, 45, 56, 95, 137, 204, 206, 208, 248, 249, 252, 283
Bland, 47
  Elza, 47, 236
Blount
  John T., 209, 248
Bogert, 42, 53, 54, 72, 149, 187, 226, 248, 263
Bond
  John, 135
Bonner, 42, 220
  S. R., 22, 200, 211, 247, 250
  Seymore R., 87
  Seymour R., 5, 43, 75, 182, 184
Boon
  John R., 5
Booraem, 202, 203
Boren
  William E., 248
Bostwick, 38, 290
Boswell
  J. J., 258, 259, 260, 261, 262

John J., 83, 89, 99, 158, 190, 228, 258, 259, 260, 284
Boudery, 240
Boudre
  Lucian A., 22, 246
Bowdery, 240, 241
  L. A., 242
  Lucian A., 252
  Thomas J., 243, 249
Bowdre, 212, 214, 219, 241, 243
  Hays, 192
  L. A., 181
  Lucian A., 181, 201, 212, 214, 215, 216, 217, 218, 219
Bowen
  Thomas W., 134
Boykin
  James, 40, 88, 96, 99, 199, 228, 284
  Jas., 205
  Samuel, 228, 271
Boynton
  Edward, 102, 157
Bradford
  James, 280
  James A., 80, 247, 280
Bradley
  E., 48, 49, 50, 52, 103, 102, 204, 236, 246, 250
  F., 48, 49, 50, 52, 102, 103, 204, 236, 246, 250
Brander, 210
  James L., 210
Brannon
  A. F., 37, 287
  Alfred F., 58, 201
  Alfred T., 8
  Bridges, 236
  T. A., 14, 111

Thomas A., 34, 71, 111, 161, 238, 242
Thos. A., 18, 98, 202
Brazil
  William, 16
  Wm., 251
Brewster, 121
Bridgland, 103
Brinkley
  Benj. H., 202
Brittain
  Emanuel, 229
Britton
  Patrick H., 120
Broadnax
  John H., 240
  Robert E., 80, 163
Brodnax
  Jno. H., 47
Brokaw
  Isaac A., 134, 140
Brooking
  Ann H., 163
  Francis, 163
Brooks
  Martin, 117, 150, 184, 228, 251, 271, 277
Brother, 100, 112, 241
Brothers, 163
Brown, 67, 77, 100, 112, 163, 233, 241, 272, 278
  ___, 103
  Augustus J., 240
  Daniel, 5, 8
  E. A. D., 249
  E. G., 77
  Enoch G., 77, 81
  Ephraim, 201
  George A., 165

George W., 229, 271, 281
J., 138
John, 165
John U., 204, 205
Joseph T., 233, 241, 243, 282
Thomas A., 230
Thomas W., 140
William B., 199
Browning
  Perry, 157
Bryan
  Theophelus, 175
  Theophilus P., 7
  Thephilus, 201
  Thomas, 201
Bryant
  James D., 241
  Thomas, 201
Buchanan
  Revarius H. L., 88
Buchannon
  Revarius H. L., 245
Buckler, 163
  S. E., 276
  Saml. E., 103
  Samuel E., 101, 240
Buckley
  C. W., 36, 65, 122, 240, 242, 246, 247, 251, 252
Bucklu, 114
Buckner
  Lorenzo D., 78, 266, 267
Bullock
  Balock, 252
  Blalock, 229
Bunn
  Bennett, 201
Burch, 161
  Gerard, 18, 25, 32, 33, 39, 47, 55, 65, 79, 80, 81, 101, 122, 123, 148, 170, 171, 194, 197, 215, 222, 227, 234, 235, 254, 255, 257, 258, 276
Burford
  Wm. P., 98
Burges
  Joseph L., 205
Burs
  Joseph D., 243
Burton
  Jonathan, 230
  Joseph, 246
Bush, 144
Butler
  Zachariah, 271, 281
Butran, 103
Butt
  Moses, 228
Butts
  James B., 200
  James R., 240, 244, 276
  Samuel W., 230
Cairnes
  Lucy Elizabeth, 196, 206
Cairns
  William D., 196, 206
Caldwell
  Allen, 209
  M. G., 239
  Maginnis G., 73
  McGinnis G., 239
Calhoun, 23, 24, 31, 37, 38, 60, 83, 85, 97, 100, 104, 127, 171, 193, 194, 199, 241, 246, 247, 265, 266, 267, 268, 270, 273, 279
  J., 234, 235
  J. S., 28, 73, 241

James C., 208
James S., 22, 23, 36, 37, 41, 56, 77, 91, 157, 179, 182, 185, 209, 228, 234, 247, 252, 262, 264, 266, 268, 269, 271, 276, 279
Js., 262, 263, 265, 266, 267, 268, 269, 270
Camp
  Joseph T., 135
Campbell, 12, 21, 41, 47, 63, 68, 81, 114, 115, 124, 126, 131, 132, 142, 145, 150, 183, 184, 185, 190, 211, 221, 223, 226, 272, 289
  Archibald, 134, 140
  Daniel C., 249
  George, 231
  J. H., 151, 152, 154, 167, 282
  J. P. H., 144
  J. W., 184
  James H., 7, 23, 60, 126, 151, 167, 184, 272, 282
  John A., 37, 252
  John W., 149, 184
Canty
  John, 289
Carlton, 204, 205
Carnes, 10, 82, 90, 93, 162, 242, 245, 246, 247, 249
  Robert W., 90, 201, 246, 247
Carpenter, 202
Carter
  George, 185
Cartledge
  Jerre, 230
Cary, 27, 202
  Edward, 24, 31, 40, 57, 60, 78, 83, 91, 149, 180, 186, 202, 237, 242, 264, 267

  Edwd., 31, 57, 181, 264, 267
Cashan
  Lodwick R., 250
Cebra, 187
Chambers
  James M., 228, 271, 277
Chandler, 208
  Frederick W., 229
Chatfield
  George, 164
Cheatham
  Obadiah P., 209
Cheesman
  Joseph, 246
Chipley
  William S., 5, 8, 44, 148, 175, 174, 228, 271
  Wm. S., 149
Chisholm, 38, 66, 105, 113, 162, 163, 241, 242, 243, 244, 246, 247, 248, 250, 251
  Malcom A., 242
  Murdock, 242
Church
  David, 252
  S. P., 10, 247
Clapp, 208
  Benj. W., 103
  Benjamin W., 243
Clark, 202, 203, 243, 248, 251
  Cullen, 230
  John C. F., 241
  Michael N., 215
  Thomas J., 230
  William, 7, 175, 228
Clarke
  M. N., 19
  Michael N., 54, 98, 202, 216, 286
  William, 5

Clarkson
  Shotwell B., 250
Clifton, 235
Cobb, 240
Code, 118, 142, 143, 144, 145, 146, 147, 203, 204
  John, 118, 142, 144, 148
Cole, 67, 163
Coleman
  Joseph, 204
Colemon
  Benjamin F., 228
Colfax
  ___, 103
Collins, 38, 66, 105, 113, 162, 163, 239, 241, 242, 243, 244, 246, 247, 248, 250, 251
  Jacobus T. S., 220
  Timothy, 22, 23, 42, 45, 80, 100, 101, 124, 148, 179, 229, 233, 240, 243, 244, 246, 248, 250
Colquit, 75, 112, 113, 121
  Walter T., 75
Colquitt, 27, 48, 59, 81, 104, 106, 109, 122, 163, 187, 204, 211, 238, 239, 273, 289
  John H., 5, 8
  John T., 252
  Walter T., 9, 14, 184, 187, 201
Colson
  Wm. W., 251
Cook
  Levi, 112, 247
  Marcus, 228
Cooke
  James, 229
Cooper
  George, 28
  John, 242

Corley
  Elijah, 42, 63, 74, 148, 160, 202, 204, 234, 235
  John C., 120
Corlius, 252
Corry
  James, 270
Cosby
  B. A., 22
Cowart
  John, Jr., 38, 103
Cowdery
  Lester L., 269
Cox
  Darias, 243, 271
  Darius, 228
  J., 103
  T., 103
Craft
  J. T., 204
  W. E., 204
Crane, 82, 249
  Elias B., 14, 150, 151, 201
Crawford, 15, 19, 38, 103, 270
  Daniel, 229
  Daniel C., 93
Crews
  R. J., 160
  William, 79
Crogan
  Patrick, 230
Cropp
  Benjamin, 249
Crowell
  Jno., 214
  John, 157
Culpepper
  Willson, 5, 8
Cumming, 187

Cunningham, 108
   Jacob, 82, 141, 174
Cushman, 77
   D. A., 233, 242, 272, 278
Dancer
   Madison, 134, 231
Daniel, 240
   James K., 119, 192, 245, 248
Davidson
   J., 59
   Joseph, 36, 40, 59, 85, 115, 119, 155, 163, 201, 205, 240, 242, 243, 245, 247, 249, 250, 251
Davie
   Jonathan, 242
Davies
   L. J., 277
   Lewis J., 201, 252
Davis, 79, 125
   A. B., 114
   Allen, 39, 123
   Arthur B., 79, 125, 161, 162, 240, 247
   Daniel, 20
   John E., 45, 67, 89, 101, 239, 250
   L. J., 102, 249
   Lewis J., 12
   Price, 6, 8, 58, 117
   Thomas, 204, 228
   William B., 288
Dawson, 79, 141, 203, 205, 240, 252
Day, 27, 202
   John, 149
De Graffenried
   E. L., 116, 241, 243, 257
   Edwin L., 191, 257
De Graffinried
   Edwin L., 155, 235, 237

DeGiles, 243
DeGilse, 244
Dekeman, 109
Delany
   Edward, 34
   Howell, 230
Delony
   Edward, 17, 20, 100, 110, 193, 228, 271
Dennard
   John C., 230
Dennison, 252
Densler
   Henry L., 228
Dent
   M. L., 65
   Michael L., 64
Dewell
   Nancy, 202
Dickerson
   John, 251
Dikeman, 38
Dikerman, 245
Dill
   Augustus A., 236
Dillingham
   G. W., 237
   Geo. W., 195
   George W., 64, 195, 196, 206, 236
   John, 43, 64, 100, 167, 195, 203, 206, 229, 236, 237, 241, 244, 246, 247, 251, 290
   John G., 251
   Lucy, 195
   Lucy E., 196
   Lucy Elizabeth, 195, 206
Dimmock, 77, 100, 278
Dimock, 233, 241, 272

Dodge
　Daniel K., 206
Doe
　John, 39, 48, 49, 123, 282, 289
Dolliver, 103
Doremus, 115, 162, 247
Dougherty
　William, 32, 33, 238, 239
Dowdle
　Lewis, 15, 16, 251
　Lewis J., 40
Dozier
　Prior, 228
Duncan, 250
　F., 103
　John, 247
　John S., 228
Dunlap
　John G., 200, 233
Dunn
　Jerre, 230
Eagan
　William J., 231
Echols, 27, 48, 59, 75, 81, 104, 106, 109, 112, 113, 118, 121, 122, 187, 211, 238, 239, 273, 289
　Absalom, 35, 76
Eckert
　Thos., 242
Ector
　Wiley B., 204
Edwards
　Sterling, 27, 247
Eley
　Seaborn, 6, 8, 117, 120, 205
Elijah
　Wm., 137
Ellis
　Benjamin F., 165, 166, 167, 170

Devenport, 134, 140
　William, 165, 166, 167, 170
Ely
　Seaborn, 58, 106, 108, 240, 241
English
　John, 55, 248
Evans, 118, 144, 145
　E., 231
　Josiah, 282, 289
　M., 22, 23, 37, 73, 78, 83, 93, 102, 178, 179, 182, 248, 262, 263, 265, 267, 268, 270, 286
　Mathew R., 193
　Matt R., 24, 45, 77, 83, 127, 194, 257, 258, 265, 270
　Matthew R., 60, 186, 189
　T., 22, 23, 37, 73, 78, 83, 93, 102, 178, 179, 182, 248, 262, 263, 265, 267, 268, 270, 286
　Tho. C., 7, 89, 257, 258, 262, 270
　Thomas C., 21, 22, 46, 60, 77, 83, 87, 88, 125, 127, 186, 189, 192, 208, 245, 248, 257, 258, 261, 265, 275
　Thos. C., 24, 80, 128, 205, 276
Ezekel
　Emanuel, 7
Ezekiel
　E., 205
　Emanuel, 5, 55, 174, 175, 251
Fairchild
　Frederick A., 226
Fairchilds
　F. A., 205
Falconar, 95
Falconer
　A. H., 40
　Abraham H., 237

Farmer
  Marcellus, 100
Favors
  Henry, 228
Fellows, 11, 103, 202, 251
Fetner
  James S., 230
Field
  George, 37, 38, 105, 215, 216, 217, 250, 286, 289
Fleming
  James, 135
  Thomas, 54, 249, 250
Flemming
  James, 230
Flewellen
  Eaton, 201, 251
Flin
  John, 230
Flournoy
  John M., 251
  Samuel W., 228
Fogle, 12, 235, 236, 243, 250, 251, 281
  Jacob, 16, 201, 243, 246, 250
Fontaine, 20, 125, 243, 245, 247, 248, 249, 250, 251, 275, 284
  Jno., 154
  John, 17, 37, 70, 152, 228, 241
Forbes, 226, 248
Ford
  Gardner, 40
Fort, 36
  Benj., 244
  William, 73, 77
  Wm., 73
Fortson
  Tavner W., 185

Foster, 12, 235, 236, 243, 250, 251, 281
  N. P., 231
  T. F., 66, 168, 210
  Thomas F., 25, 131
  Whitly, 239
  William, 241
Fowl, 66, 163
Fowle, 247
Fox, 107, 108, 117, 144
  John, 61, 104, 106, 107, 108, 116, 129, 134, 135, 150, 156
Freal
  Hugh, 64
Fuller, 190
  Hiram, 5, 7, 67, 162, 175, 203, 241, 247
  Spivy, 281
Funderburk
  Jacob, 125, 203
Furgerson
  Aaron, 120
Gaither
  Eli E., 83
Gaithwaite, 246, 249
Gallaghar, 210
  Charles H., 210
Gamage
  T. T., 290
Gambril
  Launcelot, 275
Gammage
  T. T., 38, 204
Gardin, 103
Garland, 167
  William A., 43, 167, 168
Garrett, 180
  Henry B., 135
  Moses, 244

Gathwaite, 100
George
  John, 103
Gibson
  Felix, 170
Gilbert
  A., 205
  Abraham, 11
Glen, 118, 119, 150
  Dow, 150
  Lorenzo Dow, 116, 117, 150, 156
Glenn, 107, 117, 118, 119
  Dow, 107
  James E., Jr., 244
  James U., 287
  James W., 37, 250
  Lorenzo Dow, 26, 61, 105, 106, 117, 139
Godwin
  John, 81
  Wells, 81
Gold
  Theodore S., 244
  Thomas R., 29
Goldsmith
  E., 78
  Samuel, 78
Goldstein, 219
Golightly
  D., 25, 79, 101, 119, 121, 168, 171, 289
  David, 25, 78, 101, 171
Golstein, 213
  David, 251
Gordon
  T. G., 252
  Thomas G., 13, 22, 28, 58, 97, 113, 123, 179, 193, 194, 269
  Thos. G., 29, 41, 56, 58, 85, 91, 92, 104, 124, 179, 180, 182, 185, 189, 269, 276, 279
Gordy
  William, 8, 58
  Willson, 6, 8
Gorman, 243, 244
  Alexander, 243
  James, 249
Gould
  Thomas R., 252, 253
  William T., 115, 162, 247
Grace
  Bird, 209
Graham
  James, 6, 7
Granberry
  George, 204
Grant, 112, 163, 187, 204
  Augustus L., 240
  Mary P., 25, 131
  Thomas, 25, 58
Grantland
  Seaton, 194
Gray
  Affa Maria, 130
  B. M., 205
  Benoni, 57
  Hillery, 230
  Richard, 230
Greaves, 133
Green
  J. B., 22, 190, 245
  Joseph B., 120, 182, 232
  Rhodam A., 228, 271
  William, 250
Greenway, 38, 106
Greenwood, 25, 58, 240

E. S., 10, 20, 38, 131, 228, 240, 244
Eldridge S., 109
James D., 242, 247
Thomas B., 199, 284
Greer
  George, 134, 140
  Richard, 229, 271, 281
Gregory
  Elliott W., 79, 122, 150, 238
Grieve, 34, 110
Griffin, 202
  Andrew B., 64
Grimes, 246
  Josiah, 228
Grosvener
  S., 190
Grumman, 244
Guedron
  John B., 31, 248, 249, 250, 252
Guerry, 200
  J. M., 58, 258, 260
  Jacob M., 29, 31, 34, 56, 84, 89, 110, 186, 243, 244, 247, 249, 250, 252, 258, 260
  Peter V., Sr., 22, 182
  William, 229
Guyard, 167, 284, 286
  Robert P., 43, 167, 168
Habermann
  H., 177
  H. C. A., 176
  Henry Charles, 175
  Henry Charles Adolphus, 175, 176
Halcomb, 246, 251
Hall, 58, 85, 86, 87, 90, 92, 93, 95, 97, 184, 196, 204, 239, 249, 265, 267

Fewtrall, 201, 251
Harvey, 81
Harvy, 196, 197
Henry, 140, 156, 242
Hervy, 231
Matthew, 135
Thomas H., 66, 115, 163, 247
Thos. H., 163
Hallenbeck, 180
  Garret, 34, 249
  Garrett, 56, 87, 88, 110
Hamilton, 67, 163, 240, 252
  Lemuel H., 38, 109, 110
Hamlin, 242
Hammock
  Joseph, 229
Hammond
  William, 230
Hamner
  Horton W., 201
Hand, 29, 53, 56, 252
  J. W., 204
  Joel W., 236
  Tho. J., 252
  Thomas J., 202, 251, 276
  Thos. J., 36
Hannay, 239
Hardie
  John, 201
Hardin, 252
  Edward J., 231, 239, 241, 244
Hargrave
  Sophia W., 139, 140
  William D., 139, 140
Hargraves
  George, 29, 199, 207, 208, 243, 245, 251, 252, 268
  George, Jr., 228, 271
  William D., 249

Wm. D., 139, 140
Hargrove
  Wm. D., 242
Hargroves
  William D., 36
Harned
  Michael, 38, 109
Harp
  John L., 228
Harper, 95, 97, 249
  William H., 228
  Wm. H., 19, 203, 281
Harrial
  James, 246
Harriel
  James, 251
Harril
  James, 8
Harris, 11, 100
  James, 230
  James W., 200
  Little Berry, 230, 281
  Wiley, 98, 99
Hart, 250
Hartsfield
  William S., 89, 94, 96, 97, 115, 162, 202, 239, 246
  Wm. S., 37, 93, 204, 205, 247, 249, 251, 287
Harvell, 117
  West, 107, 117
  Western, 141, 142, 144
Harvey
  Thomas, 64
Harvil, 108, 132
  Western, 132
  William, 132
Harvill, 133
  West, 132

Western, 135
Harwell, 107, 143, 144, 145, 146, 147, 148
  W., 144
  Western, 61, 62, 105, 106, 116, 134, 135, 139, 140, 141, 142, 145, 146, 148, 150, 156, 194
  Weston, 129, 143
  William, 61, 105, 120, 129, 134, 135
  Wm. H., 107
Harwells
  Western, 142
Hasting
  B., 141
  W. B., 141
Hastings
  B., 79
  William B., 79
Havil
  William, 132
Hawkins
  Benj., 137
Hawley, 212
  Benj., 240
  Hezekiah, 212, 249, 277
Hawly
  Hezekiah, 209
Hawthorn, 72, 149
Hay
  Jossas, 229
Haynes
  Nathan, 230
  William, 230
  Wm. P., 163
Haytt, 103
Hayward
  Augustus, 5, 7, 93, 175, 249
Hazleton

Pinkney, 150
Head
  Richard, 241
Heard, 240
  George W., 246
Heine, 78, 202, 213, 219, 243, 244, 247, 272
  A. L., 54, 113, 115, 231, 244, 247, 248, 252, 259
  Adolphus L., 78, 103, 113, 163, 209, 239, 242, 244
Hemphill
  Samuel, 229, 271, 281
Henley
  Slaton, 241
Henly
  Slaton, 13, 16, 205, 249
  Slayton, 135
Henry, 38, 106
  Thomas, 69
Hepburn
  B., 222, 265
  Burton, 30, 43, 48, 86, 90, 91, 139, 149, 189, 191, 206, 208, 209, 221, 222, 242, 248, 251, 252, 262, 265, 283, 284
Herndon
  J. H., 229
Herron
  S. J., 237
  Seaborn J., 205, 235, 236, 239, 240, 243
Heyer, 246
Hiatt
  Hannah, 126
Hickey
  James, 228
Hickok, 244
Higdon

Robert, 5, 8
Higginson, 118
  Marks, 118
Hight
  Charles H., 230
Hightower
  Daniel, 98, 245, 252
Hill, 79, 141, 200, 203, 205, 240, 252
  Abner, 8, 58, 106, 108
  Ed, 200
  Edd., 200
  Hampton W., 10, 246
  Henry K., 5, 8, 145, 175, 228
  Jas. J., 19
  Wade, 46
Hines
  Richard K., 276
Hitchcock
  J. P., 284
  James, 100
  Jesse P., 42, 64, 66, 284
  John, 246
  John G., 100
  Mathew M., 226
  Matthew M., 248
Hodge
  George C., 38
Hodges
  George C., 288
Hoell
  Nathaniel W., 54
Hoffman, 248
  John B., 226, 246
  Michael, 54, 248
Hogg, 12, 54, 205, 243, 246, 247, 251, 282
  James V., 241
  Jas. V., 55

Holcomb, 8
Holland
  James, 202
  James C., 66, 240
  William, 261
  Wm. C., 163
Holmes
  Julius, 239, 240
Holstead
  W. S., 204
  William S., 163
Holt, 27, 48, 59, 75, 81, 104, 106, 109, 112, 113, 121, 122, 133, 187, 211, 238, 239, 273, 289
  Hines, Jr., 136
  Thads. G., 77, 78
Hooper
  R., 85, 210
  Richard, 15, 22, 36, 84, 85, 180, 241
  Samuel, 14
Hopkins, 202
  James M., 230
Horton
  H. B., 205
  Henry B., 55
Houghton
  James K., 236
How
  Calvin, 167
  Calvin W., 167
  Fisher, 167
Howard, 39, 67, 130, 163, 165, 183, 223
  Augustus, 19, 54, 240, 263
  Benj., 204
  Benjamin, 42, 63, 74, 148, 202
  C., 230
  Claiborn, 202
  George, 202
  James W., 84
  John H., 149
  John T., 228
  Nicholas, 102, 205, 241, 275
  Nicholas L., 55, 67, 112, 283
  T. B., 53
  Thacker B., 24, 180
  Theobald, 9, 23, 28, 99, 126, 184, 200, 223, 224, 248
  Thomas, 62, 139, 140, 141
Howell, 100
  Elias, 6, 8
  Elias D., 58
  John D., 12, 23, 44, 60, 100, 101, 126, 246, 250
  Maberry, 61, 129, 134, 135, 142, 143, 145, 146, 194
  N. W., 241, 243, 249
  Nathaniel W., 161
  William, 143
Howland
  John, 205
Hoxey
  Thomas, 5, 7, 17, 21, 23, 68, 71, 126, 175, 177, 236
Hoyt, 100, 101, 276
Hudson
  Cicero D., 41
  David, 149
  Jonathan A., 229, 281
Hughes
  Joseph D., 243
Hungerford, 66
  D., 11, 28, 38, 50, 92, 105, 122, 202, 250, 251, 255, 256, 269
  Dana, 22, 23, 66, 79, 86, 130, 163, 179, 181, 182
Hunt

Anderson, 5, 7, 175
  Thomas, 41
  Thos., 41
Hunter
  Henry M., 240
Hurd, 252
  Homer, 27
Hurlbert
  E. D., 290
Hurst
  Henry, 229
Hyatt, 202
Hyde, 244
Ingersol
  Stephen M., 233
Ingersoll
  Stephen M., 194, 200
Ingoldsby, 94, 95, 97, 242
Insler, 247
Irwin, 58
Iverson, 200, 212, 214, 215, 216, 218, 219
  A., 214, 258, 259, 261
  Alfred, 9, 12, 46, 47, 57, 58, 60, 89, 151, 154, 165, 170, 183, 214, 222, 258, 259, 260, 261, 283
  B. V., 58, 89, 138, 259, 260, 261
  Benj. V., 57, 259
  Benjamin V., 89, 100, 186, 222, 258, 261, 283
  J. H., 248
  James H., 57, 212, 213, 214, 215, 216, 217, 218, 242, 243, 249
  Jas. H., 249
  Robert, 260
Ivey
  Magirt, 54, 129, 130
Jackson

  J. P., 19, 54, 65, 110
  James, 235, 254, 255
  Jonathan P., 5, 7, 34, 110, 163, 175, 208, 236, 243
  S. M., 284
  Sam M., 284
  Samuel, 48, 49
  Samuel M., 240, 242
  William N., 277
Jacobi, 59, 78, 113, 163, 202, 240, 241, 243, 244, 247, 251, 272
  John C., 208, 242, 244, 245, 250
Jacobus, 100, 246, 249
James, 133, 243
  Thomas, 98, 133, 243, 245, 252
  Thos., 99
Jaques, 247
  John B., 232
Jenkins
  John H., 230
Jepson
  Benjamin, 87, 88, 229
  Francis, 8, 13, 15, 54, 58, 87, 88, 106, 107, 117, 120, 207, 248
  Lemuel, 21, 30, 55, 65, 163, 197, 198, 251
  Thomas, 52
Jernigan
  James, 6, 8, 58, 116
Jeter
  William L., 5, 175
  Wm. L., 8
Johns
  Jesse B., 246
Johnson, 100, 241, 246
  Arthur, 120
  Caswell, 89, 226, 240, 241, 243, 251
  Creswell, 248

Daniel, 226, 248
Jacob, 6, 8, 58
Jacob M., 38, 109, 229, 240, 242, 256
John, 7, 18, 112, 175, 228
Johnston
  John, 5
Johson
  John, 72
Jones, 42, 220
  Amasa A., 236
  Andrew P., 21
  George W., 236
  J. H., 248
  J. R., 32, 33
  James H., 236, 249
  James H., Jr., 32, 35, 201, 231, 236, 243, 246, 250
  James R., 32, 33, 36, 40, 239
  James, Jr., 243
  Jas. H., 203
  John, 121, 250
  John K., 230
  Morgan, 14, 46, 85
  Moses, 235
  Randal, 32
  Richard, 22, 43, 80, 244
  Richd., 182
  S., 276
  Seaborn, 19, 37, 42, 45, 46, 53, 54, 59, 63, 72, 73, 74, 78, 90, 91, 95, 118, 186, 187, 188, 199, 241, 242, 262, 264, 265, 267, 279, 286, 289, 290
  Wiley E., 85, 205, 245
Jordan, 284, 286
  Charles N., 44, 52
  John D., 22, 27, 44, 45, 175, 182, 229

Junius, 290
Jordon
  John D., 7
Kagan, 163
Keeler, 41
Kellogg
  Edward, 64, 66, 67, 114, 162, 163, 232, 233, 243, 247, 248
Kellum
  E. J., 229
Kelly
  Edmund, 5
  Edward, 8
Kemp
  James, 271, 281
Kendall
  Henry, 251, 281
  Thomas, 271, 281
  Thomas H., 229
Kenedy, 149
Kennedy, 235
Kenney
  Benjamin G., 111
Kenny
  Benjamin G., 34
Kensey, 14
Kent
  James, 229
Killgore
  Joseph T., 237
Kimbrough, 95
King
  Charles, 5, 7
  Henry, 21, 80, 207, 231, 244, 251
Kingsland, 130
  Richard, 67, 184
Kinney
  B. G., 111
Kirk

William, 77, 81, 228
Kirkpatrick
  James, 229
Kirksey
  James, 58
Kirlin
  James, 29, 30, 55, 56, 100, 228, 249, 252, 266
Kirtland
  B. B., 73, 239
Kneeland, 42, 53, 54, 187, 263
Knight
  George, 239, 241
Kopman
  William, 203
Lamar
  Phillip, 49
Lamb
  Green E., 230
  Jacob, 231
Lampkin
  Sampson L., 250
Landrum
  James M., 228, 248
Landsberg
  Alfred, 240, 244, 245
Langford
  Henry N., 240
Lanier
  Sampson, 236
Lasseter
  John F., 230
Laurence
  Augustus G., 230
Lawhon
  Allen, 236, 251
  Henry Allen, 251
  Quincey A., 241
Lawrence, 252

Aug. G., 252
Augustus G., 242, 252
Leavitt
  J. W., 27, 131, 188
  R., 27, 131, 188
Lee
  Bartlett, 231
  Burrell, 230
Leonard
  James C., 165, 166, 167, 170
Lestarget
  Henry L., 201
Lestarjett
  Henry L., 244, 248, 251
Levi
  Anthony, 246, 249
Levie
  Anthony, 52, 242, 250, 251
Levingston, 97
Levison
  Abraham, 160, 271
Lewis, 143, 144, 145, 148
  Felix, 42
  J. L., 23, 64
  Jno. S., 227
  John, 145, 148
  John L., 65, 127, 211, 258, 268, 273, 279
  John Langdon, 279
  John S., 227
  Nicholas, 174
  Nicholas M., 37, 246
  Stephen, 145, 147
  Ulysses, 239
  Wiley, 55
  William H., 174, 226
  Wm. H., 242
Liggon
  Alexander, 228

William, 271
Lively, 28, 38, 86, 255, 256, 272
  Geo. W., 245
  George W., 243
  Wm. T., 185
Livingston, 95, 249
Livly, 256
Lloyd, 223, 224
  Jno. R., 80
  John R., 48, 54, 80, 114, 162, 200, 201, 220, 221, 223, 224, 246, 247, 248, 249, 250, 251, 252
Locke
  John, 184, 186, 187, 241, 242
Lockhart
  David, 231
Lockwood, 240
Loften
  Daniel, 251
Loftin
  Daniel, 201
Logan
  John, 34, 42, 111, 200
Loisie
  Francis A., 250
Lord
  Seth, 137, 138
Lott, 236
Love
  John H., 194, 240, 242, 256
  Seth, 48
Lovejoy
  William H., 74, 246
Loyd
  John R., 100
Lucas
  B. V., 204
  John H., 204

Luckie
  Samuel, 92
  William F., 228, 271
Ludlum, 242
  Nicholas, 103
Lycugus, 173
Lyon, 94
Lyons, 145
  James R., 34, 35, 82, 141
Lytle
  John, 229
  Samuel, 21, 35, 274
M.
  William P., 9
Mackenzie
  Kenith, 128
Maclay, 78
Maddin
  D., 230
Maitland, 149
  Robert, 287
Malone, 210
  B. F., 203
  Benjamin F., 203
  W. P., 128, 181
  William P., 5, 17, 18, 21, 68, 69, 71, 84, 101, 128, 131, 148, 175, 181, 210, 238
  Wm. P., 8, 84, 148
Maltby, 100, 246
Man
  David, 79
Mandell
  Ephraim, 201, 250
Mangham
  John C., 241, 282
Manly
  Hiram, 248
  Richard, 231

Mann
  Henry, 39, 123
  Jesse, 79, 251, 252
Manning, 100, 101, 276
Marler
  George C., 244
Marshall, 57, 259
  A. G., 203
Martin
  Geo. W., 122
  George W., 122
  John, 170
Mason
  Henry L., 204
Massy
  B., 229
Mathews
  Noel, 190, 274
Mathewson
  Bernard, 100
Matthews
  H., 284
  Henry, 13, 32, 35, 246, 249, 251
  Noel, 204
Matthewson
  Bernard, 192, 193, 204, 232
McAlpin
  Robert, 253
McBride
  William, 14
McBurney, 202
McCarthy
  Thomas, 244
McCarty
  Thomas, 283
McClary, 12, 243, 246
McColl
  John, 236
McCook
  Joshua R., 149
McCoy
  Henry G., 285
  Jeremiah, 7, 97, 175, 252
  Reuben H., 285
McCrary, 28, 38, 86, 204, 255, 256
  P. R., 97, 256
  Robert, 255, 256
  Timothy G., 24, 63
McCurdy
  John, 134
  William, 134, 140
McDaniel
  Benj. F., 239, 240
  Benjamin F., 240, 241, 244
  H. H., 230
McDougald, 12, 21, 41, 47, 63, 68, 81, 114, 115, 124, 126, 131, 132, 150, 183, 184, 185, 190, 211, 221, 223, 226, 272, 289
  A., 200, 211
  Alexander, 8, 75
  D., 43, 103, 136, 137
  Daniel, 24, 34, 43, 44, 102, 126, 183, 244
McDuffy
  John, 231
McGebony
  James C., 74
McGee
  Ann, 242
  John, 252
  William, 37, 201, 229, 232, 240, 241, 245, 247, 248
  Wm., 244, 252
McGibbony
  James C., 271
McGibony
  James C., 281

McGilory
  James C., 246
McGinty
  Thomas, 228, 271
McGough
  Jno., 11, 12, 13, 14, 15, 16, 19, 20, 21, 25, 26, 27, 28, 29, 30, 31, 32, 35, 36, 40, 41, 46, 48, 49, 50, 51, 52, 53, 55, 56, 62, 63, 72, 73, 74, 75, 86, 98, 103, 105, 108, 109, 110, 114, 115, 116, 117, 119, 120, 121, 123, 124, 126, 127, 128, 130, 131, 135, 177, 178, 179, 184, 185, 186, 188, 189, 190, 191, 192, 193, 238
  John, 5, 8, 9, 10, 14, 16, 39, 75, 106, 107, 117, 120, 135, 177, 179
McIntosh, 224
McKee, 97, 201
McKeen
  Alfred, 239
  James, 239
  Thomas C., 13, 22, 94, 112, 161, 163, 195, 238, 242, 244, 247, 251, 252, 253
  Thoms. C., 238
  Thos. C., 94
  Van L., 195, 238
  William P., 32, 33, 36, 58, 59
  Wm. P., 9, 32, 33, 90
McKenzie
  Kenneth, 24
  Kennith, 252
McKim, 15, 19, 38, 103, 270
McKinny
  Simeon, 84
McKinstry
  E., 244
McKinzie, 138
  Kenith, 128, 275
McKisson, 38, 104, 109
McKnight, 187, 193, 248
McLain
  Peter, 208
McLaren
  Peter, 204
McLarin
  Peter, 100
McLary
  T. C., 229
McMillan
  William J., 244, 249
  Wm. J., 247, 250
McMullin
  William J., 54
McMurphy
  Cullen, 236
McMurran
  John, 65
McMurren
  John, 64
McNair
  Neill, 285
McNeal
  D., 230
McNorton
  James T., 203
McQueen
  Robert, 53, 149, 239, 249, 250
Measels
  David, 75, 102
Meidzilski, 59
Merz
  John, 168, 169
Metcalf
  V. D., 230

Vernon D., 134, 141
Middlebrook
  G. L., 243
  George vL., 13
Middlebrooks
  Hiram, 235
Miedzielski, 113, 240, 241, 244, 247, 251
  Paulin, 81, 103, 140, 239, 240, 242, 243, 244
Miedzilski, 163
  Paulin, 80
Miers, 212, 214, 216, 218
Miller
  T. V., 68, 69, 71, 72, 112
  Thomas V., 8, 88, 106, 107, 117, 120, 135
  Thos. V., 58, 59, 81, 82, 83, 84, 86, 87, 88, 89, 90, 91, 92, 93, 94, 95, 96, 97, 98, 99, 125, 128, 180, 182, 183
Millikin
  H. B., 236, 282
Mills, 38, 109, 245
  Colbumbus C., 206
  Columbus, 200, 240
  Rufus K., 54, 252
  William O., 250
Mims, 190
  A., 246
  A. S., 68
  Allen, 42
  Allen J., 38, 103, 246
  C. E., 79, 122, 204
  Charles E., 122, 150, 201, 238
  H., 17, 18, 19, 63, 69, 71, 79, 88, 96, 122, 130, 131, 189, 201, 204, 251, 288

  Henry, 5, 8, 18, 23, 42, 69, 71, 102, 122, 127, 150, 175, 238
Mitchell, 259
  Bird B., 6, 54, 58, 106, 107, 117, 236, 240, 251
  Isaac, 12, 17, 18, 22, 25, 38, 58, 64, 71, 110, 124, 162, 189, 201
  James, 68
  James H., 259
  James M., 31
  John, 80
  R. G., 251
  Robert G., 80
  William H., 70
  Wm. H., 18
Moffett
  Henry, 279
Moffit
  Henry, 74
Moffitt
  Henry, 98, 99
Monk
  James, 230
Monroe
  James, 277
  Patrick, 209
Montross, 100
Moody, 240
Mooney
  Isaac, 47
Moore, 23, 24, 38, 108, 163, 164, 178, 203, 223, 239, 242, 243, 244, 246, 247, 248
  Chesley, 229
  James S., 220, 223, 224, 226, 245
  Robert, 120
  Thomas, 26, 161, 242, 243, 290
  William C., 230
Moorefield

Joseph, 135
Morgan, 78, 101, 246
  John, 138
  John W., 229
  W. M., 229
Morris
  Jacob, 230
  R. W., 205
  Richard W., 40, 226
  Thomas, 87
  Thos., 87
  William C., 6
Morton
  L. C., 244
Moses, 85, 86, 87, 90, 92, 93, 95, 97, 184, 204, 239, 249, 265, 267
  Jacob J., 228
Moss
  Alexander, 37, 287
  E. G. A., 203
Motley
  Thomas, 6, 8, 39, 58, 106, 107, 117, 120, 123
Moy
  Hardy, 11
Mulford
  John G., 11, 38, 109, 112, 123, 187, 202, 232, 243, 245, 246, 247, 248
Murphy
  John, 230
Murray, 210
  Hamilton, 210
  P. J., 137
  Patrick J., 121, 250
Myers, 215, 218, 219
  David R., 204
  George, 233
Myrick

John T., 246
  Wm., 252
Neal
  James, 260
Nelms, 59, 125, 242, 251
  William, 29, 121, 244, 245, 253
Nelson, 204, 205
  Charles, 201
Nichols, 242
  William W., 242, 246
  Wm. W., 51, 242, 244, 246, 249, 252
Nickolson
  John, 230
Nickson
  Samuel, 289
Niles
  J. T., 78, 101, 243, 244, 246
  Jona., 250
Nisbet
  F. A., 276
  Franklin A., 276
Nix
  Thomas, 229, 271, 281
Nixon, 115, 162, 247
  Saml., 282
Norman
  James S., 34, 52, 111
  Jas. S., 249
Normon
  James S., 50
Norris
  Geo. A., 5
  George A., 8, 94, 175
  William, 5
North, 100, 101, 276
Norton, 203, 259
  E. S., 242, 243

Elisha S., 21, 36, 80, 201, 208, 236, 239
Nuckolls, 100, 241
  George B., 85
Nuckols, 100
  George B., 228
Nutt
  John, 235, 248, 250
Odom, 119, 144, 145, 150
  Aaron, 228
  Abraham, 119, 150
  Avery, 61, 62, 129, 134, 135, 139, 140, 141, 142, 144, 147, 194
  John, 143, 145, 230
Odum
  Dempsey, 230
  Hubbard, 244
Olcot, 104, 109
Olcott, 38, 246
Orman
  Thomas, 241
Osborn
  Wm. C., 98, 99
Osteen
  Jessee, 271, 281
Owen
  Henry, 229
Owens
  An, 87
  Ann, 205
  Jno., 205
  John, 88
  John J., 99
  Richard A., 96
  William, 203, 236
Ozment
  Thomas B., 26
Pace

William, Jr., 14, 44
Wm., Jr., 44
Packer, 11, 248
Painter, 45, 89, 250
  Jefferson, 246
Parish, 259
Parker
  Jeremiah, 229
  Zephaniah, 120
  Zepheniah, 5, 8, 106, 107
Parks, 107, 117
Parmer
  John, 230
Parrish, 57
Patrick
  John M., 51, 241, 243, 249
  John M., Jr., 51, 246
  John M., Sr., 246
  William, 251
Patterson
  John, 135
  R. C., 229
  Robert C., 271, 281
Pattillo
  James, 228
Patton
  Alexander E., 235
Paul
  Jacob D., 15, 245
Peabody, 143
  C. A., 82, 100, 101, 114, 162, 202, 235, 236, 246, 248, 249, 251, 252
  Charles A., 203, 233
  G. H., 82, 100, 101, 114, 162, 202, 235, 236, 246, 248, 249, 251, 252
  George H., 233
  J. B., 250

Jno. B., 67, 183
John B., 23, 66, 82, 163, 183, 209, 246, 247, 248, 249, 250, 254, 255, 276
William, 77
Wm., 77
Peacock
　Samuel E., 163, 247
Peal
　James, 231
Pearry
　Michael W., 35
Peck, 236
Perkins, 202
Perry, 133
　Hamilton, 107, 117, 132, 211
　M. W., 158
　Michael W., 76, 158, 160
Peteet
　Simeon, 119, 245
Peters
　Daniel, 235
Phelps, 203, 251, 252
　H. C., 23, 62, 241, 244, 245
　Henry C., 15, 16, 88, 228, 251
　Joseph, 5, 8, 106, 107
Phillups
　Joseph, 230
Pickett
　John, 57
　William, 229
Pinhorn, 239
　Geo. W., 9
　George W., 10
Pitman
　Noah, 203, 251
Pitts
　Hannah S., 233
Plant

J. C., 248, 249
Plott
　Hiram B., 135
Pollock
　John, 229
Pomroy
　Chancey, 139
Pool, 28, 38, 86, 204, 255, 256, 272
　Mathew H., 117
　Matthew H., 135
　Pool, 256
　W. W., 256
　William W., 5, 135, 287
　Wm. W., 97, 125, 185
Pooll
　Wm. W., 24
Porter
　J. C., 230
　William, 230
　William G., 38, 108, 241, 246
Portervint
　James, 235
Powell
　G. W., 231
　Norborn B., 149
　Norborne B., 206
Powers, 92
　Edward E., 243
Poythress
　Joseph, 18, 71
Prentice, 11, 248
Prescot
　Leroy, 231
Preston, 59, 125, 242, 251
　Thomas, 271
　Thomas, Jr., 120, 121
Prickett, 97, 201
Pride
　William, 66, 135, 246, 271, 281

Wm., 163
Pryor
  C. S., 241
Purklin
  George, 244
Quinn, 203, 204
Ragan, 112, 187, 204
  Abraham B., 94
Ragland
  Raney C., 248, 250
  Rany C., 229
Rainey
  William V., 243
Randolph, 248
  Carter J., 240, 249
Randolphs, 164, 232
Randolps, 232
Raney
  Wm. D., 241
Rankin, 34, 110
  James, 24, 34, 36, 111, 180, 249
Raymond, 244
Read, 23, 178, 188
Reaves
  Pryor, 247
Redd
  Charles A., 240
Reed, 103
  Thos. J., 35
Reese, 205, 208, 251, 276
Reeves
  Geo. W., 79
Reid
  Alfred P., 250
  Ann, 42, 63
  Anne, 148
  Elisha, 228
  Ezra C., 244
  Templeton, 88, 159, 205, 245

William, 134, 141
Reynolds, 20
Rhind
  James, 89, 121, 199, 240, 244, 245, 252
Rhodes
  Bunion, 134, 140
Richards, 212, 214, 218, 219, 240, 241, 243
Richardson
  William T., 251
Richds., 130
Richster
  Frederick, 272
Ridenhour
  Daniel D., 25, 271, 281
Right
  Edward W., 193
Rinaldi
  John W., 29, 56, 236
Ritch
  David, 126
Robbins, 45, 89, 250
  C., 204
  E., 204
Roberson, 8, 36
  Bird F., 55, 161, 163
  M. D., 36, 42
  Mathew, 203, 228
  N. M. C., 229
  Nat, 143
  Nathaniel M. C., 55
  William B., 29, 55, 125
  Wm. B., 177, 178, 191
Roberts
  E. C., 244
  H., 78
  Josiah, 20
  William M., 226, 246

Robertson
  A. J., 136
  Bird F., 28
  John S., 21
  John T., 279
  M. D., 242
Robinson, 53, 56, 118, 192, 241, 246, 251, 252, 253
  B. T., 203
  Henry, 275
  Henry G., 204
  M. D., 68, 240, 246, 248, 285, 287
  Manoah D., 209
  Menoah D., 202, 204, 281
  W. B., 10, 45
  William B., 63, 119, 201
  Wm. B., 23, 186, 205, 244
Robison, 29
  Bird F., 66
  M. D., 276, 283, 284
  Menoah D., 271
  N. M. C., 84
  William B., 80, 96, 274
Rockquemore
  V. P., 289
  Vincent P., 271
Roe
  Richard, 39, 48, 49, 123, 282, 289
Rogers
  Edwd. G., 130
  J. C. W., 229
  William, 38, 105, 187, 250
Ropes
  A. B., 103
Roquemore
  Vincent P., 230, 281
Rorie
  James J., 230, 242
Rose, 187, 193, 248
Ross, 107, 145, 146, 147
  Geo. W., 92, 270
  George W., 101, 199, 207, 208, 249, 250
  William, 108, 142, 145, 146, 147
  Wm., 118
Roswell
  William, 30, 33
Rounds
  John, 37, 252
Rowel
  Richard, 8
  Umphry, 8
Rowell
  Richard, 5, 244
  Seaborn, 48, 49
  Umphrey, 5, 42, 48, 49, 63, 106, 108, 117, 120
  Umphry, 251, 271, 281
Ruse
  Francis N., 229
Russel
  James M., 7, 175
Rutherford
  A. L., 87
Ryals
  James, 5, 8
Ryder, 38, 105, 241, 250
Rylander
  William J., 23, 62, 229, 271, 275, 276, 279, 281, 285, 286, 287, 288, 290
  Wm. J., 273, 282, 284
Sackett
  Prentiss, 103
Sage
  Orrin W., 240

Samford
  Henry, Jr., 252
Sanders, 92
  Bewford W., 230
  Bluford, 20
Sanford
  Henry, 54
Sanky, 220
  Richard T., 228
Sapp
  Madison, 229
Sarenet
  James, 51
Sarsnett
  James, 227
Saulsbury
  Wm., 242
Saydams, 162
Schley
  Geo. H., 142, 160, 161
  Jno., 66, 215, 217, 285
  John, 38, 39, 65, 113, 135, 216, 219, 279, 288
  Phillip T., 162, 232
  William K., 229
Scoggins
  Fielding, 206
Scott, 232
  Samuel C., 252
  Talifear, 252
Scurlock
  William, 229
Seals
  James, 138
Seaman, 114, 162, 248
Sears
  George, 244
Sebring
  Wm. L., 176

Sewell, 103
  Francis S., 274
Seydams, 115
Shaham, 20
Shaw
  James, 228
Sherwood, 41
  George C., 208
Shipman, 82, 249
Shivers, 53, 70, 165, 180, 185, 188, 288
  James S., 228
  Thomas J., 228, 271
Short, 14, 114, 163
  G. W., 111, 252, 276
  George W., 34, 111, 145, 271, 279
Shorter, 79, 125
  Eli S., 16, 24, 25, 40, 42, 43, 49, 62, 72, 126, 127, 171, 183, 192, 193, 226, 245
  James H., 16, 21, 22, 24, 25, 40, 43, 49, 53, 62, 63, 72, 94, 123, 124, 125, 126, 127, 128, 171, 177, 178, 179, 180, 181, 183, 192, 193, 226, 239, 245, 253, 268, 269
  Jas. H., 245
  Sophia H., 16, 24, 25, 40, 43, 49, 62, 72, 126, 127, 180, 183, 192, 193, 226, 239, 245
  Sophiah H., 171
Shottles
  John, 243
Simkin
  Edmund, 229
Simmons
  John, 203
Sims

John, 245
Skinner
  Benajah, 79, 252
Slave
  Ben, 142, 144, 145
  Bill, 213, 219
  Hal, 213, 219
  James, 213, 219
  Jim, 145
  Joe, 213, 219
  Mack, 213
  Mark, 219
  Rosanna, 213
  Rosannah, 219
  Sovereign, 108
  Stephen, 213, 219
  William, 213, 219
Sloan
  James E., 28, 244, 250
  James R., 249
Smead
  P. H., 75, 76
  Patrick H., 240
Smith, 94, 103, 130, 165, 183, 239, 244, 246, 250, 252
  C. A., 229
  Elam W., 80
  Geo., 203
  George, 7, 175, 248
  H. S., 67
  Hampton S., 9, 10, 17, 67, 70, 163, 202, 228
  J. S., 87, 201, 205, 247
  James Y., 77, 233, 241, 242, 249, 251, 272, 278
  John J., 204
  Joseph, 226
  Joseph S., 201, 236
  N., 103
  N. L., 123
  Newitt L., 123
  Rhode L., 5, 8
  T. H., 59
  Thomas, 212
  Thomas H., 209, 212
  William H., 9, 250
Sneed
  A. W., 20
  Alexander W., 20
Snow
  Wm., 229
Solomon, 121
Sorsby
  B. A., 65, 98, 121
  Battle A., 23, 25, 26, 65, 98, 102, 113, 116, 120, 124, 155, 162, 163, 178, 184, 188, 245, 247
Southern
  John, 59
Southugs
  Robert, 166
Spear
  Anderson, 250
Spencer
  Richard P., 230
Spiller
  Charles F., 120, 245
Spillers
  Charles F., 8, 220
Spire
  J. P., 103
Spivey
  E. B. W., 236
  Eli B. W., 15, 26, 42, 63, 148, 228, 289
Spofford, 121, 189
Stanley
  Celia, 133

Starr, 100, 205, 208, 246, 251, 276
   Edward W., 228
Stebbins, 240
Stephen, 252
Stephens
   Green B., 231
Stevens
   Adrew, 103
Stewart, 20, 125, 243, 245, 247, 248, 249, 250, 251, 275, 284
   Charles D., 34
   Charles H., 79, 110, 252
Stilwell
   Silas B., 274
Stocks
   Thomas, 241
Stoddard
   Ezekiel B., 192, 253
Stout, 94, 95, 97, 242
Stovall, 242
Stratten
   Calvin, 164
Stratton
   Calvin, 164, 165
Sturgis
   Joseph, 5, 6, 7
Suddith
   James, 30, 33
Sullivan, 38, 105, 241, 250
   Alexander, 242
   Dennis, 184, 232, 249, 251, 252
   William, 41
   Wm., 204, 242
Sutton
   Jesse J., 134, 141
Suydam, 247
Swan
   Charles, 250
Swift

Sheldon, 102, 248
Taggart
   Thomas E., 240
Talbot, 23, 178
Talbott, 188
Tarver, 23, 24, 38, 108, 163, 164, 178, 202, 203, 223, 239, 242, 243, 244, 246, 247, 248
   Benj. P., 22, 23, 220
   Benjamin P., 53, 124, 160, 223, 224, 234, 245, 248, 249, 252
   Elisha, 102, 244
   Milton J., 203, 220, 223, 224, 226, 252
Tatum, 10, 82, 90, 93, 162, 242, 245, 246, 247, 249
   Seth, 6, 233
Taunton
   Newsome, 46
Taylor, 38, 252, 290
   Edward T., 228
   John, 28
Templeton
   Thos. J., 204
Terry, 118
   Alfred M., 18, 72, 107, 112
   G. B., 243, 252
   Garland B., 26, 195, 228, 236, 250, 251, 271, 279
   Joseph M., 82, 83, 228
   N., 252
   Nathaniel, 279
   Thomas J., 75, 76, 240, 246
Thomas, 53, 70, 165, 180, 185, 188, 288
   G. E., 245, 272
   Grigsby E., 202, 243
   Ivey, 248
   Owen, 139, 140

Penina, 157, 158, 273
Peter M., 202
Stephens, 273
Stevens, 157, 158
Thompson
  John W., 229
  Samuel, 38, 104, 268
Thorn
  Seaborn, 53, 260, 273
Thorne
  Micajah A., 244
Thornton, 95, 97, 249
  Hudson A., 5, 64
Thorp
  A., 247
  S., 247
Thorpe
  A., 202
  S., 202
Thorton
  Nathaniel M. C., 228
Thurmond
  Jerre, 230
Thustand
  Thomas, 26
  Thos., 32
Thweatt
  M. W., 24, 37
  Micajah W., 180, 273
Tileston, 121, 189
Tiller
  Paul H., 199, 211, 248, 250
Tillery
  Randol, 5, 100, 202
Tilleston
  Wm. M., 240
Tillory
  Randol, 8
Tillotson, 103

Toby
  Frederick, 5, 7, 175, 208
Toney
  W., 9, 37, 38, 99, 103, 104, 106, 109, 121, 131, 202, 251, 270, 274, 288
  Washington, 55
  William, 9
  Wm., 37, 38, 99, 103, 104, 106, 109, 121, 131, 202, 251, 270, 274, 288
Torrance, 23
  Mansfield, 26, 35, 61, 62, 82, 102, 116, 170
Torrence, 124
  Mansel H., 27, 247, 250
  Mansfiel, 7
  Mansfield, 5, 29, 129, 130, 175
  William H., 165
Towns
  G. W. B., 248
  George W. B., 208, 248
Townsen
  Lewis, 273
Townsend, 36
  J., 203
  John, 243
  M., 203
Townsley
  Victor S., 236, 243
Tozier
  John C., 59, 106, 108
Traywick
  William, 229
Treadwell, 247
  Adonarian, 240
  Adoniran, 57
Trice
  John P., 170

Turentine, 16, 251
  George W., 135
Turner, 119
  A., 13, 241
  Aaron, 119, 150
  Abel, 241, 242
  John W., 260
Turrentine
  George W., 87
Tyack
  William, 204
Tyson
  G. W., 245
Underhill, 164, 232, 248
Underwood, 23, 124
  Wm. H., 242
Urquhart
  John A., 22, 179, 208
Van Ness
  James, 55, 236, 245, 248, 250
Vance
  John, 135
Vanderpool, 103
Vanzant
  L. S., 244
  N. S., 230
Vessels
  John F., 240
Wacker
  James L., 230
Wade, 250
  R. J., 174
  Richard Johnson, 203
  William, 208
Wadsworth, 11, 202, 251
  James, 229
Wainwright
  Eli, 164, 247
Walker

A. M., 81, 90
Amasa, 113, 162, 248
Austin M., 77, 245
Benjamin, 231
David E., 42, 240
James L., 103
James S., 38
John T., 24, 49, 54, 80, 99, 178, 251, 274
Wall
  David, 229, 271, 281
  Sewell F., 235
Walling
  Daniel, 50, 233, 239
  William, 233, 242
  Wm., 239
Walsh
  Henry C., 241, 243
Walton, 58
  John L., 229, 271, 281
Ward, 114, 162, 248
  David Z., 250
  George, 195
  James, 271, 281
Ware
  John H., 10, 24, 86, 92, 127, 187, 228, 268, 270, 271
  Robert A., 72, 228
Warren
  Jno., 181
  John, 18, 23, 70, 117, 181
Watkins
  Asel L., 100
  Cornelius, 250
  William H., 129
  Wm. H., 228
  Zachariah, 229, 271, 281
Watson, 12, 16, 21, 63, 68, 81, 108, 114, 115, 124, 126, 131, 132,

150, 183, 184, 185, 190, 200, 211, 221, 223, 226, 251, 272, 289
J. C., 222
James C., 34, 48, 131, 132, 170, 185, 200, 206, 221, 222, 242
Jno. H., 241
John H., 78, 161, 184, 204, 242, 290
Robert, 197, 198, 203
Way
  Geo. W., 163, 171
  George W., 79, 232, 247, 249
Weatherford
  Alfred, 231
Weathers
  William, 230
Webb
  Isaac, 8, 106, 107
  Isaac H., 5, 117, 120
  J. B., 149, 190
  Joseph B., 86, 245, 248, 250, 251
Webster, 146
  Joseph E., 230
Weems
  Walter H., 17, 70
Wellborn, 174
  Alfred, 204
  Johnson, 138
  Marshall J., 7, 27, 30, 36, 44, 73, 80, 86, 89, 94, 104, 116, 128, 129, 142, 149, 150, 152, 153, 154, 155, 156, 157, 160, 161, 167, 169, 177, 224, 231, 234, 239, 254, 258, 271, 274, 278, 280
  William, 48, 138
  William W., 92
Welles, 143
Wells
  Benj., 141
  Elbert, 144, 235, 254, 255
  S. G., 164
  Stephen G., 164, 165
Westcott
  John, 137
Wetherel, 247
Wetherell, 66, 163
Wetmore, 37, 97, 249, 287, 288
  R. C., 251
  Robert C., 209, 212
Wheelock
  E., 115, 247
  Ephraim, 156, 163, 196, 197, 231
Wheler
  Asa, 239
Whilte
  Henrietta, 111
White, 202
  Henrietta, 34
  J., 247
  J. S. W., 249
  John S., 34
  John S. W., 111
  N., 247
Whitehead
  D., 138
Whiteside, 133
Whitesides
  John, 53
Whitfield
  James, 82, 84, 85, 88, 249
Whitney
  Joseph, 246
Wicks
  Bartlett, 271, 281
Wiggins, 252
  Joel C., 242, 252
Wilder

William H., 242, 249
Wm. H., 242
Wildman
  N. H., 241
Wilkerson
  James, 230
Willard, 103
  N. P., 33, 137
  Nathan P., 33, 81, 156, 196, 197, 240
  Nathaniel P., 231
Williams, 36, 192, 241, 253
  D. H., 230
  Jacob, 230
  John, 242
  John H., 243
  N. S., 273
  R. H., 137
  Richard S., 66, 163, 247
  Turner, 54
  W., 59
  Wiley, 200
Williamson, 133
  James E. L., 241
  William, 35, 76
Willis
  James, 250
Willson, 240
  J. J., 89, 111
  John J., 34, 36, 37, 158, 245, 247, 249, 250, 252, 273
Wilson, 118
  J. J., 111
  John J., 111, 209
  William H., 103
Windham
  John, 201
Winstell
  W., 137
Winthrop
  Thomas C., 101, 246
Wister
  John, 243
Witmore, 82
Wittich, 25, 39, 58, 67, 130, 165, 183, 240
  Lovick L., 241
Wittick, 163
Womack
  John, 230
Wood, 212, 214, 215, 216, 218, 219
  E., 240
  James, 242, 248
Woodard
  James, 200
Woodland
  J. M., 73
  James M., 77
Woodruff
  Carnot, 5, 25, 62
  Philo D., 10, 15, 20, 25, 62, 79, 100, 125, 228
Woods
  N. G., 243, 244, 274, 275
Woodson
  Green J., 240, 244
Worsham
  A. B., 20
Wray
  Farris, 230
Wright, 11, 94, 100, 130, 165, 183
  Edward W., 17, 195, 238
Wynn
  William L., 88, 90, 247
Yarborough
  Richard, 204
Yonge

Hiram, 6
William P., 248

Young, 99, 100, 244, 246, 250, 252
Hiram, 228

www.ingramcontent.com/pod-product-compliance
Lightning Source LLC
Chambersburg PA
CBHW060350080526
44583CB00012B/248